THE WALL BEHIND CHINA'S OPEN DOOR

The Wall Behind China's Open Door

Towards efficient intercultural management in China

Jeanne Boden

Cover design: David Hyde, Celsius (www.celsius.eu.com)

Cover photograph: Jeanne Boden

Book design: David Hyde, Celsius (www.celsius.eu.com)

Photography: Jeanne Boden

Map on page 15: James Greig

Print: Flin Graphic Group, Oostkamp, Belgium

© 2008 ASP nv (Academic and Scientific Publishers nv)

Ravensteingalerij 28

B-1000 Brussels

Tel. ++ 32 2 289 26 50

Fax ++ 32 2 289 26 59

E-mail info@aspeditions.be

www.aspeditions.be

ISBN 978 90 5487 464 5

NUR 812 / 800

Legal Deposit D/2008/11.161/008

Contents

Foreword
by Zhao Yining

Twelve years ago when I was a project manager at a multinational corporation in Shanghai, I worked daily with a fleet of American expatriates who all carried pocket-size books like 'Doing business in China 101' to meet with local Chinese business partners. Interestingly enough, I sometimes had to play the role of intermediary to bridge the language as well as the cultural gap. I had to answer questions like: "Why do the Chinese never say 'no' to me but rather 'we need to look into it'?" or "Isn't it true that China is a very homogenous society? Why then are business practices in Beijing so different from those in Shanghai?" Despite my detailed explanations, their facial expressions suggested they were confused by what their books said and how reality presented itself to them.

Twelve years later, I flew from New York to Shanghai with two Western executives sitting next to me, who were reading books like 'Guanxi' and 'Myths about doing business in China'. Frequently, they turned to me, asking questions such as: "Isn't it true that Chinese culture promotes loyalty? Why then is the job turn-over rate in China so high?" I could sense their confusion about the modern outlook of this mystical Asian country, changing so fast in the last decades that it has brought about not only prosperity and opportunities but also doubts and uncertainties. China today has a new modern face. For many foreigners it is a colorful but at the same time a confusing and complex country.

Outside the window, the cloud was so thick that I could not even tell if the plane was moving, while my memory was flying back to 1996 when Jeanne and I first met in Ghent, Belgium after which we became close friends and began our collaboration.

In her warm and bright study, Jeanne was working on introducing contemporary Chinese culture into the Western world. During those cloudy and rainy afternoons, we would hold interesting discussions or even debates on a wide range of cultural phenomena and social topics that are having a profound impact on the current and perhaps future business environments in China. Initially, we tried to link different business etiquette, common practices and behavior with their cultural roots, putting these puzzles together and digging deep into the social and historical sources. Gradually, a picture was vividly emerging in Jeanne's mind.

In many traditional Chinese houses a 'Shadow Wall' behind the front door blocks the outsider's view of the interior of the house, preventing them from seeing what's going on inside while the door is open. This is a perfect image to represent China today, a country where many contradictions coexist, Confucianism and communism, contemporary and convention, East and West, etc.

The idea of unveiling the interrelation of Chinese cultural roots with its modern society and demystifying Chinese business behaviors and evolution has strongly motivated us. The ambitious goal of allowing people to see through the wall and to figure out the truth about China is successfully achieved in this book.

Yining Zhao PhD, MBA
Strategy Management Pfizer Inc.
Cambridge, MA, USA
December 2007

Introduction

Now that globalization has turned every inhabitant of this planet into a global citizen, we find ourselves confronted with on the one hand the similarities between all human beings, and on the other, the considerable and persistent differences in cultural backgrounds.

Working in an environment with people from different cultural backgrounds is exiting and stimulating, but it is not always easy. Intercultural environments require an open attitude in which all members are motivated to learn from each other. A Westerner working in China will be confronted with a reality that might at first sight look modern and 'Western'. Most of China's cities have been largely built over the past few decades. Modern architecture and brand new infrastructure give China a new, international, global face. The economy has been booming for decennia in China. Since 1978 China has become a new country. Communist structures have been partly dismantled, leading to radical social changes. In many ways China has gone through a liberalization process since 1978. The so-called westernization of China however is no more than a superficial layer. Age-old Chinese thinking did not change at the same speed as the outward image of China. Under the new surface, China remains China.

The arrival of a few hundreds of thousands of Westerners in China – if there are that many – will not fundamentally change a culture that has thrived for millennia. Several times in history foreign influences have led to the renewal and revival of Chinese culture. Today this is happening again. During the last few years, China has entered the global scene with immense power. This power has been building up over the past decennia in China, and has now burst onto the international scene. The Chinese have always been strongly entrepreneurial and they control businesses in many countries. They have spread throughout the world in Chinatowns for hundreds of years. In Communist times under Mao the entrepreneurial force of the Chinese people was suppressed in a totalitarian society. After the opening up of the country, the genie came out of the bottle. In 1978 every single Chinese person started to work day and night to build a better life for himself and his family. For about thirty years now, most of the Chinese have lived only to work, and they have succeeded. The projects China has realized over the past decennia are among the biggest and most impressive in the world: the Three Gorges Dam, the train connection between Beijing and Lhasa running over the Tibetan high plateau, the fastest train in Shanghai, the longest bridge connecting Shanghai and Ningbo. How on earth could the Chinese realize all these things and many others in just a few decennia? How can a country be strong enough to transform into a modern society from scratch in such a short space of time? What is the power of China? What gives China the drive to do what it succeeds in doing? And how do we as foreigners fit into that picture?

After the death of Mao Zedong, totalitarian communism came to an end. Deng Xiaoping implemented the reforms, the four modernizations being agriculture, industry, science and technology, and defense. One of the priorities of Deng Xiaoping was also that the Chinese Communist Party should stay in power. Since 1978 political reforms have taken place but the Communist Party stays in control.

In this book we will try to understand the blend that Chinese society is today, a mixture of traditions and international influences. We will explore how China is influenced by three traditions: Confucianism, communism, and the increasing interaction with international companies and influences from abroad. We will analyze the impact of these influences in Chinese society, and more specifically in corporate culture, communication and trading today.

Confucian values affect work ethics, leadership styles, and conflict management. Many characteristics of the functioning of Chinese companies belong to the legacy of the Communist planned economy: low productivity, lack of efficiency, quality problems, nontransparent financial management, unclear time management, and so on. We explore these issues from an intercultural point of view. By providing insight in underlying cultural factors, we pave the way towards effective intercultural management.

This book wants to be a manual for people working with the Chinese in China or elsewhere. Its focus on the historical, ideological and cultural background of Chinese corporate and commercial culture will help people working in China and working with the Chinese to understand many aspects of intercultural interaction and intercultural cooperation.

In this book we make a number of deliberate choices.

Chapter four, 'Contemporary China', starts with an overview of China's recent history: the end of the Chinese Empire, the establishment of the Republic of China in 1912, the establishment of the People's Republic of China in 1949, and evolutions after opening up in 1978. In each period, we highlight the political evolutions, but more importantly, we focus on the intellectual climate. To understand China today one needs to be aware of the fact that radical changes in China mainly took place over the last hundred years. Scientific methods were introduced at the beginning of the twentieth century. They were to replace the Confucian centralist worldview that had reigned for two thousand years, but until this very day we claim that China is a mixture of ancient Chinese knowledge and Western scientific knowledge.

Another choice is the structure of the book. In the first part, we search for underlying cultural aspects of contemporary Chinese culture while in the second part, we cover practical aspects of corporate and commercial life today and of working with the Chinese. This results in two different writing styles, the first leaning towards the academic, while the second is more practical.

I would like to thank all the people who continuously encourage me and assist me in my quest to understand China and the Chinese, for helping me and for sharing their friendship with me: Kong Xiangjun, Zhao Yining, Rong Haojing, Peng Jiayu, Zhang Xinrong, Ouyang Jin, Zhang Xiaojia, Li Xiaojian, Zhang Derong, Zhou Yanrong, Zhu Jun, Liu Lixin, Ma Li, Fan Yedong, Bai Xuesong, Yang Changrong, Qian Xiaorui, Yang Rui, Sun Lulu, Yang Enhong, Victoria Lu, Wang Jiaxin, Xi Chuan, Zhang Lei, Huang Meicui, Dirk Van Braeckel, David Hyde and Frenny De Frenne.

I invited a number of people, both Chinese and Westerners, to share their experience in China with me. Their contributions serve as illustrations of everyday life in China. The statements and views of the contributors are their own. We will notice that each contributor experiences the Chinese reality from a different viewpoint. Some tend to focus on the frustrations in their daily work situation in China, perhaps sometimes viewing the situation too much from a Western perspective and trying to lecture the Chinese; others find harmony in China. The different views represent various areas of cooperation: governmental, education (state organized and private), business (multinationals and medium-sized companies), legal, and trading.

Throughout the book we read contributions by Bernard Pierre, Belgian Ambassador in Beijing; Liu Lixin, professor of Chinese language at Beijing University; Michael Conen, Instructor and advisor at CIBT Beijing; Mike Cooper, Vice President Asia Rogers Corporation; Peter Verstraeten, CEO United Fashion; Kong Xiangjun, Lawyer at Dahwa Law Firm Shanghai; Bart Dauwe, Sinologist and director ChinAdvice; and Zhang Xiaojia, student of Economy at Beijing University. I want to extend my special thanks to all of them.

I also wish to thank the people from the editorial board who took the time to read through the manuscript and who provided me with invaluable comments: Els de Jong, Trainer/consultant Intercultural Awareness and International Business Development with a focus on China at KIT, Amsterdam; Duncan Freeman, Research Fellow at Brussels Institute for Contemporary China Studies at the Vrije Universiteit Brussel; Anneleen Verstegen, Sinologist KHM; Marieke Reichwein, Sinologist and consultant China Consult Beijing; Zhao Yining, Strategy Management Pfizer Inc; and all the Chinese and American business people in China and in the USA who were invited by Zhao Yining to provide their comments.

I wish to thank David Hyde, Celsius for his beautiful book design and for the many projects we have done together over the years. I would also like to thank Gert De Nutte and the other people from ASP for our pleasant collaboration during the publishing process of this book.

And last but not least, I want to thank my daughters Jono and Nuna Pili Van Belle for sharing a passionate interest in ten thousand things.

For the transcription of Chinese words and names the pinyin standard is used throughout the book. Only where relevant another transcription standard was used, for instance for Sun Yat-sen (pinyin: Sun Zhongshan) or Chiang Kai-shek (pinyin: Jiang Jieshi) whose names became world famous in this transcription. A Chinese character list in simplified Chinese characters is provided at the end of the book.

Jeanne Boden
February 2008

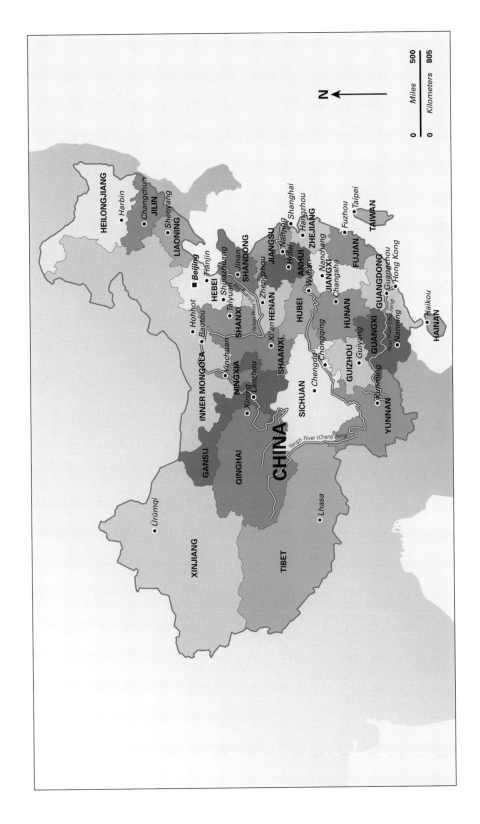

A Symbolic Title: 'The Wall Behind China's Open Door'

In 1978, Deng Xiaoping decided to open China's doors to attract foreign investment. In spite of the efforts made by the Chinese government to create an attractive investment climate for foreign companies, it is not always easy to deal with China. Great flexibility is required to succeed in China. Insight into Chinese culture and traditions and the functioning of Chinese society are needed to avoid the pitfalls and to get past 'the wall behind the door' that many foreigners bump up against.

China likes walls: traditional living compounds are surrounded by walls, temples are surrounded by walls, Communist work units are surrounded by walls, cities in the old days were surrounded by walls, modern villa compounds are surrounded by walls, and even as a country China has the Great Wall. These walls suit the idea of insider and outsider that we will elaborate in this book.

Gates give access to these walled complexes. Only insiders can freely move in and out. In traditional Chinese architecture, immediately inside the entrance gate a wall blocks the passage, forcing people to move either to the left or to the right in order to get around the wall. This 'screen wall' (*ying bi qiang*) is in fact designed to keep bad spirits out. The Chinese have always believed that dead ancestors continue to have influence on people on earth. When someone dies and the necessary rituals to accompany the soul to the hereafter are not observed, the soul will become a bad spirit or *gui*. *Gui* fly everywhere, but their mobility is limited: they cannot fly around a corner. To build a wall inside the open entrance gate thus protects a building from *gui* flying inside. It keeps the bad spirits out.

Coincidently some of the terms Chinese use to describe foreigners have this *gui* in them. *Guilaoer* (the old spirit), *yangguizi* (the spirit from across the water) are both terms the Chinese use for foreigners.

It's not easy to get past the Chinese wall as a foreigner. A Westerner might sometimes feel he is not really welcome in China, or that he will always remain an outsider.

We hope this book will help people to gain insight, and to achieve the flexibility that is required to fly around the corner to really get inside.

Eight Chapters

1 Confucianist China

China wants to be the best, the strongest, the biggest, the highest. Striving to be the one at the top of the world comes from Confucian hierarchical centralist thinking. Talking about China today is impossible without first explaining Confucianism. That is why we start this book with a first chapter on Confucian philosophy.

2 Coherent China

The universe is a coherent system where complementary forces are at work. Everything is connected to and interacts with everything else. To understand the Chinese we need to look into Daoism, concepts like *yin* and *yang*, and *qi*. These concepts influence every aspect of Chinese culture.

3 Communist China

Since 1949, China has adhered to Communist ideology. Although many things have changed over the last decades, understanding China today requires an understanding of the totalitarian Communist society and the planned economy that were in place before 1978.

4 Contemporary China

For a general understanding of contemporary Chinese society, we take a look at recent history since the nineteenth century, with a focus on the intellectual emancipation movements at the beginning of the twentieth century (First Enlightenment) and in the eighties (Second Enlightenment) and the introduction of scientific thinking in China. We look at politics today, at media and information, at the education system in China today, and at some aspects connected to Chinese society.

5 Communicative China

Aspects of communication like language and body language are dealt with in this chapter, but also communication patterns, indirect communication, *guanxi*, face, and insider-outsider ethics. To be able to communicate effectively, cultural understanding may be even more important than language skills.

6 Corporate China

Corporate culture in China is influenced by Confucian traditions, by communism and by Western management techniques. We explore the move from planned to market economy and the impact on corporate culture. We focus on the influence of culture in general on corporate culture. We look at aspects of working with Chinese employees, the labor market, time management, and conflict management in China.

7 Commercial China

We take a look at some changes in doing commerce after the move from planned to market economy, like business communication, promotion and advertising, trading ethics, and negotiations. We put copyright in China into the context of law in general in the People's Republic of China.

8 Conformist China

In the last chapter we focus on Chinese etiquette, which is connected to hierarchy and harmony. Doing business, trading, and human interaction in general require insight into etiquette issues. To be polite (*keqi*) goes a lot further in China than having good manners. To be polite is connected to holistic thinking.

Eight is a lucky number in China. We hope these eight chapters will help you to work harmoniously with the Chinese.

1 Confucianist China

1 Confucianist China

"Let the prince be a prince, the minister a minister, the father a father, and the son a son" [1]

1.1 Introduction

Professor Yu Dan recently published a book on Confucianism that swept across China.[2] In just four months, more than three million copies were sold, beating the bestseller Harry Potter.

Initially the Chinese Central Television (CCTV) created a forum[3] to promote Chinese traditions and history. Yu Dan was already a very successful lecturer. The publication of the book followed. Today she gives lectures all over the country and on CCTV. Yu Dan explains Confucianism and links Confucius' teachings to contemporary China.

Confucianism has been blamed for being backward at the beginning of the twentieth century. Communists tried to erase the Confucian heritage. Since the eighties there is a renewed interest in Confucius' teachings, and today Confucius is widely popular again amongst the people and in the Chinese Communist Party (CCP). The same CCP that once tried to destroy it now promotes Confucianism. Maybe one of the secrets of the strength of China lies in its Confucianist heritage.

Yu Dan explains: "He teaches love and tolerance, for example, and not to force others to do what you would not want to do yourself, how to develop harmonious interpersonal relationships. Are these ideas really that out of date? Are these not useful to our lives today?"[4]

President Hu Jintao is promoting a 'Harmonious Society' based on Confucian values of unity, morality and respect for authority. Confucian hierarchical and centralist thinking are the reason why the Chinese in today's China tend to exaggerate their personal position in society (adopt high titles, claim diplomas), or their product in the ranking of products, or the position of their company in the ranking of companies. It is the reason why one constantly hears people or companies claiming they are the 'best', 'top two', 'top three', the 'best in the province'.

Confucian thought is so pervasive in China that it is useless to say anything about doing business or education or trading without making the link with this way of thinking.

1.2 Main Characteristics of Confucianism

1.2.1 Confucianism: Hierarchy and Harmony

Confucius lived in the 5th century BC. This period was called the period of the Warring States; it is also referred to as the period of the 'hundred philosophers'. What was typical for Chinese thinkers of the time was that they sought ways to establish peace and harmony on earth, in society. Confucius developed a kind of society organizational model. He is not concerned with the supernatural; he focuses on human life, on humanism.

According to Confucius the key to maintaining order in society is correct public behavior, the rite or *li*. These rites existed during the Zhou dynasty (1000–221 BC). Confucius secularized them to ethical and aesthetical rules for public behavior. These rules form the basis of his philosophy for society.

Confucian society is hierarchical. It is a vertical structure with the ruler on top. The ruler displays the right public behavior; he sets the good example, he is the role model. He must behave properly and carry out the correct ceremonies. The population will then automatically be tranquil and peace loving. Through correct behavior the ruler will ensure harmony (*he*) between the world and the universe. He is the link between both and connects the microcosm with the macrocosm. He has the Mandate of Heaven.

The welfare of society does not depend solely on the charisma of the ruler. The whole of society has to be based on 'reciprocity'. The true ruler must be a father figure and an example to his subjects who in turn must remain loyal to him. The ruler's ministers must have a noble personality; they must be *junzi*. The nobility develop their virtue, *de*. Their virtue is *ren*: 'to be human'. To Confucius, *ren* means the embodiment of nobleness. A *junzi* embodies virtue in such a high measure that he serves as an example to others. The virtue of the gentleman is a social virtue through interaction with others. A noble person does not expect from others that which he does not wish upon himself. At the same time he must be loyal, *zhong*. His duty is to 'do his best for others'.

The ideal society comprises harmony whereby all role models are in tune with each other. As long as everyone respects his position, harmony will prevail. The virtue of the gentleman is displayed by how he applies justice, righteousness, *yi*.

Confucianism does not make a distinction between the public and the private realm. There is only one holistic realm: that of the humane or societal order. The family is part of the larger realm of the societal order. Within the family, Confucian values rule behavior. Order in the family is mirrored in order in society. Focus lies on moral integrity rather than on imposing of laws. Everything belongs to the societal order. Government, education, and business are all part of it. A person should be virtuous and observe Confucian values in any situation. A person high up in society should show his position not only at work; in every circumstance he should conduct himself according to his status.

1.2.2 Filial Piety

"Filial piety is the first principle of heaven, the righteousness of earth, and the code of conduct for the people. The principles of heaven and earth are eternal, and the people take them as their precept, imitate the brilliant luminaries of the heaven over the universe, and make full use of the benefits afforded by the earth so as to harmonize all under heaven. Thus the teachings are successful without being severe, the government is stable without harsh measures. Seeing how the teachings could work wonders in remolding the people, the ancient emperors set an example of universal love for all, as a result nobody neglected his parents; they promoted virtue, humanity and justice in order to influence people, and the people readily practiced them; they took the lead to show respect and courtesy, and the people had no quarrels with one another; they showed the people what was worth loving and what would be loathed, and the people knew the prohibitions and committed no crimes." [5]

'Filial piety' (*xiao*) is central to Confucius: "Filial piety is the foundation of all virtues and the fountainhead from whence all moral teachings spring" [6]. It is the duty of a son (*filius*) to obey his father. In turn, the father obeys his father. The younger must obey the older. A younger brother obeys his older brother. A woman obeys her father when she is young, her husband after marriage and her son when her husband has passed away. [7]

1.2.3 Order According to the Situation

Correct conduct does not mean following rigid rules. It does not recognize fixed rules; rather it depends on the context within which a person is acting. Correctness therefore depends on the situation at hand. Pragmatism is consequently a strong Chinese characteristic. People have to adapt to new situations continuously. In each situation someone acts as the role model, the others follow. The highest in social status will be the one who is followed by the others. This implies that all Chinese learn to follow the role model, but in any situation they themselves can become the role model. This means that everyone learns to obey and everyone learns to be a leader.

1.2.4 Social Status

When the master said, "He who holds no rank in a State does not discuss its policies," Master Zeng said, "A true gentleman, even in his thoughts, never departs from what is suitable to his rank." [8]

Confucius did not believe in laws to maintain social order. He believed in correct public behavior whereby everyone has a fixed position, a status in society and behaves accordingly.

An individual's and a family's social status (*shehui diwei*) are therefore of extreme importance. The Confucian state exams, organized throughout the centuries, were open to everyone, regardless of wealth. The exam system provided officials in service of the emperor. Confucius put great emphasis on study and on the cultivation of moral character. This is a system of meritocracy. A person can climb up by studying and by moral cultivation of the self.

Confucian society is hierarchical. It traditionally comprises four classes:
● The ruler is at the top. He is the son of heaven;
● Under him are ministers, officials, and intellectuals;
● Followed by the farmers;
● Merchants are at the bottom of society.

The ruler at the top would be so virtuous that instead of imposing proper behavior by law, people would automatically follow his virtuous example. The merchant class ranks last because its members are seen as driven by greed; they fail to bring their desires in line with the requirements of a societal order.

Social status was made explicit in many ways. The hierarchical status of lettered people in old China was displayed in their clothing: embroidered symbols, hairstyles, hairpins, hats, etc, all reflected the status of a person. The gate of a living compound showed the status of a family: size of the entrance gate, symbols on the stones at the gate, number of beams, number of inside and outside gates and so on. The dragon and the color yellow symbolize the emperor. No one in the empire could use that symbol or color without being punished. A person belonging to the military class had a tiger embroidered on his clothes; ordinary citizens had a bird as their symbol.

1.2.5 Hierarchy in Society

In Confucian society, all social relationships are hierarchical. There is the relationship between the ruler and his minister, between a prince and his subjects, between father and son, between the old and the young, between man and wife. Only the relationship between friends is less hierarchically oriented, though it may still play a role in certain circumstances, like in determining the relationship between young and old friends.

Hierarchical thinking is reflected and perpetuated in the way society is organized. Throughout the centuries, the family has been the basic unit in society. The patriarchal family structure is reflected in architecture. A family or clan lived in a

Government Shenzhen 2006. The size of the plants in between the people reflect the ranking in hierarchy between them (Confucianism); the round room creates harmony between the people (Daoism).

walled complex consisting of several buildings and courtyards. The simplest module is a building with four sides, a *siheyuan*.[9]

Big families, including servants, inhabit large complexes. Each group within the complex gets allocated a living space according to hierarchical position in the family. The first building usually has a formal or official character. Here, the master of the house receives his guests. The family quarters are at the rear. The architecture reflects and consolidates the social status of the inhabitants. A surrounding wall defines the family's unit in the community. There is a definite distinction made between what is situated within the walls and the outside. This provides for a system of groups with insiders who are (sometimes extremely) loyal to each other, and outsiders who do not belong to the group, and for whom consequently no responsibility exists.

The organization of a city in turn reflects hierarchy. The former Chang'an (present day Xi'an) is an example of this. The city was designed in 582 AD during the Sui dynasty. For three centuries, Chang'an, at that time the world's largest city with more than a million citizens was the capital of the Tang Empire. The streets divided the city into grids. The administrative centre with the palace behind it was located in the north of the city, facing south. Thus, anyone visiting the palace passed via the north–south axis. The north–south axis runs right through society. The North Star symbolizes the emperor. He sits on his throne in the main building facing south. Similarly, the official of a city sits in the main building facing south, and the head of a household sits in the main building of the living complex also facing south. The position of the emperor on his throne is reflected at the lower levels in society, right down to the household.

In the traditional Chinese capital there was no area provided for public gathering, unlike European cities where the market place was essential to political life. In hierarchical Chinese society everything had order and structure. There was no need for public meetings because information filtered throughout the hierarchy according to a predetermined pattern.

Hierarchy and the centralist organization of society is reflected in everything: in traditional architecture and the way people live, in seating positions in official gatherings, in the system of titles used to address one another within families, and so on.

1.2.6 Classification of Things

In hierarchical Chinese society not only people are ranked but all things are also classified and ranked.

In the Daoist system there are the 'Five Elements' (*wu xing*), in traditional Chinese medicine there are the 'Five Organs' (*wu zang*), in traditional painting there are the 'Three Friends of Winter' (*sui han san you*), in Chinese food there are the 'Five Flavors' (*wu wei*), in ideological campaigns we see the 'Hundred Flowers' (*bai hua*), and the 'Four Olds' (*si jiu*), in policy we see the 'Four Modernizations' (*sige xiandaihua*), and the 'Three Representatives' (*sange daibiao*). The term for the 'common people' or 'civilians' literally means the 'Hundred Names' (*lao bai xing*), and so on. Everything is counted and named.

Equally important is that all things in life are put into a hierarchy. In the centralist ranking it is always important to be the best, to rank the highest possible. Even today Chinese rank everything into a hierarchical system. There is the ranking of schools, of universities, of government departments, of factories, of museums, of products, and so on.

1.2.7 Doctrine of Zhongyong

"While there are no stirrings of pleasure, anger, sorrow, or joy, the mind may be said to be in the state of equilibrium. When those feelings have been stirred, and they act in their due degree, there ensues what may be called the state of harmony. This equilibrium is the great root from which grows all human acts in the world, and this harmony is the universal path, which they all should pursue. Let the states of equilibrium and harmony exist in perfection, and a happy order will prevail throughout heaven and earth, and all things will be nourished and flourish." [10]

The *Zhongyong*, translated as the 'Doctrine of the Mean' or the 'Invariable Medium' is one of the Four Classical Books in China.[11] It pleads for moderation in all aspects of life and in all situations. Thinking, feeling, and acting with moderation results in equilibrium, and that is the way to harmony. Throughout the ages, the Chinese have adopted the golden mean as a way of life. This doctrine focuses on the balance between the extremes in action and in thinking.

The scholar Lin Yutang[12] contrasts the focus on moderation with the focus on logic: "An educated man should, above all, be a reasonable being, who is always characterized by his common sense, his love for moderation and restraint, and his hatred of abstract theories and logical extremes." This leads to an attitude that differs from Western scientific thinking. The absolute truth does not exist in Chinese culture. Everything is relative. A typical Chinese judgment is: "A is right, and B is not wrong either".[13]

1.3 Confucianism throughout History

1.3.1 Origins of Confucianism

Many of the Chinese philosophies like Confucianism, Daoism, Legalism, and Mohism were formulated during the period of the Warring States (475–221 BC). China consisted of several states headed by a king, who had to perform the right rituals. One of those states was Lu (contemporary Shandong), where Confucius was born.

During the Zhou Dynasty (1045–256 BC) the concept of the 'Mandate of Heaven' was developed. A ruler was in position because he had the Mandate of Heaven. Once Heaven would no longer agree with a ruler, it would take away the mandate and the ruler would be replaced. To keep the mandate it was crucial that the ruler performed the right rituals as described in the *Zhou Li*, a scripture about ritual and etiquette. When Heaven took away the mandate, revolutions would break out, earthquakes, drought, floods would take place. Revolutions and natural disasters were consequently interpreted as signs from Heaven.[14]

Confucius (551–479 BCE) secularized the rites in his philosophy.[15] Confucius was a thinker, political figure, and educator. His teachings were put down in the *Lun Yu* (The Analects). He prescribed how the ideal man should educate himself and should behave, how an individual should live and interact with others, and how society and government should be organized.

Restoration of the Confucius Temple Beijing 2007

1.3.2 Confucianism in the Chinese Empire

In 221 BC, Qin Shi Huangdi unified the various states of China and declared himself the First Emperor of China. This was the start of the Chinese Empire that would last for two thousand years. In his short but totalitarian reign, the first emperor introduced a centralist bureaucracy. Ideologically he adopted Legalism, a philosophy focusing on strict rules, discipline and severe punishment. Assisted by his Minister Li he standardized legal codes, developed a new way of writing (Li script), standardized coins, measures and weights, and the length of the axis of vehicles. To diminish criticism of his policy and to consolidate his power, he cleared away dissident intellectuals and burnt dissident scriptures.

He built the Great Wall to protect China from intruding Northern tribes. The administrative division he introduced in his Empire would remain intact for two thousand years.

After the Qin dynasty (221–206 BC) several dynasties succeeded one another: Han (202 BC–220 AD), Sui (589–618), Tang (618–907), Song (960–1279), Yuan (1271–1368), Ming (1368–1644), Qing (1644–1912).[16] Several times in the course of history the Empire decentralized, but after some time it was centralized again.

From the Han Dynasty onwards, Confucianism became the dominant ideology in the Chinese Empire.

1.3.3 Confucianism as State Ideology

After the short reign of the Qin, the Han dynasty (202 BC–220 AD) followed, divided in the Earlier and the Later Han, with a very short interregnum in between. The Han dynasty gave the name to the Han Chinese people. More than 90% of the Chinese today are Han.

In the Earlier Han (202 BC–23 AD) consolidation of the bureaucratic centralization of the Qin took place. Chang'an (contemporary Xi'an) was the capital. Confucianism, mixed with legalist elements became the state ideology. Emperor Wu established the Confucian exam system in 2 AD. This system provided a strong official apparatus to keep the empire administration running in a stable and constant way. The exams were organized on different levels. The best students of the country were recruited. Only the very best reached the highest level, in service of the emperor. This system made China a meritocracy where in principle everyone could climb up the social ladder. The Confucian scholar had a prominent status in traditional society.

A fixed curriculum was taught in the central tradition. From the Han onwards people studied the Five Classics (*Wu Jing*). Two of the Five Classics can be seen as historical works: the *Shujing* (Book of Records), speeches from the rulers from the Zhou, and the *Chun Qiu* (Spring and Autumn Annals), a chronicle of the State Lu where Confucius was born.

As well as historical works, the Five Classics contain the *Shijing* (Book of Odes), a compilation of songs for ritual use at the court of the Kings of Zhou, and the *Li*

(Rites) divided in the *Zhou Li* (Rites of Zhou), the *Yili* (Rules and Rites) and the *Liji* (Records about Rites).

A fifth scripture is the *Yijing* (Book of Changes) that tries to formulate the cyclical changes of the cosmos. The *Yijing* was mainly used for divination. The focus in the Classics lay on history and rites. Apart from the Five Classics a lot of importance was attached to history and philosophy. In the *Shiji* (Historical Records), the dynastic histories were always written by the successor, based on archive material. Philosophers were also part of the curriculum: Confucian philosophers, Daoists, etc.

The Confucian exam system and the Confucian tradition were used over the ages by the different dynasties. A few times China decentralized, but each time upon reunification the Confucian exam system and the centralist organization was reinstalled. During the Song Dynasty (960–1279) Neo-Confucianist Zhu Xi adapted Confucianism with elements of Buddhism and Daoism. Zhu Xi's philosophy became the orthodox version of the official ideology for all the following dynasties.

The curriculum of the central tradition evolved over the ages, but the core always stayed the same until 1905, when the Confucian exam system came to an end.

1.3.4 Tribute System

In the Han Dynasty, territorial expansion along the Silk Road and south of the Yangzi began. To keep peace with the new territories the Han Emperors developed the tribute system. The basic idea of this system was that the Chinese Emperor was at the head of the central Chinese Empire, and consequently at the center of the universe. He had the Mandate of Heaven; he was responsible for the harmony between the cosmos and the people on earth. All citizens in the Chinese Empire were subject to the emperor and the same accounted for the people outside the borders of China. Under the tribute system, 'barbarians' from outside China, had to come to the Chinese court and subject themselves to the emperor. The subjection was demonstrated in the performance of the *kowtow*. Performing the *kowtow* meant bowing your head to the ground three times, in recognition of the supreme power of the emperor. 'Barbarians' also needed to offer tribute to the emperor in the form of gifts and presents. In return they received a seal and a calendar from the emperor.

The tribute system resulted in the fact that non-Chinese states could keep their autonomy in exchange for recognition of the sovereignty of the emperor. Relationships with foreign nations were always hierarchical relationships in which China considered itself at the top, and the foreign nation at a lower level.

In 1689 a conflict with Russia ended in the Treaty of Nertsjinsk. It was the first time in history China signed a treaty on an equal basis, and not on the basis of the tribute system. The tribute system existed until the establishment of the Republic of China in 1912.

Today the Chinese sometimes seem to believe that foreigners should still perform the *kowtow*. Imperial times are long gone but even so, today the idea of China being at the top of the centralist pyramid has become stronger again, for the first time since the middle of the nineteenth century, and it becomes more prominent every day.

At the end of Imperial times in the nineteenth century and the beginning of the twentieth century, Confucianism came under strong criticism being blamed for China's military weakness. During Mao Zedong's reign, severe attempts were made to destroy the old way of thinking. Today Confucianism is once again promoted.

1.4 Confucian Values in Contemporary Chinese Culture and Corporate Culture

Confucianism dominates many aspects in Chinese culture today. Ethics in society, at school, in corporate culture are all influenced by the Confucian values.

In the middle of the eighties, Michael Bond at the Chinese University of Hong Kong, and his group of researchers known as the Chinese Culture Connection, developed a detailed survey, called the Chinese Value Survey. Before this survey was developed interpretations of Chinese values were made from a Western perspective. Michael Bond engaged Chinese social scientists to list basic values for Chinese people. On the basis of this, he developed his survey aiming to examine how Hofstede's theoretical assumptions of national culture correspond to the orientations of cultural values derived from a Chinese point of view.[17] Questions in the survey involved filial piety, ancestor worship, obedience to parents, self-cultivation, moderation, following the middle way, observation of rites and rituals, benevolent authority, saving face. Some of these aspects, like rites and rituals, may sound strange to Westerners in connection with corporate culture and business. In Western culture the search for truth during life is highly valued. In Eastern cultures, however, the search for virtue prevails.

Several scholars have conducted research based on Bond's Chinese Value Survey. B.M. Matthews argues that Confucian values are still an essential contemporary construct, engendering parental respect as well as respect for tradition, honoring one's ancestors and financial support for parents.[18] The reciprocation of greetings and favors and saving 'face' are also still very important in a society that operates from an inner core of close relationships, which, in turn, are surrounded by more casual but still significant personal links. In the People's Republic of China, she points out a number of aspects related to Confucianism: the system of *guanxi* is an integral part of existence itself, often viewed by Westerners as a form of corruption; moderation or following the middle way is another value leading to harmony and stability, supporting the collective, extended family rather than the individual; non-competitiveness is another Confucian value, which may seem strange because the Chinese are perceived as highly competitive.

Peng Shiyong relates the Chinese survey to Hofstede's theoretical conception. Analysis of the collected data in his research generated four dimensions: integration, moral discipline, human-heartedness, and Confucian dynamism.[19] Of these four dimensions, integration correlates with Hofstede's individualism/collectivism, moral discipline with Hofstede's power distance, human-heartedness with Hofstede's masculinity-femininity, but 'Confucian dynamism' does not correlate with any of Hofstede's dimensions. This shows the need to evaluate cultural values within the setting of the Chinese social value system, and not only from theories based on Western perceptions.

The system of hierarchy and harmony penetrates every single aspect of contemporary life in China. It dominates relationships and human interaction, it is responsible for the specific way of indirect communication the Chinese use, it rules group dynamics, the concept of face is connected to it, and rules of etiquette stem from it. Etiquette is linked to hierarchical positions in society. When working with the Chinese, the importance of insight into hierarchical Confucian thinking cannot be overestimated.

---

[1] 'Jun jun chen chen fu fu zi zi': Yang Bojun, Waley Arthur, *Lun Yu. The Analects. 12.11* Hunan People's Publishing House, Foreign Language Press, 1999, pp 130–131

[2] Yu Dan, *Yu Dan "Lun Yu" Xin De*, Beijing Zhonghua Shuju, 2007

[3] CCTV 10 Lecture Room, Bai jia jiangtan (Literally: A hundred schools of thought forum)

[4] *LA Times*, 7 May 2007

[5] Fu Genqing, Liu Ruixiang, Lin Zhihe, *The Classic of Filial Piety*, Shandong Friendship Press, 1998, p 11–13

[6] Ibid, p 2

[7] In the People's Republic of China the traditional relationship between men and women as prescribed by Confucius has changed under the influence of communism. Women in today's China can study and occupy high positions in society. However, the relative absence of women in government positions and in high management positions in Chinese companies, and the preference for a male child over a female child show that China is still male-dominated and that traditional values still reign.

[8] Zi Yue: "Bu zai qi wei, bu mou qi zheng" Zengzi yue: "Junzi si bu chu qi wei.": Yang Bojun, Waley Arthur, *Lun Yu, The Analects*. Hunan People's Publishing House, Foreign Language Press, 1999, pp 162–163

[9] The modular hierarchical organization of living complexes and traditional Chinese architecture in general is well described by Lothar Ledderose: Ledderose Lothar, *Ten Thousand Things*, Princeton University Press, 2001, pp 107–117

[10] Tze Tze, *The Doctrine of the Mean*, translated by James Legge, Clarendon Press, 1893, Chapter 1

[11] The Four Confucian Classics are the 1 *Da Xue*, Great Learning; 2 *Zhongyong*, Doctrine of the Mean; 3 *Lun Yu*, Analects of Confucius; 4 *Mengzi*, Mencius

[12] Lin Yutang (1895–1976), famous for his critical articles and essays in the 1920s and 1930s in China, moved to the USA in the middle of the 1930s where he started to publish in English. See: Idema Wilt, Haft Lloyd, *Chinese Letterkunde. Een inleiding*. Amsterdam University Press, 1996, p 276

[13] Lin Yutang, *My Country and My People, Wu Guo yu Wu Min*, Foreign Language Teaching and Research Press, Beijing, 1998, p 108

[14] The disastrous earthquake in the North Eastern Chinese city Tangshan in 1976, the year that Mao Zedong died, was interpreted by some people according to the same concept.

[15] Dates of Confucius birth and death: http://plato.stanford.edu/entries/confucius/#ConLif

[16] Dates from: Wilkinson Endymion *Chinese History: A Manual, Revised and Enlarged*, Harvard University Asia Center for Harvard-Yanching Institute, Cambridge, London, 2000, pp 10–12

[17] The theory of Geert Hofstede will be elaborated upon in the paragraph on Understanding Cultures and Corporate Cultures. Hofstede Geert, *Cultures' Consequences, Comparing Values, Behaviors, Institutions and Organizations Across Nations*, Sage Publications, Thousand Oaks, London, New Delhi, 2001

[18] Matthews, B.M., *The Chinese Value Survey: An interpretation of value scales and consideration of some preliminary results*. International Education Journal, Vol 1, No 2, 2000, p 117–126

[19] Peng Shiyong, *Culture and Conflict Management in Foreign-invested Enterprises in China. An Intercultural Communication Perspective*. Peter Lang, European University Studies, Vol. 369, 2003 p 51

2 Coherent China

2 Coherent China

2.1 Introduction

Although this book mainly focuses on Confucian and Communist influences in corporate culture and business in China today, we also touch upon Daoism and holistic thinking in Chinese culture and in Chinese society. Holistic thinking links human life to nature or to the universe. Everything that is happening in life belongs to a coherent system in which all phenomena are linked to each other and interact with each other. The Daoist ideas of relativity of all things, the unity of opposites, and the attitude to discard extremes and strive for moderation continue to exert influence on daily life in China today. Chinese food, medicine, martial arts, garden layout, architecture, calligraphy, art, aesthetics, and many other cultural aspects are based on it. But its influence also reaches into the realm of business culture. Coping with information (the absolute truth does not exist), negotiating tactics, leadership styles, or the translation of brands and company names can all be seen as exemplary.

In the context of this book we limit ourselves to introducing the basic concepts of a furthermore extremely complex philosophy. Insight into holistic thinking will put certain features of business culture today into a larger context and explain that many of the symbols or ceremonies used in business culture are not related to superstition as Westerners tend to think, but to a holistic interpretation of the universe.

2.2 Main Characteristics of Daoism

2.2.1 Daoism and Holistic Thinking

Daoism, like Confucianism, originated in the 5th century BC and Laozi (author of *Daodejing*) and Zhuangzi are considered to be the founders.

Daoism originates from the term *Dao*, 'the Way'. *Dao* is the way of everything, the driving force of the world; it precedes and creates everything. The balance of macrocosms (universe) and microcosms (human beings) is kept by following the *Dao*. Laozi describes the *Dao* as follows:

"There was something undifferentiated and yet complete, which existed before Heaven and Earth. Soundless and formless, it depends upon nothing external, operating in a circular motion ceaselessly. It may be considered the root (Mother) of all beings under Heaven. I don't know its name, and call it *Tao*.[1] Inadequately giving it another name, I call it the Great. The Great moves on, the moving-on becomes remote, the remote returns to the original point. Therefore *Tao* is great, Heaven is great, and Man is great. There are four great things in the universe, and Man is one of them. Man follows the way of Earth, Earth follows the way of Heaven, Heaven follows the way of *Tao. Tao* follows the way of itself."[2]

2.2.2 Laozi and the Daodejing

Laozi's work *Daodejing* has a cryptic character, which both Chinese and Westerners alike have tried to interpret and understand. Each translation or interpretation differs from the previous one. The title *Daodejing* is translated as 'The Book of Way and Virtue'[3], 'The Way and its Power'[4], or is simply left un-translated as *Daodejing*.[5]

The Way or *Dao (Tao)* and the Power/Virtue or *De* are the two basic principles of Laozi. The *Dao* is the principle of the origin of all things through which everything exists and is what it is, but *Dao* itself does not belong to the things. The *Dao* is called 'empty'. It is the non-existent that makes existing things exist. A wheel may have spokes but it is the space between the spokes that gives the wheel its shape. It is the emptiness in a barrel that makes the barrel useful. Door and windows are cut out of a room, but it is upon the vacancy within, that the use of the room depends.[6]

Dao is invisible but it exists in reality and produces a myriad things. *De* is the working of the *Dao* in the thing, the way that individual things develop. Everything has its proper nature and its own virtue, *De*.

The *Daodejing* wants to be a guide for actions. The working of the Way is described in metaphors. *Dao* is the valley towards which everything flows; *Dao* is the water, which is soft but triumphs over everything.

The movement of the *Dao* is called 'withdrawal' or 'reversal' *(fan)*. The thought behind this is that all opposites are complementary and capable of meeting each other. One only needs to push a thing to its limit in order to meet its opposite. The wise man does not therefore strive to achieve what he wants; he simply approaches from the opposite direction.

Because opposites create each other, non-action or *wu wei* is advocated. *Wei* is conscious action. The term *wu wei* does not imply inactivity per se but suggests that an objective be pursued unintentionally: "*Dao* invariably does nothing, and yet there is nothing left undone".[7] *Wu wei* means interfering as little as possible with the processes as they take place spontaneously. One must not allow one's own actions to be controlled by goals, but simply participate in the spontaneity of the way.

The Daoist strives to live in accordance with the order of nature, with the natural order of things. He wants to allow things to happen like they happen for themselves, according to their own spontaneity. He is only a minuscule component of nature, therefore how could he possibly influence or change it?

2.2.3 Appreciation of Zhuangzi

According to Zhuangzi[8] people should withdraw from society rather than concern themselves with it. He advocates an individual way. Freedom can be achieved by letting go of conventional values. Good and beautiful only exist because we also know bad and ugly, both are mere interpretations of the same thing. Even the distinction between life and death is relative. Zhuangzi promotes the total relativity of values.

Dao is the manner whereby things happen automatically. Zhuangzi uses the term 'spontaneity'. The wisdom of the wise is to go with the natural course of things and not to go against it. Every creature has its own natural way and spontaneity that may be incomprehensible to others.

The wise man does not regard himself as an independent being but simply as a part of a greater entity, subject to the same changes as everything else. All things are continually mixed up and are, as it were, not themselves.

2.3 Daoist Concepts

2.3.1 Yin and Yang

The symbol known in the West as *yin* and *yang* is in fact called the *taijitu*, the 'diagram of the Great Ultimate' or the 'diagram of the universe'. The concept is derived from the *Yijing*, the 'Book of Changes' that according to legend originated thousands of years BC. Many of the concepts adopted by the Daoists originated in earlier times.

The *taiji* or 'Great Ultimate' is divided into two principles: *yin* and *yang*. The opposite powers are complementary, the one does not exist without the other and they balance one another: male – female, positive – negative, warm – cold, sun – moon, light – shadow, active – passive.

The interaction between *yin* and *yang* produces the *wu xing*, the five elements or five phases: wood, fire, metal, earth and water. From these five elements originate the 'ten thousand things', *wan wu*, or 'everything in existence'.

The diagram of the universe is the basic principle of traditional Chinese philosophy, science, astrology, and fortune telling. It is composed of, and held together by two complementary forces: *yin* and *yang*, negative and positive, cold and warm etc.

Yin and yang, surrounded by the Eight Trigrams from the Yijing, surrounded by the Twelve Animals

The opposing forces *yin* and *yang* occur in all aspects of nature and need to be in harmony so that the world can function in an orderly fashion. Harvest, peace, or health, are all subject to the working of these powers. The interaction between these two powers sustains life and determines the cosmos and the cycles of nature.

2.3.2 Qi

Qi is the vital force of life, the spiritual energy. Zhang Dainian who analyzes Chinese philosophical concepts as they are interpreted by different Chinese scholars over the ages, translates the concept of *Qi* as Einstein's e = mc2, because it embraces both matter and energy.[9] The concept of *Qi* is associated and connected to *yin* and *yang* and to the Way: "*Qi* transforms and flows, generates again and again unceasingly; therefore it is called the Way."[10]

Chinese philosophy underlines the movement of the *Qi*. *Qi* is both what exists and what is able to become. It is the life principle, but also the stuff of inanimate objects. It encompasses the physical and the spiritual. The movement of the *Qi* is one of the most important aspects in traditional aesthetics and art. It is the basic concept in martial arts. It is one of the main issues in Chinese massage, and in many other cultural forms in China.

2.4 Sixty Year Cycle

The sixty-year calendar is a cycle with 10 heavenly stems and 12 earthly branches. A pair of 1 stem and 1 branch names each year. A complete cycle is sixty years. The heavenly stems are associated with *yin* and *yang*, and with the five elements. The earthly branches are associated with the twelve animals. In order they are rat, ox, tiger, rabbit, dragon, snake, horse, sheep (or goat), monkey, rooster, dog, and pig.

China today uses the Gregorian calendar in everyday life. Besides that it still uses the sixty-year calendar, as we will explain in the paragraph on Calendar Use.

2.5 Pursuit of Harmony with Destiny

"It is the human mind, which possesses the ability to think, that gives life a meaning. What can be perceived within space and time is nothing but superficial reality. The ultimate reality is always kept unknown. Ultimately all things belong to the Universal Oneness."[11]

According to holistic Chinese vision, an individual is part of the universe. The life of an individual is connected with a greater whole that has its own working. To ensure harmony with nature, the moment of birth of an individual is an anchor point. In the sixty-year cycle, two Chinese characters (Heavenly stem and Earthly branch) mark the year, month, day and hour of birth, which together add up to the 'eight characters' or *bazi*. These eight characters determine a person's fate or *ming*. Fate is fixed at birth. One can only accept it. Chinese people very often refer to fate in life and in business life. When two people meet each other they call it *yuan fen*: 'it is fate that brings us together'.

A person's fate is determined, but natural circumstances will also exert influence on an individual's life. These circumstances can be prosperous at certain moments in life; these are the moments of 'luck' or *yunqi*.

Specialists initiated in Geomancy[12], fengshui[13], the study of the 'eight characters', and the whole complexity of Daoist thought that relates life of an individual to the working of the *Dao* are consulted for all kinds of advice. Their advice can decide a prosperous time or space for a certain occasion, for instance a wedding or a day to depart on a journey or to open up a production line in a factory. The geomancer gives advice on lucky days, or on days to avoid taking action, on name giving for a baby, etc, so that harmony can be obtained between the moment of birth and the influence of nature.

To maintain the balance between an individual and nature, it is necessary to consider time and space. A moment in time can be positive or negative; space where an action takes place is also significant. For example the place where someone is buried will affect the spiritual peace of the deceased.

The art of Geomancy uses the sixty-year cycle, star constellations, the eight trigrams of the *Yijing, yin* and *yang*, the five elements, the twelve animals, the five directions, and so on.[14] In principle it all boils down to taking the forces of the natural elements into account in relation to the life of an individual. Man is just a small part of nature and takes part in the cyclical movement of nature. Everything is connected and interacts with everything else.

2.6 Daoism and Holistic Thinking in Contemporary Chinese Culture and Corporate Culture

Discussing the subject of Daoism and holistic thinking in relation to doing business in China might seem a bit strange to a Westerner at first sight. Underlying many actions in China, however, lies the age-old holistic thinking. Even the most rational Chinese person may consult a geomancer. Western people tend to view this as a kind of superstition. There is however nothing superstitious or religious about it; it is purely about the position of an individual in the whole of universe and their mutual interaction. For a Westerner it is difficult to grasp the impact of it. The fact that Westerners tend to label ceremonies, rituals or actions linked to holistic thinking as superstition may explain more the Western non-holistic thinking, divided into religious and non-religious.

Confucianism and Daoism coexisted throughout the ages in Chinese thought. They should not be seen as religions that people believe in or adhere to. Both of these systems of thought permeate Chinese culture thoroughly. They are both holistic: they associate human life with the universe. Confucian thinkers also use concepts like 'the Way' or *Dao*.

[1] *Tao* is the Wade-Giles transcription of the equivalent in pinyin transcription: *Dao*

[2] Ren Jiyu, *A Taoist Classic. The Book of Lao Zi*, Foreign Languages Press, Beijing, 1993, p 41 Heaven (*tian*), Earth (*di*) and Human beings (*ren*) interact with each other.

[3] Duyvendak J.J.L., *Tau-Te-Tsjing. Het boek van Weg en Deugd*, De Driehoek, Amsterdam, 1980

[4] Waley, Arthur, *The Way and its Power. Lao Tzu's Tao Te Ching and Its Place in Chinese Thought*, Grove Press, New York, 1958

[5] Beck Mansvelt, *Laozi, Daodejing*, Servire, Utrecht, Antwerpen, 2002

In harmony with the universe: practicing calligraphy with water instead of ink purely to cultivate one's spirit

[6] Ren Jiyu, *A Taoist Classic. The Book of Lao Zi*, Foreign Languages Press, Beijing, 1993, p 25

[7] Ibid, p 55

[8] The CCTV10 *Bai jia jiangtan* forum set up to reintroduce the Chinese classics to the Chinese people led to several publications by Yu Dan. Apart from the publication on Confucius, Yu Dan also published a pocketsize book on Zhuangzi: *Yu Dan 'Zhuangzi' Xin De*, Zhongguo Minzhu Fazhi chubanshe, Beijing, 2007

[9] Zhang Dainian, *Key Concepts in Chinese Philosophy*, Foreign Language Press, Beijing, Yale University Press, New Haven, London, 2002

[10] Formulation of *Qi* by Mencius: Zhang Dainian, 2002, p 25

[11] Sheh Seow Wah, *Chinese Leadership. Moving from Classical to Contemporary.* Times Editions, Singapore, 2003, p 85

[12] Geomancy is the study of the natural elements according to the Daoist system.

[13] In 2007, for the first time, the original Chinese treatise on the Art of Scheduling and Positioning was translated from the Classical Chinese into English: Aylward Thomas F., *The Imperial Guide to Feng Shui & Chinese Astrology. The only authentic translation from the original Chinese*, Watkins Publishing, London, 2007

[14] More on Geomancy and the related symbols in: Chang Chao-Kang, Blaser Werner, China. *Tao in der architektur. Tao in Architecture*, Birkhauser, Basel, Boston, 1987, p 48

3 Communist China

3 Communist China

"The mystical 'great harmony' of old changed into the scientific 'great harmony' of Communist society, and the passive subordination under heaven changed into active commitment to the collective; but the impersonal and authoritarian hierarchy, datong (the great togetherness), was preserved. Content and attitude changed but not the structure. Where once practical actions were accompanied by Confucian ceremonies, they were now accompanied by quotations of Mao." [1]
J. Loewenstein

3.1 Introduction

Confucian and Daoist traditions continue to exert influence on Chinese culture today, but it is equally important to understand the impact of communism in China.

In 1949 the People's Republic of China was established. This Communist centralist organization was perfectly compatible with what China had known throughout the ages. In former times, the emperor and his literati ruled over China in a centralist administration. When the Communists took control of China, they installed a centralized Communist system across all the country's institutions: politics, media, culture, education, law and legislation, judicial system, and the economy. The same organizational form was used in all areas and organizations.

But not only Communist organizational structures were comparable to what China had known in former times; the Communists also adopted other influences from Confucian tradition, for instance, the concept of the Confucian role model was replaced by the Communist role model.

In the past, Chinese Communists tried to erase traditional Chinese culture; today they are promoting it again. A revival of Chinese traditions has become more and more apparent over the last decades. Under the influence of communism, society in Mainland China was thoroughly changed, and although the Communist heyday may be over and Chinese Communist Party ideologies adapted to contemporary evolutions, communism continues to influence many aspects of life and business life in China.

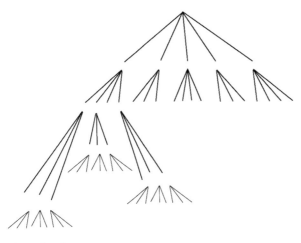

Centralist Structure

3.2 The Chinese Communist Party

3.2.1 The Chinese Communist Party in Control

Since 1949, China has been under the control of the Chinese Communist Party (CCP).[2] Until 1978, Communist ideology dominated Chinese society to extremes. Today the CCP remains in power and Communist structures continue to dominate many aspects of life in China. The Communist ideology, the Thoughts of Mao Zedong, The Reforms of Deng Xiaoping are taught in schools. The CCP recruits new members nation-wide via the Youth League, which is present in all schools and universities.

The CCP decides on all policies in China. The Chinese government and its ministries execute these policies and thereby follow the leadership of the CCP. The CCP has a hierarchical centralist structure: central (national), provincial, and local (several levels). It has branches down to the very lowest level of society in basic units of enterprises, rural areas, government departments, schools, scientific research institutes, communities, mass organizations, companies of the People's Liberation Army and other basic units.[3] The provincial level follows the central level; the local levels follow the provincial level. Next to the CCP there are eight 'democratic' political parties in China. They belong to the so-called United Front led by the CCP and their influence is limited to an advisory function.

3.2.2 Democratic Centralism

The CCP works according to the principle of democratic centralism. This means that all party members can participate in and contribute to the debate before the leadership decides on its view. Once a decision has been taken, everyone has to follow the CCP line.

The Hall of the People on Tiananmen Square where the Chinese Government holds Congresses

During Mao's reign, he alone decided everything and led the debate at the highest level. During the Reform, Deng Xiaoping launched the 'Four Cardinal Principles' (*si xiang jiben yuanze*). One principle to be adhered to was the maintenance of the leadership of the CCP. The principle of democratic centralism was maintained. Opposition to the party was labeled as 'bourgeois liberalism' (*zichan jieji ziyou zhuyi*), especially between 1986 and 1989. In July 1990, the People's Daily (*Renmin ribao*), the official newspaper

The Party is founded for the interest of the People (Li dang wei gong)

of the CCP, published an editorial that denounced 'bourgeois liberalism' once more. It stated that democratic centralism was necessary, that the CCP must implement centralism on the basis of democracy and that democracy must have the guidance of the centralist leadership.

3.2.3 Committees and Commissions of the CCP

- The National Congress of the CCP is held every five years. Each congress elects its own Central Committee that gathers in plenary sessions or Plenums. In a Plenum the most important decisions of the People's Republic of China are taken.

- The Central Committee of the CCP is the highest authority of the Party. The Central Committee includes the leading figures of the Party, the state and the army. The first Plenum of the Central Committee of the CCP is held immediately after the elections. In this Plenum the Political bureau or Politburo is elected.

- The Politburo is the executive organ of the Central Committee and is responsible for policy in between meetings of the Central Committee.

- The Central Committee also elects the Standing Committee of the Politburo. It is the most influential organ in China.

- The Central Committee has a secretariat led by a Secretary-General that looks after the permanent administration.

- Apart from the Central Committee of the CCP, other organs are the Central Military Commission (CMC) of the Central Committee, which supervises the link between the party and the army and the Commission for Inspection and Discipline, which observes internal control in the Party.

In 2008, Hu Jintao occupies the three highest functions in the People's Republic of China: President of the People's Republic, Secretary-General, and Head of the Military Commission.[4]

3.2.4 Work Unit

When Mao Zedong announced the establishment of the People's Republic of China in 1949, a period of profound change began in Chinese society. Socialism was introduced in different stages. While in pre-Communist China the family was the basic unit, the work unit became the basic unit in Communist society. The work unit or *danwei* controls the life of each individual belonging to it. Social control within the work unit was virtually total.

The work unit was responsible for:
- Management of household registration (people were registered in the place where they lived);
- Food;
- Medical care;
- Housing;
- Ideological education;
- Safety;
- Marriage and divorce;
- Family planning;
- Entrance to the CCP – Youth League;
- Entrance to the CCP;
- Reward for good behavior;
- Disciplinary actions.

The work unit

The architecture of a work unit was an inwardly directed walled complex. Offices, houses, schools, factories, and so on, were all located within the walls, separated from the outside world. Guarded gates in four directions gave entrance to the complex.

A person not only worked in a work unit, he also lived in it, his children went to school in the work unit, and when he got sick, he would go to the hospital of the work unit. When people wanted to get married or wanted to have a child, they needed authorization from the work unit. To change to another work unit one also needed authorization. The authorities of the work unit kept a personal file (*dang an*) on each member.

There are similarities between the group-oriented family system headed by a patriarch and the enormous impact on each individual in former times, and the Communist work unit headed by the CCP. The life of each individual was subject to the importance of the group. Personal ambition was not valued highly when it was not linked to general interests. No one should stand out from the group. One's personal intellect and competence were subject to social position. The concept of privacy has never existed in China. Nowadays, as more and more people have their own private house, this is slowly changing. Private space is new in China, and it will have consequences for society.

In Communist society during Mao Zedong's reign, the CCP had representations everywhere down to the very lowest levels of society. This assured that policies were executed in all regions and at all levels. Even at the lowest level, at every corner of the street, there was a control mechanism in place. In today's China this is still the case to a certain extent. It is more obvious in the North of China than in the South. In small streets you can still see people with a red cotton bandage on their sleeve with the characters 'Neighborhood Inspection'. In apartment buildings, someone sits in the elevator going up and down all day. In government buildings, hotels, etc, there is someone at the reception as well as people on every floor of the building. In trains you have a *fuwuyuan*, a service provider in every carriage. At the gates of schools, residential compounds, villa areas, army units, industrial parks, a gatekeeper will control each person entering.

The concept of the Communist work unit remained intact until China opened its doors. Changes in the work unit started to take place along with the reforms. It was not an overnight change, but a transitional process developing over the decades and still continuing today.

Communist Cinema Architecture

3.3 From Confucian to Communist Role Model

"What the Communists had drawn from Confucian heritage was to encourage the emulation of models. The best way to inculcate any behavior is to select a model for emulation." [5]
Qu Sanqiang

As we have seen in the chapter on Confucianism, the Chinese attach a lot of importance to the role model, setting a good example. If the ruler and the literati display the right conduct, the whole of society will be in order. In Mao's revolutionary China, the role model continued to play a crucial role, but the Confucian noble person no longer inspired it. Mao glorified the 'revolutionary hero'. Legendary heroes like Lei Feng, an exemplary soldier in the People's Liberation Army who devoted himself to Mao and offered his life for the revolution, were set up as role models. In 1963, Mao started the campaign 'Learn from Comrade Lei Feng'.

Various media inform us of the fact that the concept of the role model in Communist tradition is still alive in today's China. In 2004 the Chinese government issued a number of measurements. The state administration of Radio, Film, and Television issued thirty standards for TV spokesmen: no extravagant clothing, no extravagant hairstyle, not too naked. Their language also had to be correct: the use of English words, Hong Kong or Taiwan expressions were to be avoided.

In spite of the fact that China still claims to be Communist, China's role models today may not necessarily reflect Communist values.

In 2005 an article in the *LA Times* bore the following headline: 'Working-Class Hero? NBA Star Nets China's Proletarian Award'. World famous Chinese basketball player Yao Ming was elected as model worker of the year. The article states: "Even Yao, who has a four-year contract with the Rockets worth $17.8 million, was surprised: 'Before, I thought model workers only recognized ordinary people who worked tirelessly and without asking for anything in return. Now the award also includes someone like me, a special kind of migrant worker. That's a sign of progress'." [6]

Whether this is a sign of progress for Communist China remains a question, but the fact that China chooses a person like Yao Ming as a model worker reveals the country's aspirations to have an international face.

In 2007 Fang Yonggang was promoted as a role model by the Communist Party Working Committee in Dalian: "We should earnestly organize party members, officials and people who live in this neighborhood to study the advanced achievements of Comrade Fang Yonggang ... We should learn from Fang's spirit of studying party doctrine and exploring the truth". President Hu Jintao personally endorsed the campaign by visiting the ailing Fang in hospital and, in a front-page article in the official People's Daily newspaper on April 6, urged party members and soldiers to "learn from Fang Yonggang".[7]

Today, the concept of the role model still plays an important role in Chinese society. The teacher is the model for students, the best student is the model for other students, the best worker in the factory is the model for other workers, and the manager is the model for employees and workers. Sometimes photographs are displayed with an explanation of the merits of a role model. In train stations or restaurants you can see billboards with photographs and articles of praise about the organization, or photographs of people in the presence of important political personae.

It's not always easy being appointed as a role model. Social pressure rises and those chosen as role models stand out from the group and become an easy target for criticism. The Chinese sometimes claim, with a smile, that they like to be second in rank; they don't have the pressure of being the role model, while still being one of the best.

When Chinese people consider someone from the business or political world as virtuous and competent, they will show honor and loyalty, cooperate with him and do their best to fulfill his wishes.

Not only people but organizations also function as role models. During the first decades of communism, factories and communes served as role models. Daqing was a model commune: 'We all learn from Daqing', the slogan sounded.

Today the government issues awards at different levels to companies that are considered to do a good job, and even multinational companies are set up as role models.

3.4 From Planned Economy towards Market Economy

3.4.1 Planned Economy

To understand the forces in the Chinese economy today, we need to look at where China started off when the country opened its doors.

Chinese companies that existed before 1949 were often family businesses, ruled by the Confucian inspired hierarchical system of the family with the patriarch at the top. The fortune these businesses built up was the family fortune. In Taiwan, Hong Kong and the overseas territories this is still often the case. In Mainland China, the hierarchical organization of corporate businesses changed under the influence of Communist structures.

After 1949, China adopted the system of the centrally planned economy. The state controlled production and distribution of all commodities. The state decided what needed to be produced and it decided the price and distribution. Gradually the

Communist Architecture: Everyone has the same house

system of work units and communes was implemented all over China. This led to extreme collectivization controlled by central government. The life of each individual was totally controlled and dominated by the Communist system.

Corporate life came under the full control of central government. All enterprises and organizations were owned by central government and their management controlled by it. That management was based on goals according to a macroeconomic national plan. The organization of companies was strongly inspired by the principle of centralism. Enterprises were hierarchical pyramids and the government decided on production quotas. The enterprise itself had no ambition to make extra profit, to work more efficiently, or to minimize losses, because everything was for the benefit of the state.

Unemployment did not exist. Everyone had some kind of employment. Very often, far more personnel were employed than was necessary for efficient production. Wages in different jobs did not vary much: the salary of a doctor or university professor was not much higher than that of a factory worker. Wages could be kept low because the government provided all the daily necessities, like housing, energy, hospitals, and so on for free. Housing was limited; everyone lived in the same style of accommodation without much luxury.

Everything was centrally planned. This resulted in situations like, for example, when the government decided that the heating should not be turned on before the first of October, even if it froze outside. The first of October signaled the start of the cold season and all the shops suddenly only provided winter clothing. On the first of May, the warm

In Maoist times there was no room for diversity in society

More room for individual expression in society today

season started, and from then on shops provided only summer clothing. Energy and water supplies were provided free by the government, which led to a nonchalant attitude towards the usage of water and energy, like leaving taps running and lights on unnecessarily.

Photographs from Communist times show the absence of diversity in society. The whole Chinese population wore Mao suits in blue, green or grey. Everyone had the same hairstyle, rode the same bicycle, lived in the same uniform housing blocks. Every family strove for the same 'three essential things': a watch, a bicycle, and a sewing machine.

After China's opening up, 'three new essentials' became a washing machine, a television, and a refrigerator, or the goal was to purchase the six 'big things': video recorder, television, washing machine, camera, refrigerator and electric fan.

3.4.2 Towards a Socialist Market Economy after 1978

The so-called 'socialist market economy' or 'market economy with Chinese characteristics' that China implemented after 1978 was a shift from totalitarian communism to a more decentralized, but still to some extent centralized system. The term 'socialist market economy' refers to the control and involvement of politics and the CCP in the market economy. Corporate cultures and businesses in China today are not totally exempt from political involvement. The Chinese government keeps control over areas it thinks crucial for assuring the central authority remains in place, for example, energy supplies or telecommunications. Political involvement in corporate culture to the extent it exists in China is something Western companies are not used to. It influences decision-making, issuance of licenses, and so on.

3.4.3 Legacy of Planned Economy and Innovation in Contemporary Corporate Culture

International cooperation with China today is very different depending on the kind of organization or company (State Owned Enterprise, Joint Venture, Chinese Private company, Wholly Foreign Owned Enterprise), and on the region (stage and level of development). The development of the Chinese economy is moving rapidly but in many places it is still in a transitional stage. Several characteristics of the Chinese business environment belong to the legacy of the planned economy.

In the planned economy and homogenous society before 1978, the most important requirement was that all people in China were provided with the daily necessities. The egalitarian society did not ask for high quality or new products. People grew up in a climate where utilities broke down continuously. The result was an attitude of 'throwing away', implying lack of respect for products, but also lack of insight into production processes. Innovation and high productivity were not the first priority. In such an environment it was difficult to become acquainted with the concept of 'good quality'. With China's opening up to the outside world, this challenge grew.

The policy of employment for all in pre-1978 Communist China led to overstaffing. Overstaffing led to low productivity and did not create a challenging atmosphere. In contemporary China, we sometimes see the remnants of this policy. Many state-owned entities employ too many personnel for the work that needs to be done. Many employees have full-time jobs for work that in reality only takes a few hours a day.

Bainaohui Shanghai: huge shopping mall for electronics

Sometimes jobs seem to be invented to provide employment opportunities. Since 1984, remuneration is linked to job performance resulting in higher productivity.

To a certain extent the complex bureaucracy of former years still exists but the situation has improved considerably and transparency has risen. Professor Zhu Yunxia, analyzing the changes in business communication after the reforms, sees a move from hierarchical communication towards communication on an equal level.[8] Today, business communication is no longer solely a matter of ordering and providing. Rather it is directed towards commercial motives. We will deal with that in the chapter on Commercial China.

Multinationals in China impose their global corporate culture. We see a trend towards a more procedural culture with the systemization of rules and regulations, job analysis, performance targets, goal setting, reward and disciplinary procedures.

With its accession to the WTO, China accepted to live up to international standards. Transparent accounting and a well functioning financial system according to international standards was part of that. China has made huge improvements on this score, but it remains an issue for attention.

Sometimes the Chinese lack an understanding of research, development and production costs, and of the concept of Intellectual Property. The concept of Intellectual Property as it is internationally understood, on which we will elaborate later, was absent in Communist times. People tended to deal with prices without taking costs of development, production, transport, energy, infrastructure, or wages into account. Customer services or After Sales services did not exist in the planned economy. Today more and more companies are aware of the importance of this. Corporate culture evolves towards more operational excellence with a focus on productivity improvement, improvement of customer services, and the application of quality norms like ISO 9000. Quality is still a problem for some products, but the situation has improved spectacularly, up to the point that China produces high quality products. China has also created its own quality labels. More and more we see a development towards the installation of national and international research and development centers in China. It took a few decades before the country was ready for this, but today evolution towards innovation is taking place rapidly.

Chinese Quality Label

[1] Loewenstein, J., *Marx against Marxism*, Routledge & Kegan Paul, 1970, London, p 178 quoted in Qu Sanqiang, *Copyright in China*, Foreign Language Press, Beijing, 2002, p 31

[2] More information on history, structure and principles of the Communist Party in China: http://english.cpc.people.com.cn/66739/4496616.html

[3] Primary organizations of the Party: http://english.cpc.people.com.cn/66739/4496616.html

[4] Listing of highest ranking CCP members and general program of the Party Constitution adopted in November 2002: http://english.cpc.people.com.cn/65732/4446148.html

[5] Qu Sanqiang, *Copyright in China*, Foreign Language Press, Beijing, 2002, p 32

[6] *LA Times*, 28 April 2005

[7] *Washington Post*, 25 May 2007

[8] http://immi.se/intercultural/nr3/zhu.htm Business Writing in Mainland China: A Look at the Developments of Sales Genres. See also: Zhu Yunxia, *Business Communication in China*, New York, Nova Science Publishers Inc. 1999

4 Contemporary China

4 Contemporary China

4.1 Introduction

After 1978, opening up, pluralization, and decentralization of the totalitarian centralist Communist system took place in many areas like finance, education, media, state-owned enterprises, and social security. In this chapter on contemporary China we will focus on decentralization in a number of areas to show what happened in Chinese society during the last few decades. We will take a look at politics, media, education, and society in general.

But before we move to the evolutions in contemporary Chinese society and the decentralization of the Communist system we will take a look at contemporary Chinese history. Many scholars claim that the evolutions in Chinese society after the opening up in 1978 are a continuation of what happened in the beginning of the twentieth century. The intellectual emancipation that took place over the last decennia can be interpreted as a further development of the emancipation movement at the end of the Chinese Empire and the beginning of the Chinese Republic. Chinese people attach a lot of importance to history and have a high historical consciousness. To have an understanding of recent Chinese history will help people to interpret contemporary evolutions in a wider context.

4.2 History

4.2.1 Contemporary History: Introduction

For thousands of years, the Chinese have described their history as a continuation of cycles; one dynasty came to an end, the next one followed, consolidated, reached a height and declined again. Each dynasty wrote the history of the former, legitimizing its own power. The cyclical vision on Chinese history is still applicable today. The Chinese Empire started to decline with the Opium War in 1840 and came to an end in 1911 when the Republic of China was established. Wars and civil wars within China went on from the middle of the nineteenth century until the middle of the twentieth century.

In 1949 Mao Zedong succeeded in bringing all of China under the control of the Communists. He 'centralized' China again after a 'century of humiliation' (*chiru de bainian*) by the West, giving rise to the start of a new age, a 'New Dynasty'. In 1978 the cycle started to move upward, China was on its way to a new glorious period. As the Chinese say: "Mao Zedong made the Chinese people stand up again, and Deng Xiaoping has made them rich".

In this chapter we focus on the changes China went through socially and intellectually at the end of the former cycle and the beginning of the current one taking place today. We will try to understand the characteristics of Chinese society from the perspective of recent history.

4.2.2 The Last Imperial Dynasty: Qing (1644–1912)

4.2.2.1 Political Evolutions

The Chinese Empire that was established in 221 BC knew a continuation of many strong dynasties, Han, Sui, Tang, Song, Yuan, Ming, and finally came to an end with the Qing dynasty.

In 1644 the Manchu gained control over China and established the last Imperial dynasty, the Qing. They took over the structure of central and local governments of the previous dynasty. The Confucian state exam system, which had existed since the Han (221 BC–208 AD), continued to be used. Emperors Kang Xi (1662–1723) and Qian Long (1736–1796) were powerful and successful.

Westerners like the Jesuits Adam Schall and Ferdinand Verbiest brought Western knowledge to Beijing. Trade delegations tried to negotiate trading contracts with China, but were not very successful. The Chinese were very proud and superiority feelings towards the West were strong.

From 1800 onwards the Qing started to fall apart. The government restricted trade. Opium smuggling started. In 1839 the seizure and destruction of a stock of opium in Canton by Lin Zexu, a commissioner sent by the Chinese government, gave rise to the Opium War between China and the British Empire in 1840, which China lost. In 1842, the Treaty of Nanjing was signed between China and Great Britain, stating that Hong Kong was to become a British colony, that a number of Treaty Ports had to be opened to foreign trade (Shanghai, Canton, Fuzhou, Ningbo and Xiamen), that low import taxes had to be introduced and foreign consuls had to be allowed in China. The Treaty Ports became centers of foreign influence, especially Shanghai. Foreigners were concentrated in concession areas over which they held full power.

After the Opium War, the Qing dynasty was further weakened by a continuation of national revolts and international wars. Throughout the nineteenth century, one conflict followed another, slowly bringing an end to the Chinese Empire.

In 1894 the Chinese-Japanese war broke out. China lost and consequently Formosa (Taiwan) fell into Japanese hands. After 1895 the 'Mad Scramble for Concessions' started: different nations tried to colonize parts of China. Russia occupied Manchuria, Germany the Shandong province, France the south of Yunnan Province, England the Yangzi area. China was defeated once again in the 1900 Boxer Rebellion, an anti-Western movement supported by the Imperial Chinese court.

Around the turn of the century, Chinese intellectuals looked for ways out. They saw the weakness of the Chinese army as the main reason for continuous military defeats. A military reform with Western weapons and a naval fleet after the European model ensued. China realized it had to develop in new directions to be able to resist against the West.

At the same time, nationalism arose under the leadership of Sun Yat-sen (*Sun Zhongshan*). He established the Revolutionary League, which in 1911 turned into the Nationalist Party (*Guomindang*). In reality it was an amalgam of small political groups. In 1911 the Chinese Empire came to an end and the Chinese Republic was established with Sun Yat-sen as its first president.

4.2.2.2 Cultural Climate during the Qing Dynasty

For almost two thousand years there had been some kind of continuation of tradition, partly due to the Confucian exam system and the related Confucian scholarly culture. All scholars had the same educational background and were educated in the same classics. The Confucian exam system that had dominated Chinese culture for two thousand years was abolished in 1905 and a new education system, based on the Western model, was implemented in China.

Throughout the centuries, during periods of decentralization or dominance by foreign cultures, Chinese culture assimilated foreign cultural influences. At the end of the Qing dynasty, the West had strong influence over developments in Chinese culture. Chinese intellectuals felt the need for change. Study societies and political parties were created. Newspapers and magazines began to emerge in China. That the country was in sore need of a media to inform the people and to spread new ideas is illustrated in the following quote by John Henry Gray in 1878: "There is no important country in the world in which the liberty of press is so little recognized as in China. The ignorance, in which the people are kept with regard to passing events, whether of a trifling or a serious character, is surprising. Until quite recently there was nothing in the shape of a Chinese newspaper throughout the length and breadth of the land, except the *Peking Gazette* – now published daily – which is the official organ of a corrupt government."[1]

The Shanghai Newspaper *Shenbao* from the British businessman Frederik Major was pioneered in 1872.[2] It was the first newspaper in colloquial Chinese. Until that time, classical Chinese had been the dominant language in all official documents and literature.

In 1895 Liang Qichao established the magazine 'Become Stronger' (*Qiangxue bao*) as the organ of the reform-minded Party of Kang Youwei's Study Society for Self-Strengthening (*Qiangxue hui*), and in 1896 he established the magazine 'Contemporary Themes' (*Shiwu bao*). By 1906 China had 239 magazines. These magazines were the sign and vehicle of political, social and intellectual changes.

In spite of the drastic changes Chinese society underwent in the twentieth century, the Confucian-Daoist tradition survives until today.

4.2.3 The Republic of China (1911–1949)

4.2.3.1 Political Evolutions

The first president of the Chinese Republic, Sun Yat-sen promoted the 'Three Principles of the People' (*san min zhuyi*): the 'Principle of Nationalism' (liberation from foreign domination), the 'Principle of Power of the People' (gradual introduction of democracy in different stages: military dictatorship – gradual democratization – complete democratization), and the 'Principle of Welfare of the People' (social-economic program of the Party).

In 1925 Sun Yat-sen died. Chiang Kai-shek (*Jiang Jieshi*) took over the leadership of the Nationalist Party. He started his Northern Expedition against the warlords who had claimed regional power and within nine months he had half of China under his control.

Chiang Kai-shek also fought the Chinese Communist Party (CCP) that had been established in 1921 by a number of intellectuals like Chen Duxiu and Mao Zedong as an alternative to the Nationalist Party. In 1926 Chiang Kai-shek restricted CCP members from taking part in the Chinese leadership. In 1927 he attacked the CCP from Shanghai and established an anti-CCP government in Nanjing. By 1928 Chiang Kai-shek claimed to have all of China under his control. The government in Nanjing received almost immediate international recognition.

At the same time, the Communists organized an agrarian revolt in Hunan under the leadership of Mao Zedong. By 1927 several Communist enclaves had formed in remote areas. In 1931 the Communists united in Jiangxi, which became the basis of agrarian communism. Surrounded by the Nationalists in 1934, the Communists decided to retreat strategically. They began the Long March from Jiangxi towards the north, through the remote areas of six provinces, in total a distance of 10,000 kilometers. On the way they got hold of weapons from warlords and recruited new members among farmers. Due to continuous attacks by Chiang Kai-shek's armies, and to famine and cold in remote areas, only 20,000 of the 90,000 people who started the Long March survived. During this Long March, the leadership of Mao

Zedong, politically as well as ideologically, was established. In 1935 the Communists retreated to the mountains in Yan'an in the Shaanxi province. Until 1948, Yan'an remained the center of Chinese communism.

The conflict between the Communists and Nationalists temporarily came to a halt at the outbreak of World War II. In 1937 the Chinese-Japanese war broke out as a reaction to the occupation of Chinese areas by Japan since 1931. This was the beginning of World War II in China. During a short period between 1937 and 1945, the Communists and the Nationalists joined forces in the 'United Front' in order to resist Japanese aggression. As soon as the war came to an end, both parties started to fight each other again.

The Communists had developed successful guerrilla tactics and in 1949 they succeeded in gaining control over the whole of China. On 1 October 1949 Mao Zedong established the People's Republic of China. Chiang Kai-shek fled to Taiwan with two million Chinese and established a Chinese government in exile. Even today, Taiwan calls itself the Republic of China (ROC) and continues to use the Nationalist flag.

4.2.3.2 Cultural Climate during the Republic of China

The fascination for the West, which was very strong around the turn of the twentieth century, should be analyzed within the context of changes occurring at the time within Chinese society and politics. It was not about blindly copying Western ideas, and substituting everything Chinese with Western values. Rather, it was an active search by Chinese intellectuals for reform. The introduction of Western science (Darwin, Newton) replaced the traditional Confucian-Daoist cosmology that taught that socio-political phenomena and natural cosmic patterns are linked in a process of interdependent causation.[3]

The reform movements started at the end of the nineteenth century, continued after the establishment of the People's Republic. In 1915 Chen Duxiu, who was later to become one of the founders of the CCP, established the magazine 'Youth', later renamed as 'New Youth' (*Xin qingnian*) also carrying the French name La Jeunesse.[4]

In 1916 Hu Shi, a Chinese thinker and writer who had studied in America promoted the Eight Point Program for the reform of literature in a letter to Chen Duxiu. Following this, Chen Duxiu published an article in 'New Youth' with the title 'About Literary Revolution'. This was the beginning of the replacement of classical Chinese (*wenyan*) by colloquial Chinese (*baihua*). The use of colloquial Chinese instead of classical Chinese shows the emergence of intellectual movements in China far removed from the traditional literati culture. It was part of the democratizing process of Chinese society. Surprisingly quickly, the government supported this movement; already in 1920 the use of colloquial Chinese was introduced in the educational system.

Western influences came from different angles. Western literature, theories, scientific treatises, the Enlightenment thinkers were all systematically translated into Chinese. Chinese students studied abroad and brought back knowledge and information. The Sinocentric worldview was abandoned and the direction of New Learning (*xin xue*) inspired by Western Enlightenment was adopted.

The scholar Cai Yuanpei, who was educated at the traditional Confucian Hanlin Academy (*Hanlin Yuan*) where generations of elite Confucian scholars had been raised over the centuries, and who had also studied in Leipzig, reorganized Beijing University from 1916. He employed Western scholars and organized courses in European literature, history, science and philosophy. Cai Yuanpei devoted his life to education, the development of museums, libraries, galleries, exhibitions, literature and drama as essential elements in the development of a new China.

Yan Fu, a Chinese scholar who had studied in England, translated Darwin's work on natural selection and survival of the fittest into Chinese at the end of the nineteenth century. He also translated Thomas Huxley's 'Evolution and Ethics', Adam Smith's 'Wealth of Nations', and John Stuart Mill's 'On Liberty'. Lin Shu translated European fiction.

Zhou Zuoren, better known as Lu Xun, translated Russian literature into Chinese. Most influential were Liang Qichao and Wang Guowei. Liang Qichao was convinced of the fact that the introduction of political literature was a must for reform. To establish a new nation and to promote a new moral, a new kind of literature was needed. Wang Guowei studied Kant, Nietzsche, and Schopenhauer and tried to find inspiration in this for a new Chinese literary tradition.

Western literature by Miguel de Cervantes, Daniel Defoe, Charles Dickens, Walter Scott, Lord Byron, Shelly, Keats, Goethe, Ibsen, Victor Hugo, and so on, was introduced in China. All kinds of 'isms' were introduced in Chinese literature and art (Realism, Naturalism, Romanticism), but also in the socio-political field (Socialism, Anarchism, Marxism, Humanism), together with the concepts of democracy and science.

The introduction of scientific method shed new light on Chinese history and placed China and Chinese culture in a global context. Kang Youwei and other intellectuals felt free to incorporate traditional constructs of speculative reason into scientific approach. Yan Fu believed in science based on a methodology of verification. Economic development, and science and technology were seen as valuable for the building of a nationalist and independent state power.

Despite these emancipation movements, the introduction of science and technology, political and social movements in Chinese society, traditional values were not completely abandoned. The traditional view of Confucian and Daoist processes underlying nature, implying that the human being and his consciousness embody the same forces that move the cosmos, was evaluated against the Western concept of the physical model of the universe, implying that human beings are biological and social organisms. Intellectuals in the neo-traditionalist movement tried to explain the relationship between the essential traditional values and contemporary cultural expressions. Between 1898 and the May Fourth Movement (*wu si yundong*) in 1919, different currents of strategies to adapt Confucianism and the classical heritage to modern conditions can be seen.

Some scholars searched for 'National Essence' (*guo cui*). They explored the origins and development of national traditions from archaic roots in land, race and culture and made history serve nationalist ideology. Liang Qichao focused on 'National Character' (*guo xing*), a social morality to be found in unique Chinese norms of interpersonal relations and spiritual self-cultivation. A third trend focused on the central spiritual symbols of Confucianism as a kind of state cult or doctrine.

On 4 May 1919, students of Beijing University protested against the Treaty of Versailles wherein the victors of World War I planned to hand over German rights in Shandong to Japan (Japan had already occupied Shandong since the beginning of the war). An anti-Japan boycott was launched. Consequently China did not sign the Treaty. The 'May Fourth Movement' became symbolic of the intellectual emancipation movement China was going through. The intellectual climate that gave rise to the 'May Fourth Movement' became known as the 'New Culture Movement' (*Xin Wenhua Yundong*). It can be seen as an attack against traditional moral and social order. The New Culture was to establish 'science and democracy'.

4.2.4 People's Republic of China

4.2.4.1 The People's Republic of China: 1949–1978

4.2.4.1.1 1949–1978: Political Evolutions

In the People's Republic of China, after more than a century of political unrest, Mao Zedong brought stability and peace. Once again China went through a period of drastic change, ideologically, politically, socially, and culturally. All attention went to the farmers, workers, and soldiers under the leadership of the Communist Party. The period of Mao's reign in China is divided into the '17 years' (1949–1966) and the 'Cultural Revolution' (1966–1976).

Tiananmen Gate

Following the establishment of the People's Republic, China became socialist in every aspect of political, economic and social system. In the countryside, communes were set up with a radical form of socialization in which all economic and individual life was collective. Light industry was integrated into the people's communes. Heavy industry was reformed after the Russian model. Urban reform organized people in 'committees', which among others also had a political function. Collective institutions like kitchens, kindergartens, etc, were set up.

Mao Zedong translated his socialist ideological principles into new rules for interaction between the people, and between the people and the Party. Party members had to be free from any ties with former regimes. They were obliged to take part in agricultural or industrial work to learn ideological lessons, or they were sent to Yan'an for socialist training.

Party members had to be in close contact with the people and had to report the ideas from the masses. Those ideas were analyzed, then mixed with Communist ideas and sent back to the masses to be brought into practice. This endless process was called the permanent revolution.

Farmers and workers were brought to schools to teach. Students, artists, and writers worked in agriculture and in industry in order to remain in contact with the masses.

The marriage law was introduced, stipulating that men and women were equal. The free choice of partner was allowed, alimony had to be paid in case of divorce, and women were allowed to have their own income. Polygamy and child marriages were forbidden.

Between 1953 and 1957, China maintained good relations with the USSR. Many features of the Soviet Model were implemented in China. The Soviet Union helped China with the socialist transformation. The army was professionalized and had to self-support all its living needs. Bureaucracy was centralized. The system of the work unit and neighborhood committees was implemented. Autonomous regions were appointed for ethnic minorities.

In 1957 Mao Zedong organized the Hundred Flowers Campaign: "Let a hundred flowers bloom, let a hundred schools contend" (*bai hua qifang, bai jia zhengming*). Intellectuals were invited to take a critical stand towards the political evolutions. Mao's original idea was a constructive one. Unfortunately, when the Communist Party received too much criticism Mao changed his stance. The critics in the Hundred Flower Campaign were attacked under the Anti-Rightist Campaign (*fan you pai douzheng*) that followed, which labeled them as 'Rightist' (*you pai*).

In 1958, the Great Leap Forward Campaign (*Da yue jin*) was launched. It aimed to transform China's primarily agrarian economy into a modern, industrialized Communist society. The entire Chinese population was engaged in iron melting activities. Agricultural production failed due to several reasons. As a result, millions of people died from starvation.

As a consequence of the Great Leap Forward, relations with the Soviet Union became troubled. Opposite tendencies arose within the CCP. Zhou Enlai and Peng Dehuai criticized the Great Leap Forward. Consequently at the Lushan Conference Peng Dehuai was replaced by Lin Biao. Zhou Enlai stayed in position. Liu Shaoqi and Deng Xiaoping, who wanted a return to the Soviet Model, came into conflict with Mao Zedong and were criticized for taking the capitalist road. In July 1966 both were removed from their Party posts. After the failure of the Great Leap Forward, a radicalization of views occurred.

In August 1966, Mao announced the Cultural Revolution. He called on the youth to turn against those who took the 'capitalist road' (*zou zi ben zhuyi daolu de dang quan pai*). Red Guards born after 1949 set out to put Mao's ideas into practice. They studied Mao's Thoughts and turned against anyone not living a proletarian life. A campaign was launched to extinguish the 'Four Olds' (*si jiu*): old customs, old culture, old habits, and old ideas. A period of destruction followed. People in authority were being criticized and became the target of aggression. Schools closed down. Ancient cultural treasures were damaged or destroyed. The Cultural Revolution turned China into chaos and anarchy. When things got out of hand, the army was called in to stop the Red Guards. In 1968 a new movement started, the 'Go to the Mountainous and Rural Areas' movement (*shang shan xia xiang*). Young people were sent to the countryside to spread Mao's ideas.

In 1972 friendly relations with the US were restored when Nixon visited China.

At the Fourth National People's Congress in 1975, Zhou Enlai formulated the 'Four Modernizations' that Deng Xiaoping would later implement in 1978.

In 1976 Zhou Enlai and Mao Zedong both died. Hua Guofeng followed Mao. After Mao's death the 'Gang of Four' (*si ren bang*), four people who were crucial in policy making during the Cultural Revolution among them Jiang Qing, Mao's wife, were arrested. They were blamed for all the mishaps of the Cultural Revolution; Mao Zedong was protected from severe criticism.

In 1977 Deng Xiaoping was restored to power. Politics were changing and the Cultural Revolution had come to an end.

4.2.4.1.2 1949–1978: Cultural Climate

After the establishment of the People's Republic of China, culture came under the all-encompassing control and censorship of the Party. The Party decided on what could and should be written or created; no room was left for personal expression or creativity. All artists were members of the artists' association, writers of the writers' association, filmmakers of the film association, and the Party controlled all the associations. Film production houses or media centers were official institutes governed by the CCP. Printed media, radio, film, literature, art, and later television, all became part of the big propaganda machine: the new socialist culture.

Campaigns for the ideological reform of intellectuals and artists were organized. Culture had to serve the people and the revolution. It was the task of culture to give a "representative image of the reality in socialist evolution and it had to educate the people in the spirit of socialism".

Subjects in art and literature were limited to land reform, collectivization, industrialization, war, and the education of the people. Farmers, workers and soldiers were the heroes. Traditional culture was considered feudal, modernist art was considered bourgeois and imperialist, and religious art was considered superstition. The campaign against the 'Four Olds' during the Cultural Revolution had to extinguish all traditions. It led to the destruction of cultural treasures and to the extreme restriction of cultural production. During the Cultural Revolution, culture and life in general were completely dominated by the deification of Mao Zedong.

4.2.4.2 The People's Republic of China: 1978–Today

4.2.4.2.1 Political Evolutions after 1978

In December 1978, Deng Xiaoping officially launched the 'Four Modernizations': agriculture, industry, science and technology, and national defense. Political reforms have taken place since then, but all within the Party. With the reforms, Hu Yaobang and Zhao Ziyang, two influential and very reform-minded Party members, appeared on the scene.

Agriculture underwent de-collectivization: farmers were allowed to produce for the market. Industry and trade became more autonomous. The price system was liberalized. Small private companies were allowed to exist. China opened the door for foreign investment and Special Economic Zones were created to attract foreign investment. Many Chinese went abroad to study.

The agricultural reform of 1979 was a great success. The reform of industry that started in 1984 was more problematic and resulted in an economic crisis from 1986–1987. Hu Yaobang was held responsible for the problems and he was removed from position. Deng Xiaoping took a more conservative view and Li Peng became premier. Inflation and corruption rose to new high levels in 1988. The death of Hu Yaobang, who had become a symbol for modernization in China, on 15 May 1989, became the catalyst for the social movements that followed. When Gorbatsjov visited China in June, a number of students went on hunger strike on Tiananmen Square to protest against corruption and to demand more freedom of speech. Zhao Ziyang visited the students on Tiananmen Square to show his support. This act revealed the internal frictions within the Party. By showing his support to the protestors, Zhao Ziyang made an anti-policy statement. Until his death in 2005 he was blamed for this and when he died, he did not receive an official state funeral.

On 4 June 1989, the army was called in to put a stop to the demonstrations on Tiananmen Square; a bloody suppression followed. This happened during the visit of Gorbatsjov with the whole international media there to report it. China lost face to an extreme extent and it would take years, if not decades to overcome this.

After the Tiananmen suppression in 1989, a period of stagnation followed. Many countries froze their business contacts with China. In 1992 Deng Xiaoping gave a new impulse to the economy. He traveled to Shanghai and the Special Economic Zone in Shenzhen. During his trip, Deng gave speeches with a clear message to China: "To become rich is glorious", "to be more brave with reform". The slogans of this trip are paraphrased until today. Deng's trip had the desired effect. The economy received a new impulse. Many international companies have set up businesses in

Calligraphy Deng Xiaoping "Bring Good Fortune to Generation upon Generation"

China since 1993 and 1994. On 11 December 2001, China became a member of the World Trade Organization.

In 2002 during the Sixteenth Party Congress, Hu Jintao followed Jiang Zemin, Deng's successor, as the new President of the People's Republic of China. During the congress, to leave his trace on the political history of China, Jiang Zemin introduced his 'Theory of the Three Representatives'. He introduced his three-point plan of which one point implied that from that moment on, not only 'farmers, workers, soldiers' could become members of the CCP, but also the 'capitalists'.

Since 2002 Hu Jintao has enhanced his authority and has taken a stronger stand. In 2006 he dismissed the mayor of Shanghai, Chen Liangyu, an ally of Hu Jintao's predecessor Jiang Zemin, for corruption. In 2007 during the Party congress, several influential Party members were replaced by favorites of Hu Jintao, among them Vice President of the Standing Committee, Zeng Qinghong, who owed his position to Jiang Zemin. By eliminating the influence of Jiang Zemin and putting his own people in strategic positions he strengthened his position.

4.2.4.2.2 Cultural Climate during the People's Republic of China after 1978

After the opening up in 1978, influences from outside China, from Hong Kong and Taiwan, and from many other places abroad spread over China. The Chinese were craving for information after the extreme Communist climate. The flood of information in the eighties resulted in discussions, but also gave an impulse to creativity. The cultural and artistic output of the eighties reflects the complexity and enormous changes taking place in Chinese society. Systematic translation of Western texts caused Western authors to flood the Chinese theoretical platform and to arouse intellectual discussion. Westerners like Heidegger, Wittgenstein, Barthes, Jameson, Weber, Husserl, Sartre, Nietzsche, Foucault, and Derrida dominated theoretical discourse. The complexity of different ideologies and influences, Western and Chinese, led to heavy discussions, the so-called *wenhuare*, or 'Cultural Fever'.

China was flooded with all kinds of foreign theories, philosophies, literature, music, and all kinds of other cultural forms. It was a period of recovering from a suppressed life where there had been no room for any kind of personal feeling or individualism. Heated debates were held in symposia and magazines. The period following the opening up in 1978 is often seen as a continuation of the emancipating evolutions at the beginning of the twentieth century. It is sometimes referred to as the 'second enlightenment', the May Fourth period being the 'first enlightenment' of China.

When remembering the time and atmosphere of the eighties, people who went through this period share similar voices. Chinese people were starved in many ways and after the opening up they did not know what to consume first.

The artist Xu Bing when explaining the creation of his now world famous work *Tianshu*, 'Book from the Sky', describes the artistic climate of the time:

"I began working on 'Book from the Sky' at a time when I was constantly in a very anxious and confused mood. This mood was related to the 'cultural fever' that was present at the time in China. Culturally, Chinese people were sometimes overfed and at other times underfed. For example, during the Cultural Revolution (1966–1976) the whole nation read only Chairman Mao's Red Book. After the Cultural Revolution ended, people were starved for culture and consumed everything available. During this time I read so much and participated in so many cultural activities that my mind was in a state of chaos. My psyche had been clogged with all sorts of random things. I felt uncomfortable, like a person suffering from starvation who had just gorged himself. It was at that point that I considered creating a book that would clean out these feelings."[5]

Artist Wang Jianwei describes the situation as follows: "the void left by age-long suppression was like a dry sponge, ready to soak up anything new... I crossed the centuries spanning Tolstoy and Duchamps, Botticelli and Borges in a single night."[6]

Scholar Zhang Xudong writes: "Incredible scope and idiosyncrasy marked this Cultural Fever. Around 1987, for example, the streets of Beijing were flooded with beautifully printed albums of artistic photographs of the human body, which were sold side by side with translations of a dazzling variety of modern Western classics, as if reading Wittgenstein were just another form of sensuous stimulation, and

Marcuse or Daniel Bell represented the same inspiration and restlessness symbolized by Madonna and Pepsi." [7]

Zhang Xudong analyzes the three main schools in the discussions of the Cultural Fever. The Futurologists promoted westernization in three steps: introduction of advanced technology, strengthening of democracy and legality, and the rapid reform of the economic system, which would affect Chinese culture.

The Culturalists wanted a resurrection of the ancient Confucian tradition. Zhang Xudong sees this trend not as merely traditionalist, but rather in relation both to the intellectual movements of the 1920s and the 1930s implying Confucianism and Chinese Marxism. The main goal in the search of the Culturalists was the compatibility of the Confucian tradition and Marxist thought.

The Hermeneutic school was a younger generation of scholars, all born after 1949 who took a more radical stand towards Chinese tradition. They focused on the *Geisteswissenschaft*, adopted Western theoretical discourses, and were consequently criticized as 'wholesale Westernizers'. [8]

Despite the liberalization of the climate, political campaigns continued to be organized. In 1983 the Campaign Against Spiritual Pollution (*jingsheng wuran*) wanted to keep out foreign decadent influences. Gao Xingjian, winner of the Nobel Prize for literature in 2000 was one of the people heavily criticized during this campaign. In 1987 the Campaign Against Bourgeois Liberalization (*zichan jieji ziyou zhuyi*) followed. These campaigns however didn't have the strength and impact of the past, partly due to the influence of reform minded Party members Hu Yaobang and Zhao Ziyang who had brought modernization to a point of no return.

In 1989, the deep discussions, flourishing cultural climate, and the decade long search for identity came to a halt. 1989 can be seen as a turning point in many ways. In the nineties when economic development took off again, the cultural climate was very different from the previous decade. China became more internationalized and commercialized. Money was the new god. Many Chinese became obsessed with money. Today the Chinese government tries to shift the fixation on money towards other values. Confucianism is actively promoted again in today's China.

Developments in Chinese society have matured. After the turbulence of the eighties and the extreme focus on money in the nineties, life in China has stabilized for many people. The extreme admiration for the West has shifted to a revaluation of Chinese things. In the eighties and the beginning of the nineties, the longing for a place of global significance made the Chinese admire many things Western. In the meantime, China has become richer and stronger and Chinese people have become more and more aware of their own country's strength.

We love our country – Tiananmen Square 1 October 2007

Nationalist feelings are growing stronger; a feeling of superiority from former times has been reinforced. Over the last decades it seems that nationalism has risen along with the economic boom. The Chinese government stimulates nationalistic feelings to keep the country together. Children's toys are decorated with the Chinese flag or show missiles being launched into space.

Nationalism is at stake in all issues China can be proud of: the launch of a spacecraft, the building of the biggest dam, the longest bridge, and the highest railway, and the country hosting the Olympic Games in 2008 and the World Exhibition in Shanghai in 2010. When in 2001 the news broke that the 2008 Olympic Games were assigned to Beijing, the whole country celebrated for days. The location from where the spacecraft was launched turned into a tourist destination overnight. And the image of President Hu Jintao personally seeing off Taikonaut Yang Liwei into space dominated the front-page of the People's Daily.

Chinese people who have become very successful abroad also help to constitute the face of China today. Chinese NBA basketball player Yao Ming has become a national symbol. Filmmaker Zhang Yimou was the first Chinese director ever to win an international prize at the international Film Festival in Berlin in 1987 with his film 'Red Sorghum'. He was criticized in China at the time for making movies for a Western audience. But today he has become a national symbol. He was even appointed to create the Chinese performance at the closing ceremony of the Olympic Games in Athens in 2004.[9]

The Olympic Games in Beijing are not only about sport. They are about the face of China and the whole Chinese nation is expected to contribute.

President Hu Jintao Seeing Taikonaut Yang Liwei off into space in 2003 on the front page of the People's Daily

In preparation for the Olympic Games, more than a hundred books are being published in China to prepare the population. In these publications, nationalism and patriotism are strongly promoted: 'The Olympic Spirit. A perfect unification of the Olympic Spirit and the Chinese Spirit. A Manual the whole nation must read to cultivate the Olympic Spirit' states: "All people love their motherland and are enthusiastically patriotic. Patriotism is the glorious banner inspiring the unity of all people. It is the spiritual force driving the people of our own nation to strong development. As children of the Yellow Emperor we should learn from the Olympic athletes to stimulate the patriotic feelings in our own heart. For the honor and glory of the nation we should prepare thoroughly. When the motherland needs it, we must contribute our own part, and not bring disgrace to this glorious age. This is our greatest goal. Therefore we raise the patriotic banner high and compose a beautiful patriotic poem." [10]

Nationalism focuses on the strength of the nation, the strength of Chinese culture, a culture going back five thousand years, a culture to be proud of, and this is referred to in anything China can be proud of today. Unfortunately, nationalism is also fed by 'anti' feelings, like anti-foreign occupation, anti-Japan, anti-Korea. More often than ten years ago, in today's China you hear 'In our country, we are', 'In our country, we do'. We hear references to the 'century of humiliation', which refers to the period between the Opium War and the establishment of the PRC during which Western powers invaded China. When the US bombed the Chinese Embassy in Belgrade in 1999, a spontaneous anti-American feeling swept over China. But the strongest target for 'anti' feelings is Japan. Anti-Japanese protest occurs regularly, and spontaneous outbursts of nationalism appear on the Internet.

Emblem of China

China is becoming stronger and it is very much aware of that. Evolutions in China have an influence on the whole globe.

4.3 Politics

4.3.1 Introduction

The political structure and the structure of the CCP are relevant topics for Westerners interacting with China and working in or with China, because the CCP has branches in all areas and levels of society. Political involvement exists to a greater extent in business than people in the West are used to. This results in complex organizational forms often lacking transparency in the eyes of many Westerners.

4.3.2 Chinese People's Political Consultative Conference (CPPCC)

The CPPCC was established in April 1948. The first plenary session was held in September 1949. During the first session, the decision was made to choose Beijing as the capital of China, to use the red flag with the yellow stars as the national flag, the national anthem was chosen and the decision was made to adopt the Gregorian calendar throughout China.

During this session the president, vice-president, the members of the central government, and the members of the first National Committee of the CPPCC were chosen. Mao Zedong became the first president of the National Committee of the CPPCC. He announced the establishment of the People's Republic of China on 1 October 1949.

The CPPCC is an organization of the United Front, an organ that looks after the cooperation between the different parties under the leadership of the CCP. The CPPCC includes members of the eight democratic parties, people without connection to the Party, representatives of the different People's organizations, representatives of ethnic minorities, people from Taiwan, Hong Kong, and Macau, returned overseas Chinese, invited individuals, and CCP members.

The CPPCC has no real power; it is a forum that is used by the CCP to consult the democratic parties. In practice it is the CCP who decides. In 1954 at the first meeting of the Second National Committee of the CPPCC the constitution of the People's Republic of China was approved.

4.3.3 Parties in the People's Republic of China

The CCP is the leading party in China, but it is not alone. In total there are nine: the Chinese Communist Party (CCP) and eight so-called democratic parties (*minzhu dangpai*). Only the CCP holds real power and decides on policy. The eight other parties are the Revolutionary Committee of the Chinese Nationalist Party, the China Democratic League, the China Democratic National Construction Association, the China Association for Promoting Democracy, the Chinese Peasants and Workers Democratic Party, the China Party for Public Interest, the September Third Society, and the Taiwan Democratic Self-Government League.

The eight democratic parties are not opposition parties. In 1948 they were invited to become part of the Chinese People's Political Consultative Conference (CPPCC). They take part in the United Front and follow the leadership of the CCP.[11]

There is a lot more freedom today in comparison to a few decennia ago and freedom of speech exists to some extent. Within the borders of constraint, diversity of opinion exists and fairly open discussions on social issues and policy are allowed. One sensitive issue remains the position of the CCP. Any criticism in that direction, whatever form it may take, is absolutely forbidden. The government is very much aware of the transitional period China is going through and the problems in Chinese society. To keep everything under control, it exercises censorship.

4.3.4 The State Structure Today

Setup Diagram of State Institutions of Central People's Government

National People's Congress

Standing Committee of the NPC

President of the People's Republic of China

State Council

Central Military Commission

Supreme People's Court

Supreme People's Procuratorate

4.3.4.1 National People's Congress (NPC)

The Chinese constitution stipulates that the power in the People's Republic is in the hands of the people. The organs through which the people can exercise power are the People's Congresses at different levels, with the National People's Congress at the highest level. The National People's Congress (NPC) replaced the former CPPCC. Voting in a democratic way elects the representatives of the local People's Congresses, on county and township level. All Chinese citizens older than eighteen have the right to vote and the right to be a candidate, independent of ethnic background, gender, profession, family background, religion, or education.

The representatives of the People's Congresses at provincial level, autonomous regions, municipalities directly under the central government, autonomous prefectures, and cities divided in districts, are appointed by the People's Congresses of the following lower level.

The NPC is the highest state organ. It can be compared to a Parliament. The members are elected for a period of five years. They gather once a year for two weeks. The plenary sessions receive a lot of attention in the media because this is the period during which work reports are presented and press conferences held, also for foreign reporters. Outside of the plenary sessions, the Standing Committee of the NPC is the executive organ.

The NPC adopts and amends the constitution and has supervision on its execution. It enacts and amends laws. It elects and recruits the leading figures of the highest state organs in China, including the president and vice-president, premier and other members of the State Council, president of the Supreme People's Court, and the procurator-general of the Supreme People's Procuratorate. It approves the National Plan of economic and social development and reports on the implementation. It examines and approves the state budget. It decides on all the important national issues.

The NPC appoints special committees responsible for specific issues like ethnic issues, internal and legal issues, financial and economic issues, science and technology, culture and social welfare, foreign affairs, overseas Chinese, and so on.

4.3.4.2 Standing Committee of the NPC

The Standing Committee is the permanent organ of the NPC and reports directly to it. The Committee functions as the highest organ of state power and acts in the name of the NPC when it is not in session. The Standing Committee of the NPC is composed of the president, vice-president, secretary-general and other members chosen out of the representatives during the first session of each NPC.

Besides the CCP, the members of the Standing Committee also represent the democratic parties and non-party-related people, the People's Liberation Army (PLA), and minorities with more than one million members.

According to the constitution, the NPC and the Standing Committee of the NPC together have legislative power. The Standing Committee interprets the constitution and the laws and explains the articles that need further definition. It supervises the execution of the constitution and the working of other state organs. It appoints or dismisses ministers, and positions in the State Council. It takes decisions about important state issues like agreements with other countries, or the granting of amnesty.

During the reign of Mao Zedong, little effort was made to develop a good legal system. This policy changed in 1979 and since that time a better law system has been developing. The law is inspired by the European system, but separation of legislative, executive and juridical power still does not exist in China today.

4.3.4.3 The President of the People's Republic of China

The president of the People's Republic of China is chosen by the NPC. The function was inscribed in the constitution of 1954. In 1954 Mao Zedong was appointed as president of the People's Republic of China (since 1949 he was already the president of the Central People's Government), in 1959 Liu Shaoqi, in 1983 Li Xiannian, in 1988 Yang Shangkun, in 1993 Jiang Zemin and in 2002 Hu Jintao.

4.3.4.4 The State Council and the Premier

The State Council is the highest organ in the state administration. The heads of all the central government departments and organs are seated on it, in all about fifty. The Standing Committee of the State Council includes the premier, four vice-premiers, five state advisors and the secretary-general. The full council gathers once a month, the Standing Committee of the State Council once every two weeks. The council is presided by the premier. He is appointed by the president of the NPC and can stay for two terms of office lasting five years. He is usually a member of the Standing Committee of the Politburo of the CCP. The premier is the equivalent to a first minister in a parliamentary democracy. He executes the daily leadership of the government.

Since 1954 the following premiers have occupied the position: Zhou Enlai in 1954, Hua Guofeng in 1978, Zhao Ziyang in 1980, Li Peng in 1988, Zhu Rongji in 1998, and since 2002, Wen Jiabao.

The vice-premiers are selected by the premier and appointed by the president of the People's Republic of China. Each vice-premier has supervision on a certain domain of the government. The secretary-general leads the office that executes the daily affairs of the State Council.

In principle the State Council works under the authority of the NPC. In practice, it is rare that the NPC does not accept the decisions of the State Council. The State Council is closely connected to the CCP. Most of the members in the State Council are high ranking CCP-members.

4.3.4.5 Central Military Commission (CMC)

China has a Central Military Commission (CMC), of the state and of the CCP. The CMC of the state is elected by and in theory reports to the NPC. The CMC of the state was established with the constitutional changes in 1982, with the formalization of the role of the army within the state structure as a goal.

The CMC of the CCP is elected by the Central Committee of the CCP and supervised by the Politburo of the CCP and the Standing Committee of the Politburo. Both CMCs have power over the Chinese army, the PLA (People's Liberation Army). The Chinese army does not fall under the authority of a Ministry of Defense. China does have a Ministry of Defense but it only serves for international contacts, and has no control over the army.

The Army in control of Beijing

4.3.4.6 Chinese Justice System

The Chinese justice system comprises four institutions: the People's Court, the People's Procuratorate, Public and State Security, and the judicial administrative departments. The Public and State Security organs and the judicial administrative departments depend on the government. The People's Court and People's Procuratorate are in theory independent organs.

The People's Court is responsible for jurisdiction. The People's Procuratorate is responsible for the approval of arrests and for initiating prosecutions. The Public Security organs are the police departments in China. They are responsible for the investigation of crimes and for the conservation of public order. The State Security is responsible for the secret agents and the investigation of espionage. Judicial administration services are responsible for the administration of lawyers, notary, people's conciliation, arbitration and detention.

The People's Court has four levels in the centralist structure: local, intermediate, higher, and supreme. The Supreme People's Court is the highest juridical organ in the People's Republic of China. Apart from these four levels in the People's Court, a military and special court exists.

The higher level supervises the lower levels. Each level can appeal to the level above. The Supreme People's Court supervises the whole judicial system. The Supreme People's Procuratorate is the highest organ at national level that can act as a prosecutor in the People's Republic of China. It is responsible for jurisdiction at the different jurisdiction levels and for the execution of the law. The Supreme People's Court and the Supreme People's Procuratorate make judicial interpretation. Their decision in a process is final; no higher appeal is possible.

Justice in China is often arbitrary. Punishment is designed to frighten people off. The death penalty is executed on a very regular basis. Some regions may work better than other regions. A change in the system is noticeable, but it is very complex and changes are slow.

Hong Kong and Macau have a separate juridical system due to their statute of Special Administrative Region (SAR).

4.3.5 Administrative Division of China

Between 1949 and 1952, political and administrative reform took place. The country's administration was organized into provinces, municipalities, and autonomous regions.

Schematic Diagram of Administration Division

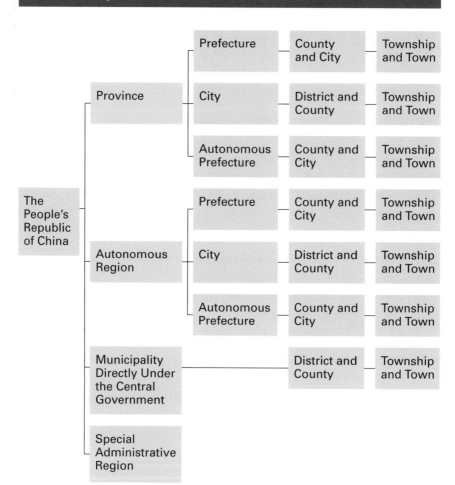

The Chinese provinces are Heilongjiang, Jilin, Liaoning, Hebei, Shanxi, Shandong, Jiangsu, Anhui, Zhejiang, Jiangxi, Fujian, Henan, Hubei, Hunan, Guangdong, Hainan, Shaanxi, Gansu, Qinghai, Sichuan, Guizhou, Yunnan, and Taiwan.

A number of these provinces are named in reference to their specific location. Along the Yellow River or *'Huang He'* there is Hebei 'North of the River' and Henan 'South of the River'. Shanxi and Shandong respectively mean 'West of the Mountains' and 'East of the Mountains'. Hubei and Hunan respectively mean 'North of the Lake' and 'South of the Lake'.

Four cities or municipalities in China reside directly under the control of central government: Beijing (capital of China), Tianjin, Shanghai and Chongqing.

Five areas in China are considered as Autonomous Regions in which people other than Han Chinese live: Tibet (people: mainly Tibetan), Xinjiang (people: mainly Uygur), Inner Mongolia (people: mainly Mongol), Ningxia (people: mainly Hui) and Guangxi (people: mainly Zhuang).

There are two Special Administrative Regions (SAR): Hong Kong and Macau. In 1997 Hong Kong changed from a British Crown Colony to SAR of the People's Republic of China. The agreement dictates that starting from the transfer in 1997, Hong Kong can keep its own political system for another fifty years. Macau changed from a Portuguese Colony to SAR of the People's Republic in 1999.

The relationship between Mainland China and Taiwan is complex. The People's Republic considers Taiwan as a province of China. In Taiwan, voices calling for independence are heard. Since the establishment of the PRC, the relationship between Taiwan and the PRC has been problematic. Taiwan has developed its own political organization and uses a democratic system since the 1980s. Taiwan is not internationally recognized as an independent country. This is a sensitive issue between China and the United States because the US tends to support Taiwan.

4.3.6 Regional Government

The highest level of regional government is the province. Local government in the province is a mirror reflection of the central governmental structure. Each province has it's own People's Congress and Standing Committee. The provincial People's Congresses have their own authority to stipulate local legislation on condition that it is not contradictory to central legislation.

Since the constitution in 1982, the following administrative units exist below the provincial level: autonomous prefectures, counties, autonomous districts, cities, municipal districts, townships, nationality townships, and towns.

The townships replace the former communes. The autonomous prefectures and counties are self-governing. Each of these units has different administrations, adding to the already complex bureaucracy in China.

4.3.7 Decentralization after 1978

The reforms, especially after 1984, have led to decentralization in many areas. Political decentralization resulted in more autonomy for the regional administrations and in a greater diversity of laws and regulations in different regions in China. The control of central government has loosened; regional differences have become a lot more outspoken over the last decennia.

Cutting down central subsidizing for media and education has led to a diversity of institutions. To some extent, the media is still under the strict control of central government, but more diversity is allowed. In the educational system, decentralization took place, private schools have emerged and with them the possibility to offer alternative curricula to that provided by central government. Decentralization of the economy also took place. We will elaborate further on that in the chapter on Corporate China.

4.3.8 International Politics

China takes a strong stand towards Taiwan: in 2005 the constitution was adapted to provide the opportunity for China to use military force against Taiwan if it declared itself independent.

The attitude towards Hong Kong is also becoming stricter: Tung Chee-Hwa, who was appointed by central government as Chief Executive of Hong Kong in 1997, was dismissed by Beijing in 2005, and replaced by Donald Tsang.

At a global level, the relationship between the United States and China remains ambiguous. Criticism interchanges with alignment. Already in 2002, Hu Jintao, who was still vice-president at the time, visited the United States for no particular obvious purpose, just a few months before he was elected as president. In 2007 he visited the White House as president.

Europe mainly uses a charm offensive to strengthen its ties with China. Premier Wen Jiabao and President Hu Jintao both travel to Europe and European officials continuously visit China. For the sake of economic relationships, diplomatic missions are lining up in China. Europe and China both seem to seek alignment. At the same time, severe economic conflicts can take place between Europe and China, for instance about textiles. These discussions will continue to exist without any doubt for some time to come.

Other regions and countries are also intensifying their relations with China. China is investing in Cuba. China and India have become partners. The relationship with Russia is restored. Argentina gives China free market status and Brazil declares that China belongs to the free market.

The relationship with Japan remains very difficult. In 2005 there was conflict between the two countries. China blamed Japan for distorting recent history about the China-Japan conflict in World War II and for washing over their war crimes. China strongly opposes Japan's request to sit on the UN security council. In 2007 premier Wen Jiabao visited Japan and pleaded for improvements in the relationship between China and Japan. However, economically the two countries certainly approach each other.

In terms of energy, China depends strongly on coal supplies, covering about two thirds of the domestic need. China belongs to the world's top three coal producers. The supplies available in the ground are estimated to be a few thousand billion tons. Estimates of petrol supplies differ widely, but are thought to be billions of tons in the sea and on land. The production of oil is not sufficient; significant quantities of oil products and gas need to be imported. Coal, oil, and gas provide more than 85% of China's primary energy needs. The production of hydropower has risen with the building of dams.

China is one of the biggest producers of raw steel in the world. The iron ore supply in China is huge. But Chinese steel is not always of the best quality; to satisfy the need for millions of tons of high quality steel, China needs to rely on imports.

Although China has huge energy reserves, it is striking how the country conducts an international policy focused on the sourcing of energy from abroad. China sets up good connections with countries that have oil reserves. This is the case with many African countries. Walden Bello, executive director of the research and advocacy institute Focus on the Global South, puts it concretely: "If not yet the biggest external player in Africa, China is certainly the most dynamic. It now accounts for 60% of oil exports from Sudan and 35% of those from Angola. Chinese firms mine copper in Zambia and Congo-Brazzaville, cobalt in the Congo, gold in South Africa, and uranium in Zimbabwe." [12] As a result, Western countries often criticize China for making agreements with countries that violate international conventions and human rights.

In December 2006, the President of South Africa, Thabo Mbeki, warned against a colonial relationship between China and African countries.

4.4 Media and Information

4.4.1 Freedom of Speech and Censorship

"China has long been regarded as a state with a tradition of highly centralized power. For thousands of years, no matter which dynasty was in power, official authority always rigorously controlled the flow of information and ideas for the maintenance of feudal rule. Free dissemination of information and ideas was therefore strictly controlled."
Qu Sanqiang[13]

Since the nineteenth century, the media in China have widely developed, but one constant factor has remained: government control. After the collapse of the Chinese Empire, control on information flow continued to exist in the Republic of China between 1911 and 1949 and through the People's Republic of China after 1949 until today.

The constitution of 1982 guarantees freedom of speech for Chinese citizens. Article 35 states "Citizens of the People's Republic of China enjoy freedom of speech, of press, of assembly, of association, of procession and of demonstration." Chinese reality however is complex, and the media and culture are censored.

The media is structured as a centralist hierarchy. Centralized media, under the direct control of the Propaganda Department of the CCP, supervises provincial and local media. This is the case for printed press, radio and television. Depending on the media format, more freedom exists locally, or control is more central.

Today, the Chinese government runs all the largest media organizations. The central television CCTV, the People's Daily (*Renmin Ribao*) newspaper, and the *Xinhua* (New China) News Agency are all under the rigorous control of the government.

Inside China there is no clear outline or list of censored subjects. There are some sensitive issues that everyone knows are not tolerated. The following subjects are banned from publications and blocked on the Internet:
- Advocating independence or self-determination for territories that Beijing considers under its jurisdiction;
- Public challenges to the CCP's monopoly in China;
- References to democracy;
- Free Tibet movement;
- Taiwan as an independent state;
- Certain religious organizations;
- Anything questioning the legitimacy of the Communist Party of China.

The government uses a variety of approaches to maintain control over the media. Newspapers need to be registered and attached to a government ministry, institute, research facility, labor group, or other state-sanctioned organization. Magazines are shut down if they publish information that is deemed sensitive. Journalists are fined or even jailed for unfavorable reporting. All journalists are part of official journalists' associations (All-China Journalist Federation). Weekly meetings are held with top newspaper editors to direct the journalists to news items they want them to focus on and which stories they want to keep unreported. A hierarchical relationship among the Chinese print and broadcast entities seeks to control the media.

Certain leaders are appointed to the most powerful media institutions, which in turn try to dominate the rest of the media countrywide.

Journalists usually exercise a kind of self-censorship. They know which subjects are sensitive. On special occasions, like in the case of the Tiananmen Revolt in 1989, or SARS [14] in 2003, journalists got clear guidance and instructions on how and what they had to report.

Yahoo Advertising in Beijing Subway: "Do you want to know?"

The state has cut down on subsidizing the media, which has resulted in decentralization and a trend towards greater autonomy and diversity, but control continues to be exercised. The media is expected to look for financial support through commercial advertising and is obliged to adapt to the market to some extent.

Television produces programs people find attractive and interesting. The loosening of the political climate and the withdrawal of government subsidies has caused newspapers and tabloids to take bolder editorial stands, sometimes even critical of the government.

4.4.2 News Agencies and Printed Media

The Xinhua News Agency and the People's Daily newspaper are the most important media in China under the supervision of the CCP. Xinhua reports to the CCP Propaganda Department. Xinhua is a huge organization controlling all the official printed media in China. It provides the information for all China's newspapers. Chinese newspapers don't have independent correspondents abroad. It is the Xinhua News Agency that has people in every country. Xinhua correspondents provide the News Agency in China with information from the country they reside in and they distribute information from China to the rest of the world. Xinhua has a monopoly on international scale media, and at national level it has correspondents in every province.

All national newspapers are set up under the control of the Propaganda Department of the CCP. The National Propaganda Department appoints the publishers, the chief editors, and all other key officials. They are the People's Daily, the Guangming Daily (*Guangming ribao*), and the Economic Daily. They feature Party speeches, announcements, propaganda, and policy viewpoints. Other national newspapers relate to the Communist Youth League, the PLA, etc. At a lower level, provincial and local Party leaders control the Party newspapers in their jurisdictions.

Magazines enjoy more freedom than newspapers. Sometimes a symbolic action takes place and a magazine is closed down, but a lot of information escapes the attention of the so-called all-seeing eye of the government. Due to internationalization and commercialization, it has become virtually impossible for central government to exert control over everything. Magazines and newspapers need to be officially registered, but the market has become too diverse to be able to check everything that is published.

Sinologist Perry Link draws attention to the political weight Chinese calligraphy can give to newspapers and magazines.[15] Mao Zedong's calligraphy still heads the People's Daily, the mouthpiece of the CCP. After 1978, Zhou Yang donated his calligraphy to the 'Red Bean' magazine, giving it a political license.

4.4.3 Television

Chinese Central Television (CCTV) is the only national network and controls television broadcasting. The CCTV falls under the supervision of the Propaganda Department and State Administration of Radio, Film, and Television. It has the monopoly on purchases of overseas programs. Local television stations are restricted to broadcasting within their own province or municipality. CCTV broadcasts news three times a day and all local stations are required to broadcast the 7 o'clock CCTV news.

Both program makers and government use television in China as a means to arouse or to stimulate national debate. In 1988 the pro-democracy series 'River Elegy' (*Heshang*), fired debate all over China. Some years ago a series showing aggression and violence between married couples, stimulated a debate on domestic violence. An example of educational television is the series 'How Can I Tell You This?' a program that wants to break down the taboo of discussing sex. It focuses on sex education for young people and provides guidance and teaching for young people on how to protect themselves against pregnancy and venereal disease. In 2002 the first set of sex education textbooks were printed in China, informing people on sexual behavior, procreation, and AIDS prevention.

The impact of television on the whole nation was also demonstrated in 'Super Girl', a Chinese version of the Western 'idol' contests, organized in 2005 and hosted by Hunan Satellite Television, a provincial television station. Li Yuchun, dressed in a boyish style and with short hair was the winner. She fascinated huge numbers of fans with her trans-gender appearance and performing style. The television show was extremely popular, watched by some 400 million people all over China. Li Yuchun was one of the people who introduced the concept of 'unisex' into China. Girls in China started to cut their hair short and wear baggy clothes. Shows like this are examples of the kind of freedom local television stations have today in China. A similar show was organized in Shanghai to select the trendiest boy in 'My Hero!' But apparently central government doesn't want to take any risks and it decided to prohibit tele-voting shows. The show 'The first heartbeat' (*Di yi ci xindong*) produced by Chongqing Television was also prohibited by government.[16]

4.4.4 Radio

Radio is equally important as television in China. It is sometimes open to a freer exchange of views than other media. Competition between radio stations results in lively coverage: phone-in programs with discussions on all kinds of issues where callers don't have to identify themselves, make it possible to discuss topics more openly than on television. Provincial radio stations have more autonomy than the central radio station.

4.4.5 Internet

Internet services come under the jurisdiction of the Ministry of Post and Telecommunications, Ministry of Electronics Industry, and the State Education Commission. Technical advances in communications are undercutting CCP efforts to control the flow of information, but the government tries to keep as tight a control as possible.

Foreign web portals like MSN, Yahoo, and Google are allowed to work in China, but only on condition they accept state control. All these foreign companies have been criticized internationally for collaboration in China's control system. Since 2005 human rights groups have criticized Yahoo for its role in turning over the e-mails of political dissidents' to the Chinese government, which were then used to prosecute and imprison them. In April 2007 two journalists, Shi Tao, Wang Xiaoning and a relative sued Yahoo for being responsible for their imprisonment due to the handing over of e-mail correspondence with pro-democracy content to the Chinese government. The lawsuit was settled in November 2007. The terms of the settlement, other than the agreement that Yahoo would pay the lawyer's fees of the two journalists, were not disclosed.[17]

Firewalls limit the content of home pages and block access to certain Internet sites through routing filters. Words like democracy, Tibet, Taiwan, *Falungong*[18], the names of dissidents, and so on, result in the blocking of the site. The on-line encyclopedia Wikipedia cannot be accessed in China because it contains too much information that is censored in China. Subscriptions to international on-line newspapers are disrupted when news about China that the government does not approve of is published.

4.4.6 Information and Secrecy

China uses an internal publication system exclusively for government and Party officials. This internal medium provides information and analysis unavailable to the general public. Internal reports contain sensitive, controversial, and investigative articles. Xinhua and other media organizations produce the reports for these internal journals.

A lot of information in China, like for instance statistical data, is deemed to be 'internal' or a 'state secret'. Therefore, it is difficult to get reliable information about China. The situation today has improved due to the presence of many international organizations in China, sometimes based in Hong Kong. But getting reliable facts and figures is still problematic.

Insider-outsider ethics, on which we well focus later, are responsible for the fact that people amongst themselves, departments in an organization or company, organizations amongst themselves, organizations towards the government and vice versa all are reluctant to disclose information on their internal functioning.

4.5 Education in China

4.5.1 Introduction

Through the ages, China had a strongly centralized education system inspired by Confucianism as we described in the section 'Confucianism as State Ideology'. In this exam system the best students climb to the top, through study and self-cultivation. The focus is not only put on knowledge but also on attitude. Education is one of the cornerstones of Confucian society. The very best students reach the highest level. Unlike the caste system in India, it is possible for anyone to climb up the social ladder in China. A person born into a poor farmer's family can become top of the class and consequently go to a better school, and he or she can climb higher and higher until the level of the very top universities. It is not social background but intelligence, persistence, the right attitude, and self-cultivation that propel a person higher up the education system and in society. Education is in principle open to everyone. Although the curriculum has changed dramatically, again and again, in the course of the twentieth century, this system of Confucian meritocracy still lies at the core of Chinese education today. The contribution of professor Liu Lixin in this chapter clearly exemplifies the focus of education in China today as inspired by Confucian values.

The different focus in education between China and the West may be rooted a lot deeper and be more fundamental than we would expect at first sight. Scholar Tang Junyi has written extensively on Chinese and Western humanism and their relationship to education. He points out that the idea of the humanities as understood by the classical tradition of Western culture, has its root in the Greek idea of *paideia*, later a derivative of the Latin *humanitas*, further incorporated in the *studia humanitas* by the humanists in the Renaissance. "The humanities are considered both as the ideal of man and as the curriculum for ideal education. The purpose of *studia humanitatis* is to educate oneself to become a free person and a good citizen." [19]

The Chinese idea of humanities (*renwen*) however originated in the *Yi Jing* and was later incorporated in the educational ideal of Confucianism. The Chinese term for humanities stresses the idea of man rather than external activities. It is connected to the interrelatedness of humans and nature: "To observe movements of Heaven (*tianwen*) so as to understand the change in time; to observe human activities (*renwen*) so as to acculturate the world". [20] The difference lies in the ways human beings see the world.

But not only Confucian values are important in contemporary education in China. The Chinese education system also adheres to the socialist cause. Article three of the Education Law states: "In compulsory education, the state policy on education must be implemented to improve the quality of instruction and enable children and adolescents to achieve all-round development – morally, intellectually and physically – so as to lay the foundation for improving the quality of the entire nation and for cultivating well-educated and self-disciplined builders of socialism with high ideals and moral integrity".[21]

The move from planned economy towards market economy forced a change in the education system in China. The reforms asked for an education system that was adequate to contribute to economic developments. At national level, decentralization took place and a diversification of education institutions came into being. In spite of the diversification, the government still wants to keep tight control. To this day, the education system in China does not fully provide the skilled people the internationalized market needs. There is a discrepancy between the methods and focus of the system and the internationalization of the economy.

4.5.2 Education Reform

In 1985 the government outlined a series of general policy guidelines to align the education system with the economic reforms. Policy was directed towards the implementation of a nine-year compulsory education system with decentralized finances and management, the increase of vocational and technical education, and the increase of the number and quality of teachers. In 1986 China adopted the Compulsory Education Law that stipulated nine years compulsory education, divided into primary and junior middle school education.

In 1992 a statewide curriculum framework was drafted. In 1993 the State Council issued the 'Program for China's Educational Reform and Development' in which many of the 1985 policies were restated in a more detailed manner. A whole series of laws regarding teachers, disabled people, community-run schools, vocational and technical education, educational finance, fund-raising, and science and technology were drafted.

In 1998 the Fifteenth National Congress of the CCP mapped out an overall plan for implementing strategies for education reform. The government realized that educational development had to be a priority: "The educational development in our country is far from being adequate. The structure and management system of education, the prevailing concepts and methods, and patterns of human resources development are yet to fit in with the demands of modernization. At present and for some time in the near future, the lack of creative talents of the highest caliber is one of the major constraints unfavorably affecting the innovative ability and competitiveness of the nation. Therefore, to invigorate education is the objective and pressing demand of socialist modernization and national revival as well as a move to accommodate the needs of the times."[22]

In 1999 premier Zhu Rongji affirmed that as long as non-state run schools operate in the context of relevant state laws and regulations they should be encouraged.[23]

The main goal of the whole reform plan was that by the year 2000, the nine-year compulsory education plan would be implemented throughout the country and that illiteracy would be largely eliminated. The system of vocational training had to be improved with training programs of all types and levels. Research and development had to be strengthened in higher education institutions to enable high-technology based enterprises affiliated with universities to contribute to economic development. Efforts had to be made to establish a basic framework for a new educational system that could meet the needs of the economic and social development in China. All this had to be accomplished by 2010.

4.5.3 Decentralization and Recentralization of finances in the Education System

After the opening up, the state no longer engaged in full responsibility and control. Education decentralization was part of a broader economic liberalization in which the state disengaged from being the sole provider of educational services. Financial reform took place, which replaced the government as the sole financial source resulting into various financial resources.

The government reduced subsidies for local schools so that education officials at county, township and village level had to pursue alternative sources of income to fund basic education, such as local taxes, tuition, overseas donations, contributions from enterprises, and so on. The system worked well in the richer areas, but was problematic in poorer areas. Which is why in 1994 a tax recentralization was implemented.

Increased fiscal responsibility at local level has led to a diversification in administrative structures of China's schools. Changes also took place at the level of the curriculum, and at the level of the management of education institutions.

4.5.4 Education in China Today

The education system has three categories. The first category is basic education comprising pre-school, primary school starting at the age of six, and regular secondary divided into academic secondary and vocational, technical secondary. The second category is higher education with short-cycle or long-cycle colleges, and universities with both academic and vocational programs. The third category is adult education overlapping the two previous categories, focusing on cadres, staff and workers, radio and TV, and so on.

The department in charge of education under the State Council decides on teaching methods, courses and content, curriculum, and the selection of textbooks for compulsory education and diplomas.

Teachers should be 'committed to the cause of socialist education, endeavor to raise their own ideological and cultural levels as well as professional competence'.

Supervision of education today is no longer a matter solely controlled by central government. It is applied through a hierarchy whereby government agencies above county level supervise, evaluate and examine the authorities at lower levels. The National Educational Supervision Agency is the highest level and supervises all the lower levels. During compulsory education, the government keeps strict control, but tolerance for diversity is greater in higher education.

The entrance exam for university is organized at national level. All eighteen year olds are under severe pressure to prepare for this. The results of this exam have consequences for one's whole career. This entrance exam decides who goes to university and who doesn't. The result of the entrance exam also decides who goes to which university. The higher your score, the better the university you can go to. The expectations of parents and families towards their only child are extremely high. In an already highly competitive Chinese society, children grow up under terrific pressure to succeed and the competition is fierce.

Following Deng Xiaoping's focus on science and technology for the development of China, the targets set for education reforms are inspired by the development of scientific and technological progress and the advancement of information technology.

Hu Jintao introduced the Scientific Development Concept (*Kexue fazhan guan*) as the official socio-economic ideology of the CCP. The ideology is dominated by egalitarian concepts involving sustainable development, social welfare, a person-based society, increased democracy, and the creation of a Harmonious Society. This strongly influences the focus of the Chinese education system today. Education is heavily oriented towards science-based technical training like engineering, computer science, mathematics, and chemical science. Another popular area is everything linked to the economy, like economics and accountancy.

Throughout China, schools have to promote the standard language, *Putonghua*. In schools where more than half of the students belong to a minority, the minority language can be used.

4.5.5 Privatization

Apart from the different forms of decentralization, privatization also took place. Non-state operated schools are allowed within the context of existing government laws and regulations. Non-governmental or semi-privatized schools have emerged. Non-state run educational institutions are financially self-supporting and can deviate from the state curriculum. Chinese families are prepared to invest a lot of money in the education of their children, which has resulted in the emergence of expensive, private schools for the elite.

4.5.6 Education Policy and International Cooperation

The economic reforms demand high quality personnel, communication and language skills, and management skills. Until today a gap exists between the supply and demand of good personnel.

Now that institutions other than state-controlled ones are tolerated, private initiatives are emerging in China, and also international cooperation between schools and universities. In the first period after opening up, the students China sent to study abroad were university graduates who went to the West to obtain a Ph.D. Since the end of the nineties, more and more young Chinese students are coming to the West to get a bachelor or master degree. More and more Western schools and universities attract Chinese students and are setting up cooperation structures. Structural cooperation results in shared educational programs in and outside of China. Western universities are also opening up branches in China. Harvard University has built a branch in Xian. China and Australia are enhancing education exchange and cooperation. A Sino-Russian University has been set up in Heilongjiang. China and Argentina are boosting cooperation in science and technology. East African Universities are pushing for academic exchange, and China is setting up Confucius Institutes in Europe.[24]

4.5.7 Main Focuses in Chinese Education Methods

The Chinese deal with knowledge and information in a totally different way from Westerners. Teaching methods differ widely from the West, for example, the Chinese have to memorize thousands of characters in order to be able to read and write. As a result, they are extremely good at memorizing, far exceeding Westerners in this respect. But it's not only the Chinese language that is responsible; the entire education system in China is based on memorization. Results are numbered and scores are based on the exact reproduction of memorized material. Detailed teaching material clearly outlines what has to be memorized. A lot of importance is also put on moral and ideological education.

Gao Ge and Ting-Toomey call the Chinese way of communicating 'listening-centered' (*tinghua*).[25] They explain that most Chinese schools focus on listening, memorizing, writing, reading, and only seldom on speaking. According to Tony

Fang, it is easy to distinguish if a Chinese student has studied in the West just by the way he gives a presentation.[26]

Having a stronger reading ability than a speaking ability becomes obvious when a Chinese person speaks in another language, for instance in English. Westerners sometimes mistakenly think that a Chinese person who has difficulty expressing himself verbally in English does not master the language, while he may only have difficulty in speaking it and be excellent at reading and writing.

Skills like individual analysis, creativity, or responsibility for individual assignments don't belong in the requirements of the official Chinese education system. The same goes for logical reasoning, motivation, and argumentation: taking a stand and arguing your case is not something the Chinese learn at school.

4.5.8 Two Views on Education: a Chinese and an American

It is interesting to read the contributions of the two people below from an intercultural perspective. Professor Liu Lixin from Beijing University, teaches Chinese to foreign students. She has a Chinese background. Michael Conen, an instructor at a private school in Beijing, teaches English to Chinese students preparing to go and study in the West. He has an American background. Both of them describe their views on and experience of Chinese and Western education. In their quite opposite statements, we can detect that they both approach the subject from their own cultural viewpoint. We learn that it is not always easy to study or work in an international environment. The difference in focus, expectations between student and teacher, the responsibilities that both parties have towards each other, the interpretation of attitudes and so on, seem to be quite different, often leading to misunderstandings. We think this is a fine lesson in intercultural communication.

Liu LIXIN is a professor of Chinese language at Beijing University. In 1996 she was a guest professor at Hawaii University. From 1998 to 2001, the Chinese National Education Committee sent her to Belgium as a guest professor at Ghent University.

'In today's globalizing world the exchange between China and the West becomes deeper and more frequent. Although it is difficult to talk about differences between Chinese and Western people, we should not ignore that each nation is deeply influenced by its traditional thinking and culture and that this is reflected in people's behavior. To cooperate with the Chinese or to provide training to Chinese students or employees in a company, you will get a better result if you understand Chinese culture. The Chinese focus in education differs from the West:

1. Moral dignity (*dao de*)

Chinese values are deeply influenced by the Confucian concepts of 'benevolence' (*ren*), and 'virtue' (*de*). A teacher should in the first place display moral dignity, be a person of high quality. Only then will he receive wholehearted respect and esteem. For students 'virtue' (*de*) is equally important. In Chinese primary and secondary schools the assessment of a good student includes 'virtue, wisdom, health'[27]. 'Virtue' is the most important. In the assessment of Chinese students 'integrity and ability' are equally important[28].

2. Diligence

'Hard-working', to be 'assiduous', to 'study hard', and to be 'persistent' are highly ranked values in China, because the Chinese believe that 'dripping water wears down a stone'[29], 'The fragrance of plum blossom origins in bitter cold'[30], 'To be able to eat the most bitter of bitterness elevates a human being to a higher level'[31], 'Only thorough skill can grind an iron pestle down to a needle'[32], 'To study the boundless sea of knowledge one needs to sail the boat with bitterness'[33]. The Chinese strongly believe that success can only be attained by never ending hard work. Western teachers should understand this attitude to be able to anticipate to it. This requires thorough preparation and rigorous practice. Contrary to this, Western people prefer experience-oriented training, which looks very light to the Chinese, but maybe the West focuses more on skills and efficiency.

3. Role and position of the teacher

China has a tradition of respect for teachers, 'When the teacher is virtuous, the respect is deep'. The teacher transfers virtue, professionalism, and resolves unclear issues; he is a model. A teacher's salary is not very high, but due to respect his social position is high. His position is higher than that of the students. He is the one who teaches, who transfers knowledge, he is the leader, the person who sets the rules; what the teacher says has to be obeyed and followed. China has teacher-centered learning, in contrast to the Western student-centered learning. Western teachers put more emphasis on the individuality of the students, and Western students are free to discuss with the teacher or propose issues different from those the teacher proposes.

4. Training methods

Interaction, performance, and experience-oriented methods are valued in Western learning situations and Western students are used to these kind of methods. Chinese students, although they sometimes like entertaining learning methods, prefer methods where an example is set, and explained word for word and clause-by-clause, ex cathedra speeches. Westerners focus more on individualism and on what each person wants, therefore in learning situations students learn to express themselves without paying too much attention to what others think. In comparison to Westerners, the Chinese are more aware of their position in the group and of what others think about them; they do anything to keep a positive image. As the saying goes 'The bird that sticks his head up is shot'[34]. Chinese don't like to speak their mind in case they lose face. Sometimes they avoid showing off their ability in a group to avoid others from losing face or they are shy to do so. But in spite of this, trainers should not be afraid of group interaction; they can work in small sub-groups where individuals feel comfortable to express themselves. In these circumstances students will take their responsibility towards the small group and perform excellently.

China also has a tradition of respect for age 'the oldest is the most esteemed, the oldest goes first'[35]. The eldest student of a group will take a lot of responsibility; he will make sure that everything goes according to plan. The teacher should show respect towards him.

The Chinese are stronger in reading skills than speaking skills; therefore they like to obtain a lot of written material to study, preferably before the training starts.

5. Evaluation System

Two sorts of tests are used to evaluate. A written test is used to check knowledge and is directed towards standard fixed answers. From childhood onwards, the Chinese learn to recite poems from the Tang and Song dynasty; in primary and secondary school they learn lesson texts by heart. The written test is a repetition of the memorized knowledge. An oral exam will be used to test further. The Chinese attach extremely high importance to results, endlessly comparing and checking meticulously and they tend to haggle over every detail. Therefore the teacher must be clear and fair about the results. Evaluations shouldn't take place in the group, but if possible on a one-to-one basis. Evaluation forms can be used as well.

To conclude, I would like to give some advice to Western trainers:
- It is necessary to show enthusiasm for the Chinese language and culture because the Chinese are extremely aware of the value of their culture;
- It is necessary to understand Chinese cultural habits, only then will you be able to establish deep relationships.

The Chinese are extremely fond of proverbs and ancient sayings; in any interaction with them it is good to know a few of their sayings. If you can use them at the right spot in your training you'll notice that people will open up to you.'

Michael CONEN, English Instructor and Advisor CIBT School of Business, Beijing

'During my eight years of teaching various English courses at a private school in Beijing, several patterns of behavior have evidenced themselves in the classroom. Of particular note, is the persistent habit of passive learning in a considerable number of pupils: passive to the point of showing little or no motivation to acquire the skills needed in order to become the competent student that can succeed at a Western-styled preparatory school in China, let alone an actual Western university or college abroad, which is where many aspire to study.

The reasons behind this 'passivity' are many, and in some cases, complex. For the most part, it can be said that differences in the social, economic and educational cultures between the Far East and the West are major factors. In spite of the fact that such passivity also exists in the Western classroom, here, social-standing and economic affluence exert a considerable amount of influence on classroom behavior, especially in such private schools. The result is that, often, such students have the attitude that they should be entitled to merely attending preparatory school and then be automatically accepted at a college or university abroad, rather than adopting the work ethic that is required to incorporate the necessary skills and aptitude for academic study that is required at higher education institutions in the West.

This attitude can be partially explained by the longstanding 'norm' which exists within nearly every level of Chinese society: 'who you know' can be much more important than 'what you know' and this approach applies to nearly every facet of life here. Single children of powerful people in particular, generally exhibit much less motivation to adapt to the new methods and study skills being introduced in their courses, relying instead on the notion that since their parents tend to be of some level of importance in their political or business careers, their futures are secured, and therefore, it should be a foregone conclusion that everything will be worked out in the end, whether or not they actually attempt to do the required coursework.

This attitude is magnified as a direct result of the rote method of education that has existed for decades now, in which educators in China are directed to make sure that everyone succeeds. This system, of course, leads to particular compromises on the part of the instructors, and to a student mindset of 'failure is not an option', especially when one takes into consideration, that at many private schools, parents are assured that since they are paying customers, their children will, as a matter of due course, finish their classes and receive their certificates, unless something extraordinary should occur. Problem-solving and its subsequent skill of analytical thinking, as thought of as primary building-blocks in Western education, have not been a major part of the Chinese education system up to this point in time.

Many students enrolled in schools which include English courses taught in a very different manner and aims by Westerners, have never really learned the skill of note-taking during classes, unless the instructor actively demands it. Nor have many developed a disciplined approach to 'advance' preparation of course books, as again, they will usually wait for the instructor to tell them everything they need to know during the class. This extends to a general lack of academic initiative and inquisitiveness on the part of the students, who rarely seek out and utilize supplemental materials that could enhance their general knowledge, skills that are integral to the Western educational process at college or university level.

Instead, these students have come to rely on their instructors to tell them 'everything' they need to know, in order to succeed at their exams and courses, and it is not that unusual for a student (and their parents, for that matter) to blame the instructors for any failures on these points. After all, in their minds, the traditional respect afforded instructors is supposed to be reciprocated in the form of seeing to it that everyone succeeds, relatively speaking, through the teacher's efforts. The perception is not what the student must do to earn their grades, but what the teacher must do to assure that they will receive good grades.'

4.6 People and Society

4.6.1 Urbanization and City Governance in China

4.6.1.1 Urban Governance during the Chinese Empire

Throughout the history of the Chinese Empire, cities fell under the administration of central government. Statecraft was considered to be merely an administrative technique rather than governance in a broader sense. All local government employees were subjects of the imperial presence himself, never citizens with specific rights and obligations. The whole country was organized according to administrative areas reflecting a five-tier hierarchy: the lowest tier was the rural county, rising to prefecture, the circuit, the province and culminating in the imperial capital itself.[36] The entire nation was built according to this unified administration ruled by the center. Each level had a city as administrative capital. Capital cities were distinguished from other cities by having imposing walls, gates, and towers, all symbols of imperial power. Within the city walls stood the walled government compound, the *yamen*, where officials worked and lived. The power of the *yamen* stretched over the designated administrative level. Central government formulated imperial policies. Provincial, circuit, and prefecture administrations acted as intermediaries between central government and the county level.

County magistrates had to maintain public order, oversee construction of public works, and collect taxes. The county *yamen* served as the justice court of the first instance in civil disputes. Magistrates' involvement with the local gentry and their efforts to make as much money as possible during their tenure, which was usually not longer than three years in any *yamen*, led to corruption. The *yamen* was disbanded after the establishment of the Republic of China.

As the administration was a top-down centralized system, there was no public space in cities. Markets with shops, drugstores, wine houses, and restaurants were walled in. They could not serve as public spaces where people gathered to form or voice a political opinion. Nor was there a space provided for such an activity. The public square that was a crucial element in the urban plan of many European cities, and which played a vital role in their political life, did not exist in the tight grid pattern of the Chinese capital. [37]

4.6.1.2 Evolutions between 1912 and 1949

After the establishment of the Republic of China, local centers of official authority were set up during a transition period between 1912 and 1928. In 1928 the central government, with Nanjing as its capital, appointed a mayor to supervise eight bureaus: public security, social affairs, public works, public health, finance, education, public utilities and land. However, central government was weak and a lot of informal governance took place in which responsibilities were shared. "While the police sought to administer the city, organizations representing merchants, lawyers, bankers, students, workers, and other groups attempted to police their own ranks and influence the behavior of other groups, including the police. In this politically complex, pluralistic process, the Beijing chamber of commerce played a critical role in handling a range of issues related to public order, from welfare policy to city planning'.[38]

Sun Yat-sen's son Sun Ke, who had studied in the US, published an essay on modern city planning in 1919. It was a manifesto for a city in which the communication needs of the future were prepared, like improvement of sanitation, and open spaces for recreational use such as urban parks. His conviction that scientific planning would force people to become modern reflects the *zeitgeist* of the beginning of the twentieth century.

Shanghai Pudong 1994

4.6.1.3 Communist Work Unit City Planning

After the Communists established the People's Republic of China in 1949, the urban planning that had been started by Sun Ke was abolished. The Communists introduced the concept of the work unit as we described earlier in the paragraph 'Work Unit'. Cities became centers of socialist production forms. All people worked and lived in a work unit under the total control of the CCP, and life was organized according to a centrally planned economy.

4.6.1.4 Restoration and Reform: Chinese Boxes within Boxes

During the reforms in the eighties, the functions of the work unit changed. In 1984 a redefinition of the municipality was formulated: the central municipality was responsible for the management of the surrounding rural areas and county-level cities. This meant that city and countryside again merged into a single administrative unit, as it had been under the Imperial Qing Dynasty. Within this framework, rural counties could be annexed to the metropolitan center raising their status to that of urban district.[39] Municipalities and urban districts thus become distinct levels of local government.

Two other levels, 'Street Offices' and 'Resident Committees', belong to the legacy of the Maoist era, although their function has changed today. Street Offices operate as a kind of intermediary between society and government. Resident Committees

Shanghai Pudong 2004

are responsible for a number of households (100–600), looking after public order, basic welfare, and in Maoist times mobilizing people for political movements. New organizations like Property Owners' Associations, or Business Owners' Associations have come into being in today's China. But in urban administration 'the old favorite model of Chinese boxes within boxes' is still alive and well.[40]

4.6.1.5 Urban Land Reform

The Constitution of 1982, amended in 1988, declared that all urban land was the property of the state, while rural land was the collective property of (administrative) villages. The right to use a parcel of land could be transferred by the local state to work units for their own use, or leased to developers on a long-term basis, usually for 75 years. As part of their lease agreement, real estate development companies can level the land and put in the infrastructure necessary for their project.[41]

4.6.2 Population

According to the population census held in 2000, China has almost 1.3 billion inhabitants. More than 90% are Han Chinese. Apart from the Han there are 55 minorities in China including Tibetan, Mongol, Hui, Uyghur, Zhuang, Miao, Bai, Dai, and Dong. Large parts of China are uninhabitable so the Chinese population is concentrated in a relatively small area, resulting in overpopulation.

Just how many inhabitants each city has at this moment in time is hard to tell due to the continuous migration of people throughout China. The number of inhabitants of Chongqing was assessed in 2005 to be 32 million, that of Shanghai 20 million, and that of Beijing 14 million.

4.6.3 One Child Policy

After the establishment of the People's Republic of China, due to a decrease in infant mortality, better health care and higher life expectancy, the Chinese population increased spectacularly. Mao Zedong believed in the system that the more Chinese people there were, the stronger China would become (*ren duo liliang da*) and thus stimulated people to have lots of children, which led to a baby boom. Already in 1953 Zhou Enlai was pleading for birth control.

In 1979, during the third session of the Fifth National People's Congress, Hua Guofeng officially announced the implementation of the One Child Policy (*jihua shengyu*): each couple could only have one child. The decision of imposing something that goes against human nature onto an entire nation is a fine example of the power central government can exercise in China.

The policy was applied with bureaucratic precision during the eighties. In the work unit, strict controls were kept. After a woman had a child, she was encouraged to have an anti-conception spiral or to undergo sterilization. Condoms were distributed in all state organizations. Those who transgressed the rules of the One Child Policy were forced to have an abortion, sterilization, and had to pay heavy fines.

From the very beginning the policy had exceptions. Farmers in the countryside could have a second child if the first was a girl, because they needed the extra manpower. The One Child Policy is only applicable for the Han Chinese; minorities can have more children.

Today, the One Child Policy has been adapted to the contemporary needs of society. After a few decennia, the Policy has led to the so-called 'One-Two-Four' problem: one child has to look after two parents and after four grandparents. To avoid demographic ageing of the population, the policy is more versatile. Today a couple in China can have two children if both partners come from a One Child family. In a few decennia the policy will lead to a shortage of labor power.

The One Child Policy has far reaching consequences. Chinese traditionally prefer a male child. This preference leads to selective abortions, child murder, abandoning foundlings, etc. To avoid these practices, it is forbidden by law to inform pregnant women of the gender of their baby. But bribery often leads to the neglect of this rule.

One child

Overpopulation and the One Child Policy are just two of the many difficult issues facing the Chinese government. The One Child Policy puts pressure on the population, but on the other hand, overpopulation leads to a heavy environmental burden.

4.6.4 Hukou

During the 1950s, the CCP introduced a system of 'household registration' called *hukou*. This system had to control the movement of the population by way of residence permits. Peasants and workers were assigned to a specific workplace. The *hukou* system ties every person to a certain location in China and it makes traveling without permission difficult.

Two forms of *hukou* were introduced at the time: an individually registered urban household (non-agricultural *hukou*), and a collective registration for cooperatives in the countryside, which can be seen as a kind of household of peasant families. An urban *hukou* was considered more valuable because food, energy, housing, health care and so on were all provided for, whereas a rural *hukou* was equated to a life of heavy work and hardship.

After the reforms in 1978, the system was relaxed and people were able to move around more freely. Major reforms in the *hukou* system took place in 1984 and in 2001. Since 2001 the government allows people with a rural residence permit to move into cities. When they find a steady job they can apply for an urban residence permit.

Migrant workers can get an urban residence permit, but if they bring their children or wife along, no provisions will be made for them. Children cannot go to school if they are not registered in the city. The social consequences of illegal migration weigh heavily on Chinese society. Millions of migrants have moved into the cities, whilst staying registered in the countryside. This makes it impossible to assess the population of cities and many cities have developed a shadow population of illegal migrants.

The *hukou* can be a burden for people with an urban permit as well. A person with a *hukou* in Chengdu, studying in Shanghai needs to return to his or her place of residence for all kinds of administrative procedures.

In 2008 the *hukou* system still exists, as well as the legal distinction between rural and urban residents, but big changes are underway. In January 2008 the traditional *hukou* registration system in Yunnan was eliminated. This reform means that millions of people can now migrate legally and move into cities for the first time. Applicants will receive a residence permit in their city of choice. This implies that people now living illegally in cities will be registered officially and population statistics will be updated to reflect reality.[42] Not only Yunnan announces changes. The rural *hukou* will also change in the provinces Zhejiang, Guangdong, Hunan.[43] It is possible that *hukou* reform will be implemented throughout the whole of China in the near future.

Since September 1985 identity cards were introduced throughout the People's Republic of China for people older than sixteen. Name, gender, nationality, date of birth and address are all mentioned on the card. Depending on the age of the person, the card expires after ten years, twenty years, or is 'long term'. China introduced this identity card system 'in order to guarantee a resident's status, make social intercourse easier for a citizen, protect social order, and guarantee the appropriate legal rights and interests of the citizen'.[44]

Before the introduction of this identity card, no unified system existed in China. Its introduction however has not led to the abolition of the *hukou* system. The *hukou* system covers more areas than the ID card. For example, it is the basis for city administrative planning; it provides identity certificates for people younger than sixteen that are required for kindergarten and school, and for public welfare.

4.6.5 Migrant Workers

Following the reforms in 1978 and consequent economic development, people started to migrate inside China. In rural areas, communes were de-collectivized. A transformation of China's villages took place. Around 900 million of the 1.3 billion Chinese are farmers, or rural residents.

The enormous cheap labor force in China is partly the result of a lack of employment opportunities in some regions, which makes many Chinese people continuously migrate to economically booming places, looking for a better life and new opportunities. The rural population – also called migrating population or migrant workers – moves to cities looking for work, leaving their official place of residence in the countryside. In the city, they live in factory dormitories or on construction sites where they work almost day and night. Once a year they usually return to their family for Chinese New Year.

According to Chinese Labor Law, a married couple has the right to thirty days family holiday a year. In reality this is often not the case and many couples only see each other for one week a year.

Different kinds of migrant workers exist. Some migrants move from their native village to the nearest town, later moving on to another place, and then to the next. This kind of migrant is sometimes referred to as a serial migrant. Another type of migrant leaves their home to look for work, after some time they return home, and then they leave again. This is termed repeated migration. Cyclical migrants are those who migrate to find a job, but they return home for every harvest. Some migrants return home after a period of time. They have saved money whilst away working and they don't leave their hometown again. Sometimes they set up a business in their hometown. Some migrants never return home. They build a new life in the place they have found a job.

The migration of workers has far-reaching social consequences. Rural people, who move to the city to find a job, sometimes only return to their village after many years. In the meantime their lives have changed and they cherish new expectations. Many rural women work for rich families in the city and dream of an equal kind of life. Returning home they take the new values they've learnt in the city back with them. Back in the countryside, they have difficulty accepting the basic existence that awaits them.

The migration of hundred of millions of people gives rise to a slackening control of the population. Rural migrants settling in cities leads to rapid urbanization. A fine example of this is the city of Shenzhen, next to Hong Kong. A few decennia ago this area was covered in rice fields; today it is a brand new city with ten million inhabitants coming from all over China.

The South Station in Beijing 2007. It will be the largest station in Asia, built by migrant workers who live on the site during construction

'Migrant villages' (*cun*) sprout up in the suburbs of many cities. People coming from the same area flock together in these so-called villages: *Anhui* village, *Xinjiang* village, *Zhejiang* village. Sometimes migrants even organize their own illegal education system.

At times, urban inhabitants perceive migrants as a dangerous class because they disturb the status quo and the peaceful, easy life of the city. Migrants are those who do the dirty work for minimum wages. Men often have jobs as scrap collectors or they work on construction sites; women often end up in garment factories, electric assembly lines or as servants to rich city families.

Migration to the city also puts a burden on rural areas. When men move away to work in the cities, the women stay behind and have to look after the farm by themselves. In this way, many families are disrupted.

Migrants are beginning to voice their sorrows and bemoan their harsh existence more and more. 'Migrant Literature' has arisen over the last decennium and in 2007, the migrant poet Zheng Xiaoqiong won the People's Literature Award for her poems relating the pain and misery of migrants' lives:

"There are over 40,000 severed fingers in the Pearl River Delta. I often think: How long will the fingers extend if they were connected one by one? But my poor words cannot restore any of the fingers..."[45]

The Chinese government is well aware of the problems facing migrants and of the harsh conditions in which they live. At the 17th National Congress of the Chinese Communist Party in October 2007, the Chongqing municipal government announced that 4 November would be designated as Migrant Workers' Day to mark the contribution of rural migrant workers to the area's social and economic development.[46]

4.7 Calendar Use and Festivals in China

4.7.1 Introduction of the Gregorian Calendar in China

The Gregorian calendar was adopted in China on the establishment of the Republic in 1911, but people also continued to use the so-called Moon calendar. After the establishment of the Republic of China, various regions stayed under control of different warlords. In 1928 Chiang Kai-shek reconstituted the Republic of China under the leadership of the Guomindang or the Nationalists. The Gregorian calendar was officially adopted from January 1929 in all areas under Nationalist control.

When the Communists took over in 1949 and established the People's Republic of China, they adopted the Gregorian calendar for business and everyday use across all of China. Until today both the traditional Moon calendar and the Gregorian calendar are used in China.

4.7.2 Moon Calendar

The traditional Chinese calendar is a combination of influences of the moon (*yin*) and the sun (*yang*). After the establishment of the Republic of China in 1911, it was referred to as the 'Old Calendar' (*jiu li*) or the 'Moon calendar' (*yin li*). After 1949, in Communist China, it was called the 'Farmer's calendar' (*nong li*). Today all three names are used.

The calendar is based on the 60-year stem-branch-cycle (*gan-zhi*), which we explained in the paragraph on the 'Sixty-year cycle'. The earliest archaeological evidence of this system is found on the Oracle bones of the Shang dynasty (1600 BC). Since the Han dynasty (202 BC–220 AD) numbers are used for naming months and days, but in official documents and records, including horoscopes, the stem-branch system was used. Historical dates according to this system are exactly determinable since 841 BC. The stem-branch system is still used for counting in contemporary China. For instance in official documents or legal contracts the system is used instead of numbers.

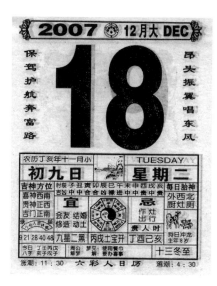

⊲ The Chinese calendar: a combination of the Gregorian and Moon calendar. On the basis of the information at the bottom, people know which days are lucky for them.

△ Newspaper heading showing both Gregorian and Moon calendar date

4.7.3 Festivals and Holidays

Festivals and folk traditions continue to be based on the Moon calendar, which is closely related to the cycles of nature. The traditional calendar is used to fix the dates of festivals like Chinese New Year, Mid-Autumn Festival, and so on; it is also used for choosing auspicious dates for a wedding, or for example, the opening of a building.

As well as seasonal festivals, there are traditional Chinese festivals related to ancestral worship, and festivals related to the world of the gods. Ancestral spirits and gods are honored to guarantee their good influence on life, and to ward off bad influences. Great attention is paid to harmony with the universe, with heaven and earth, and the unity of the family.

Many regions have their own customs and rituals and minorities in China also have their own festivals. Buddhists and other religions in China celebrate their own feasts. Every festival has its own symbols, rituals, and festive dishes.

The main festivals of the year celebrated by the Han Chinese are: Chinese New Year or Spring Festival, Lantern Festival, Clear and Bright Festival, Dragon Boat Festival, Double Seventh Night, Ghost Festival or Middle of the Year Festival, Mid Autumn or Moon Festival, Double Ninth Day, Winter Solstice, Kitchen God's Day, and New Year's Eve. Chinese New Year or Spring Festival is the most important festival of the year; it marks the beginning of a new cycle.

4.7.4 Chinese New Year

Beijing 2006: Street Vendor selling red ribbons and belts in the days before Chinese New Year

The Spring Festival is celebrated on the first day of the first month. It is the most important traditional festival, because it marks the start of a new cycle. This is the moment of the year when all Chinese return home, even those who work thousands of kilometers away. Many factories in China close down during this period.

The first day of the year is also called the 'Three mornings', this being the morning of the year, the morning of the month, and the morning of the day. Celebrations start on New Year's Day. The first thing to do at the start of a New Year is honor the ancestors. All family members, in order of seniority, will honor the oldest and most senior members of the family, parents, grandparents, or great grandparents. Traditionally, highly symbolic dishes are eaten. Red envelopes containing cash money are given to young people.

Many rituals and symbols are observed during the New Year celebrations, like one should not clean the house because good luck might be swept away; one should not use money on the first day of the year, or all the money might be lost during the year; one should not use scissors during the first 15 days of the year, because they might cut away good luck. Doors and windows are traditionally decorated with red paper cut outs or red paper bearing calligraphy with auspicious phrases, or posters are put up with symbols referring to the coming of the new spring, to happiness, wealth, longevity, and prosperity.

To protect oneself from bad influences, one should wear something red: a red belt, or red socks, etc. The character *fu*, 'wealth' is pasted on the door, sometimes upside down, which means *fu dao* or 'wealth arrives'. Regional differences exist and with globalization, traditions may fade in some areas, especially in the big cities. But Chinese New Year still means a lot more in China than New Year's Day does in the West.

Pink Christmas in Shanghai Zheng Da Supermarket

4.7.5 International Influence

Due to globalization and commercialization, Western festivals are gaining ground in China. For example, Christmas and New Year have become more popular, as have Western style weddings, but these are above all purely commercial activities. Around Christmas time, you may see Chinese people in shops and restaurants wearing a Santa Claus hat, and notice Christmas trees and music everywhere you go, but these are acts stripped of any true significance.

The introduction of Western celebrations does not mean that Chinese festivals are disappearing, on the contrary, traditional festivals are gaining new ground and the Chinese government wants to re-emphasize festivals like Tomb Sweeping Day (*qingming jie*), Dragon Boat Festival (*duanwu jie*), and the Moon Festival (*zhongqiu jie*) alongside Chinese New Year (*chun jie*).[47]

4.7.6 Official Holidays

In November 2007, the National Development and Reform Commission initiated a proposal to have seven official holidays in China. It applies as of 1 January 2008.

The 1st of May is Labor Day. The 1st of October is the national holiday, the day on which the PRC was established. The seven official holidays are: Chinese New Year (7 days), Qing Ming Festival (3 days), Labor Day (3 days), Duan Wu Festival (3 days), Mid Autumn Festival (3 days), National Day (7 days), and the Gregorian New Year (3 days).

Christmas: an imported celebration

[1] Gray John Henry, China. *A History of the Laws, Manners and Customs of the People*, Dover Publications, Inc. Minneola, New York, 2002 (first printed in 1878 by Macmillan London), pp 178–179

[2] Smith-Glintzer H., *Geschichte der chinesichen Literatur. Die 3000 järige Entwicklung der poetischen, erzählenden und philosophisch-religiösen Literatur chinas von den Anfängen bis zur Gegenwart*, München / Wien, 1990, p 485

[3] Goldman Merle, Ou-Fan Lee Leo, *An Intellectual History of Modern China*, Cambridge University Press, Cambridge 2002, p 16

[4] Smith-Glintzer H., 1990, p 503

[5] Silbergeld Jerome, Ching Dora, *Persistence/ Transformation. Text as Image in the Art of Xu Bing*, Tang Center for East Asian Art, Princeton University, 2006, p 99

[6] Driessen Chris, Mierlo, van, Heidi, eds. *Another Long March. Chinese Conceptual and Installation Art in the Nineties*, Fundament Foundation Breda, 1997, p 99

[7] Zhang Xudong, *Chinese Modernism in the Era of Reforms.* Duke University Press, Durham, London, 1997, p 268

[8] More information on the main trends in the Cultural Fever, see Zhang Xudong, 1997, pp 35–70

[9] http://www.chinadaily.com.cn/english/doc/2004-08/26/content_369162.htm

[10] Xie Weidong, *Aolin pike jingshen. Aolin pike jingshen yu zhonghua minzu jingshen de wanmei tongyi.* Zhonghua gong shang lianhe chubanshe, Beijing 2007, p 1

[11] For an overview of China Politics and Law, see Mackeras, Colin, *The New Cambridge Handbook of Contemporary China*, Cambridge University Press, 2001

[12] Foreign Policy in Focus (3/9/2007): http://www.fpif.org/fpiftxt/4065

[13] Qu Sanqiang (2002), p 49

[14] SARS, Severe Acute Respiratory Syndrome, a disease leading to quick death, broke out in China in 2003 and grew to international proportions over a period of a few months.

[15] Silberberg, Ching, 2006, p 56

[16] http://news.sina.com.cn/c/2007-08-16/020512391211s.shtml

[17] *New York Times*, 14 November 2007

[18] Falungong is a religious sect established by Li Hongzhi in 1992. It takes a clear anti-Chinese government stand. In 1999 the Falungong held a peaceful protest action outside Zhongnanhai, the Chinese central government complex. The day after this incident, the sect was forbidden in China. The Falungong has millions of members all over the world, both inside and outside China. In Hong Kong, Taiwan and in the West they regularly hold strong anti-China propaganda campaigns.

[19] Cheung Chan Fai, "Tang Junyi and the Philosophy of "General Education", in: De Bary Theodore, *Confucian Tradition and Global Education*, Chinese University Press Hong Kong, Columbia University Press, New York, 2007, p 66

[20] Ibid, p 66

[21] http://www.edu.cn/20050114/3126820.shtml

[22] http://www.edu.cn/21st_1407/20060323/t20060323_3996.shtml

[23] *China Daily*, 21 June, 1999

[24] www.edu.cn

[25] Gao Ge, Ting-Toomey, 1998, p 41

[26] Fang Tony, 1998, p 99

[27] De zhi ti

[28] De cai jianbei

[29] Shui di shi chuan

[30] Meihua xiang zi ku han lai

[31] Chi de ku zhong ku fang wei ren shang ren

[32] Zhi yao gongfu shen tie chu mo cheng zhen

[33] Xue hai wu ya ku zuo chuan

[34] Qiang da chu tou niao

[35] Zhang zhe wei zun zhang zhe wei xian

[36] John Friedmann, 2005, *China's Urban Transition*, Chapter 6 'The governance of city-building' University of Minnesota Press, Minneapolis, London, 2005 pp 96–116

[37] Ledderose Lothar, *Ten Thousand Things*, Princeton University Press, 2001, p 117

[38] David Strand, 1989. *Rickshaw Beijing. City People and Politics in the 1920s.* Berkeley UP, pp 98–99, quoted in Friedman, 2005

[39] Friedmann, 2005, p 103

[40] Ibid p105

[41] Ibid p106

[42] http://www.clzg.cn/xinwen/2007-10/10/content_965935.htm

[43] http://news.sina.com.cn/z/hukou/index.shtml

[44] Zhang Qingwu "The resident identity card and the household register" in: Michael Dutton, *Streetlife China*, Cambridge University Press, 2000, p 94

[45] http://www.womenofchina.cn/people/unique_women/17120.jsp

[46] *Asia Times* (10/24/07) http://www.atimes.com/atimes/China_Business/IJ24Cb01.html

[47] http://www.nytimes.com/2007/11/10/world/asia/10china.html?_r=1&oref=slogin

5 Communicative China

5 Communicative China

5.1 Languages and Communication

5.1.1 Introduction

The Chinese language seems to be very difficult, complex and mystical for those who are not familiar with it. In fact it is possible to gain some basic insight into the system of Chinese characters and the language in a relatively short space of time. However, after that, a lengthy process ensues, in which a Westerner will go through stages ranging from delight when at last being able to understand, read and write Chinese texts, to intervals of complete frustration with the amount still waiting to be studied or reading a sentence, recognizing all the characters, but still not understanding what is written because they can't grasp the grammatical structure. Learning Chinese is a life-long process with many ups and downs.

After many years one can reach a more or less satisfactory level in Chinese language skills. However, the challenge persists because even if one masters the language to some extent, there are still thousands of proverbs and sayings you have to learn. What Westerners initially experience as most difficult is pronunciation in the right tone, and the different meanings a character can have in different contexts.

But learning Chinese is worth the effort for anyone who works in China or with the Chinese. Speaking a few words of the language will open doors. It will help you to become less of an outsider. The higher your level of Chinese, the more you will be regarded as an insider.

Language has far-reaching consequences on intercultural communication between Chinese and Westerners.

Although a lot of research has been done on foreign language acquisition, very little has been done in the field of the relationship between language skills and leadership or language skills and conflict management for Westerners working in Chinese environments. Native English speakers frequently underestimate the extent to which mastery of language is a prime contributor to failed cross-cultural interactions.[1] Peng Shiyong pleads for empiric research in the field of language and choice of conflict style: "Would a Chinese person with a higher level of English-speaking proficiency be more likely to adopt conflict styles similar to an English-speaking expatriate? Would expatriate employees with a higher level of Chinese proficiency be more likely to adopt conflict styles similar to their Chinese colleagues? If learning a foreign language also means integrating into or adapting to a foreign culture, how does foreign language proficiency increase the cultural sensitivity of the learners and therefore, influence their way of handling conflicts?" [2]

5.1.2 Features of the Chinese Language

Chinese has no alphabet. There are relatively few grammatical rules. Verbs are not conjugated; past or future are not indicated. Chinese characters get their meaning from the context in which they appear. A character in a sentence can function as a verb, a noun or something else, and thus can have different grammatical functions.

Chinese is a tonal language. Mandarin or *Putonghua*, the standard language in the People's Republic of China, has four tones. The pronunciation of a character in a different tone, generates a different meaning: *ma*1: mother; *ma*2: hemp; *ma*3: horse; *ma*4: to curse.

5.1.3 Simplification of Chinese Characters

After the establishment of the People's Republic of China, Mao Zedong and the CCP organized literacy programs for the people. One of the measures they took was the simplification of the Chinese script. In 1956 the first list of simplified characters (*jian tizi*) was introduced. In 1964 the definitive list was published. Taiwan, Hong Kong and the overseas Chinese still use the traditional non-simplified characters (*fan tizi*). Much criticism is heard about the simplification in these areas. Simplification diminishes the aesthetic value of the character, but also to some extent the etymology and the traceability of the different constituents of a character. Despite the general introduction of simplification in the PRC, artists and calligraphers sometimes still use the non-simplified characters.

5.1.4 Mandarin and Local Languages

Since the beginning of the twentieth century the term *Guoyu* or 'National Language' was used to refer to the standard language based on the Beijing dialect. Attempts to implement a unified standard language for the whole of China have been made since that time. From 1932 *Guoyu* was the standard pronunciation of the standard language. In 1952 it was replaced by the term *Putonghua*, which is still used today, and which refers to the 'general language' or standard language based on the Beijing dialect.[3] People all over China learn the standard language, even if their mother tongue is another language like Tibetan, Uyghur, or Mongol, or any other 'local language' or 'dialect' like Cantonese or Shanghainese.

5.1.5 Indirect Grammatical Structures

The indirectness of Chinese communication stands in stark contrast to the direct manner of communication used by Westerners. Indirect communication is not limited to body language, indirect communication patterns (on which we will elaborate later), or the use of intermediaries. The Chinese language itself has grammatical structures that are indirect. That is the case for example with '*fei ... bu*' like in '*fei... bu ke*', or '*fei ... bu xing*'. *Fei* and *bu* are both negations resulting in a meaning that is strongly affirmative. Instead of saying 'You must go!' the Chinese might say 'It's not OK if you don't go'. Another example is that instead of speaking a very affirmative sentence, the Chinese might tend to ask a question. This leads to misunderstandings. A Western manager asking a question may be surprised if his Chinese employee interprets his question as a task. In the Chinese context, however, when a person higher in rank asks a question it is often interpreted as an assignment. When someone higher in the hierarchy speaks, he must be followed. A very general remark can also be interpreted as a compliment or a criticism. The Chinese also tend to make a lot of use of words like 'maybe', 'probably', 'possibly' without purposely intending to express doubt or uncertainty.

5.1.6 Working with Translators

Western people working in China very often have to rely on an interpreter. It is important to realize that the Chinese language has a completely different structure to Western languages and that translating is therefore a more difficult task than say translating between two Western languages.

Simultaneous translators are hard to find. For simultaneous translation two translators are sometimes used, alternating every twenty minutes because due to the different language structures it is an extremely tiring process for the human brain.

Even for consecutive translation, the translator should always have the opportunity to prepare. Every language has its particular technical jargon, but Chinese is even more complicated due to the fact that, as explained above, Chinese characters can have different meanings depending on the context. Usually Chinese people write out their speech or lecture beforehand and give it to the translator so that he or she can prepare. Westerners who have no insight into the Chinese language don't often realize how important it is to provide the translator with material and texts beforehand.

5.1.7 Body Language

Gaining insight into a culture and the way communication patterns reflect underlying cultural tendencies is crucial in order to achieve a deeper understanding of intercultural communication. Body language is an integral part of human communication. This is the case in cultures using direct communication patterns as well as in cultures using indirect communication patterns. People using direct communication will attach more importance to the words that are spoken; body language will have to reflect a direct open communication attitude. In highly collectivist societies like China where communication patterns are indirect and have to be interpreted in the whole context of the given situation, words carry less weight, and might even have an opposite underlying meaning. Body language is connected to indirectness and respect for hierarchy.

When the power distance between the two participants engaged in communication is high, the lower one may be reluctant to look directly and openly into the eyes of the high-ranking person. Looking away from a person who is talking to you might be interpreted in the West as 'showing no interest in the person speaking', or 'feeling embarrassed', or 'having something to hide', while in the Chinese context this is a sign of respect more than anything else.

Smiles can be interpreted as an indirect action. For a Westerner, smiling is associated with happiness (or sarcasm in some cases). A Chinese person may be very angry or frustrated and still smile, to hide or conceal his real feelings. Chinese use many different ways of smiling. A frustrated or angry smile is very different from a happy smile, but Westerners not used to this kind of body language tend to interpret situations wrongly when it comes to frustrated or angry smiling. Chinese people have a different sense of humor than Westerners. The ironic humor Westerners use is usually not appreciated or understood by the Chinese. It is difficult to pinpoint the Chinese sense of humor. Generally speaking, the Chinese laugh a lot more than Westerners in everyday life and they love to play games.

Bodily contact exists more in China than in the West and especially between people of the same gender. For example, it is normal for men to pat each other on the shoulder or on the knee. Men walk arm in arm down the street. The physical distance between people in China is smaller than in the West.

Silence may also be seen as a form of body language. Chinese have a great deal more silence in conversations or negotiations than Westerners are used to. Sometimes Chinese people really take their time to think things through.

5.2 Guanxi Networks: A Society of Circles

5.2.1 Insider – Outsider Ethics

Members of the in-group (*nei*) look after each other, share with each other, and live together. Demarcation of the group happens in several ways. The 'family' is an in-group, but an in-group can be more extensive, for instance the 'family and friends'.

The Great Wall

A superficial functional relationship exists with people outside the in-group (*wai*), but there is no real engagement. With strangers or outsiders there is no family tie and no tie on the basis of common experience. The relationship is superficial, temporary, only dominated by utilitarian motives. The relationship is instrumental, without any form of affection. One does not have responsibility for someone one does not know. Here, insider-outsider ethics rule. In difficult situations this may mean that people are not inclined to help spontaneously. A sort of fundamental distrust towards people you don't know exists in China. Chinese don't like to be involved in or take responsibility for situations over which they have no control.

People in the West with a Greek-Roman-Christian background have difficulty with insider-outsider ethics. You think you have built up a relationship with someone, and at a certain point other parties show up that seem to be more interesting and the so-called friendship seems to disappear as if it never existed.

The division in *nei*, inside and *wai*, outside recurs in all kinds of ways. Working together with the Chinese is very nice because people take their jobs seriously and you can really count on your colleagues or employees. But as soon as the professional task is finished, there is no engagement anymore. The relationship is purely functional. No matter how nice a contact is during work, it very often ends when the job ends. It can take a long time to move from the position of outsider to that of insider.

The distinction between insiders and outsiders is influential in the (lack of) information sharing between people, between departments, or in negotiations where strategies are used to make it clear to the opposite party that they do not belong. The term *neibu* is often used in this context, which means 'internal/inside/indoor'. Internal information is not shared with outsiders. Strong loyalty towards the in-group may even lead to 'inter-departmental indifference, stonewalling, and competitiveness in Chinese organizations'.[4]

Official organizations always have a *waibu*, a department responsible for 'outside' or 'external' contacts that looks after visitors. A 'region' can also be considered an in-

Walled Complex in Beijing

group. In criminality it is usually the *waidi*, those from some 'outside area' who get the blame.

An experience the author went through is exemplary of insider-outsider ethics and the refusal to share information connected to it. After receiving a scholarship in the nineties to do research on contemporary literature at the Shaanxi Shifan University, due to a number of circumstances she wrongly ended up in the history department instead of the literature department. During the welcome dinner, the history department professors introduced her to a professor from the literature department. During her month-long stay, however, it was impossible to receive any support or engagement from the literature professor or anyone else from the literature department. Whenever she phoned this professor, she always came up with some reason for why she could not help her. The author was able to do her research in the general library without any problem, but if she needed material from the literature department, she met with considerable resistance. They were unfriendly; she had to pay to consult their resources. The literature department obviously perceived her as an outsider and they made this very clear to her. Apparently, the introduction made by the history department professors did not have enough authority to transfer her from an insider of the history department to an insider of the literature department.

5.2.2 Chinese Insiders – Foreign Outsiders

Through the ages the Chinese have considered themselves at the top of the hierarchical pyramid of society, resulting in feelings of superiority. For centuries, the Chinese regarded foreigners as 'barbarians'. They were referring mostly to the 'uncivilized' Northern tribes from Mongolia. When the Chinese first met Caucasians, the idea arose that there was still another category of 'barbarians', who hadn't had the privilege of receiving a fine Chinese education. Foreigners are called *guilaoer*, 'foreign devil' or *yangguizi*, 'ocean ghost'. A commonly used expression today for foreigner is *laowai*; *wai* means 'outside', implying the position of the 'outsider'. Even though *lao* is a fairly respectful term for 'old', a foreigner in China remains an outsider. No matter how long you live in China, no matter how well you speak Chinese, you will always be an outsider.

The negative connotation of terms used to describe foreigners is linked to the bad experiences the Chinese had with foreigners. Westerners brought war, violence and frustration to China in the nineteenth century. During Mao's reign foreigners were associated with decadence and perversion.

Today the Chinese are more open to foreigners, but they are still in a separate category to which different rules apply. The image most Chinese have of foreigners is a cliché (like the image most Westerners have of the Chinese). Some Chinese divide the world into two: China and foreign countries. All 'foreign countries' and all 'foreigners' are one and the same: outsiders.

There is a kind of apartheid system in China. At universities and in schools, foreigners live in separate buildings. Control over interaction between the two still exists. Foreigners often live in the same compound in cities. Foreigners can never rent a residence opposite a government building. The government chooses the buildings in which foreigners can establish Representative Offices.

To become more of an insider, it is crucial to build relationships. Language skills can help, as can knowledge of Chinese culture and history. But perhaps the most important is showing commitment towards China.

5.2.3 Guanxi and Reciprocity

Chinese society functions on the basis of personal relationships rather than on the basis of law. Law is in a developmental stage and is gaining ground. But with no separation of power, the law and judicial system do not fundamentally protect people nor is there any possibility of dealing with conflicts on the basis of formal rights. Social relations ensure protection. This absence of an objective judicial and law system is the basis for the impact of *guanxi* in Chinese society.

The term *guanxi* is usually left un-translated in Western literature because it is quite difficult to find a word rendering the full and right meaning, as it refers to a specific kind of networking that does not exist in the West. *Guanxi* refers to long-term relationships between people, implying reciprocity and mutual obligation.

Chinese living abroad seldom rely on the society they find themselves living in. Most often they look after each other. Due to this specific way of interacting and networking or *guanxi*, Chinese all over the world are connected to each other. This gives them a certain strength that other peoples don't have.

Interpersonal transactions between Chinese are based on *renqing* and *huibao* or *bao*. *Renqing* literally means 'human feelings'. It has three layers: feelings between people, a person's natural inclinations, and interpersonal resources. *Bao* means 'to correspond', ' to repay', 'to retribute'.[5] The reciprocity (*huibao*) of a relationship is without time limit. This means that person X can help person Y today and maybe only many years later will he come to ask for help in return. When person X comes to ask for help in return, it is the obligation of person Y to fulfill it, whatever the request may be. Chinese call this 'feelings' (*qing* or *renqing*). You could say that person Y 'owes a lot of feelings' to person X.

The reciprocity is socially binding. Social interaction cannot happen in disconnection from reciprocity, from the exchange of services. The moment you ask someone for a favor, you 'owe him *renqing*' and the obligation of reciprocity exists. The obligation for reciprocity stays until one has reciprocated. In practice however this is not a one-off exchange. In reality, the more you exchange, the more you engage, the deeper the relationship becomes, and the more difficult it becomes to extract oneself. Social obligations pull you into a relationship, and since there is no time limit for the reciprocity, there is no way to escape. The nice side of it is that relationships tend to be much more long-term than in the West.

Engaging in *renqing* and *guanxi* usually also means a heavy social investment. Once one is inside the *renqing wang* ('network of feeling') or *guanxi wang* ('network of relations'), he is locked into an intricate relationship of interdependence with others. He is socially obliged to respond to any request for help from others. As such, the individual loses his autonomy and freedom.[6]

Social obligation is implied in family relations, and reciprocity towards your parents exists from the moment you are born. To honor and love your parents is part of this reciprocity. That is the reason why the Chinese are closely connected and loyal to their network. Chinese society is strongly group-oriented, contrary to Western societies that are very individual-oriented. An individual in China belongs to and depends on a group. It is almost impossible in the Chinese context to be befriended by an individual. This group-orientation results in becoming part of a network, rather than being able to establish a friendship between just two individuals.

The system of *guanxi* can be traced back to Confucius. Confucius, looking for a system to bring social harmony, departed from the fact that human beings connect to and rely on each other. An individual is not an isolated entity but operates, lives, and acts in a group, in relation to others. The Confucian social order is based on the concept of *lun*, the differentiation between individuals and the sort of relation they have.

The fundament of Chinese interpersonal relationships is based on the Confucian principles of moral behavior: loyalty (*zhong*), filial piety (*xiao*), humanity (*ren*), credibility (*xin*), justice (*yi*), and harmony (*he*). Social order and stability depend on the observance of the right role patterns and relationships between individuals. The hierarchy, rules and public behavior, as described by Confucius, need to be respected at all times.

Guanxi can originate in a relationship or in a common experience. In principle everyone you meet in the course of your life can end up as a new relationship. From the moment you are born to the moment you die, your network extends. Classmates, neighbors, friends of friends, colleagues, in principle anyone can become part of your network.

The closest link for each individual is the link with his own family. This is an obligatory relationship, a connection and commitment for life. Chinese families are closely knit, and loyalty is for life. In China after the opening up, many overseas Chinese started to restore links with their hometown. If a Chinese person has lost connection with China, and then finds relatives in his hometown in China (the Chinese government provides services to overseas Chinese so that they can trace their ancestors), he will automatically have a network he can rely on.

Between Chinese sharing the same surname there is what may be called a 'fictive' relationship, or as the saying goes: "Five hundred years ago we were one family". Sharing the same surname implies that there is some kind of a link. The Chinese also have unspoken rules, like someone called Zhang should never marry someone called Pang, because they might at sometime have belonged to the same family.

Group-orientation influences the status of an individual in society. You could almost say that in some cases the Chinese don't have an independent social status, due to the obligatory connection with their family and network. In this way, individuality is different in China than in the West. An individual always exists in relation to others and this relationship is central in individual experience. In the West, an individual is more independent. An individual is considered as an independent, autonomous entity with unique features, motivations and possibilities. Each individual organizes his life on the basis of personal, individual choice. A child in the West learns to be independent at a very young age. The education system in the West is also designed to develop individual, independent people. Even relationships are based on personal individual choice alone. A child in China learns to obey and to be subject to the needs of the family and group. Relationships in China have a deeper impact on individual life than in the West. A relationship is a goal in itself, rather than a means to reach a goal.

The Chinese have a strong tendency to divide people into categories and to treat them accordingly. This tendency to deal with people according to the relationship you have with them is what makes *guanxi* so influential. There are three distinct categories of relationships and they can be depicted as circles: the individual is the core of the circle, then comes the family circle (*jia ren*) around the individual, followed by the friends circle (*shou ren*), who can be friends, neighbors, classmates and so on. Outside the circle are strangers (*mosheng ren*), those people one has no connection with. Each of these three categories implies different social and psychological meaning for those involved and different ways of dealing with each other.

Chinese Sociologist Fei Xiaotong who studied social science in the US was one of the first Chinese people to claim Western theories as irrelevant to the study of Chinese society. In 1938 he established the first school of sociology in China. After the Communist takeover in 1949 the school was outlawed by the CCP and it moved to Hong Kong.

Fei Xiaotong represented Chinese society as circular waves like those that emanate from throwing a rock into the middle of a pond. The waves form a perfect circle around some central invisible point and, as they move further from that point, become weaker. Fei Xiaotong argued that while people in Chinese society display no distinct individualism like in Western societies, Chinese society exhibits more egocentrism than Western society.[7] The boundary between the self and the group is relative and elastic. The term *jia*, 'family' is an elastic entity; it sometimes includes only members of a nuclear family, but it may also include all members of a lineage or a clan. The term *zi jia ren*, 'one's own family' can refer to any person one wants to include; it is entirely up to the individual to contract or expand the boundary of the concept of *jia*.[8]

5.2.4 Guanxi Networks versus Relationships Based on Individual Choice

 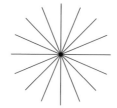

Guanxi, insiders-outsiders or Relationships based on individual choice

Fei Xiaotong contends that Western society consists of individuals who volunteer their loyalty to groups they choose, with reciprocal guarantees that the groups recognize the individuals' inherent rights. In Chinese society, the individuals, forever at the center of their worlds, generate waves that begin with themselves and expand through a series of bipolar relationships into their families, lineages, localities, provinces, and countries. Waves closer to the center elicit stronger relationships, and hence greater loyalty.[9]

Due to the fact that all Chinese are indebted to each other, they establish networks in which everyone is obliged to help everyone else. If only one Chinese person befriends me, it is virtually possible to do many things. I will ask my friend for help. If he cannot help me, he will ask a friend (who owes him), if he cannot help his friend will ask the next person (who owes him), and so on. In the end, it may be the eighth person in line who helps me. The social capital people build up in the course of their lives makes it possible to get whatever you need at whatever time. The counterpart is that you need to be ready to help your friends out at any time they need you.

If we compare Chinese relationships (the circle), with relationships in Western societies, it may be appropriate to depict relationships in the West as star-shaped. The individual finds himself in the center of the star. He builds relationships with all kinds of people; relationships can result in high commitment and loyalty. But in the West, relationships are made on the basis of individual choice. If person A has a good relationship with person B, this does not imply that his wife or father also has a good relationship with person B. They may not even know each other.

Individualist societies assure great freedom for the individual, but this implies that the individual cannot always count on the help of other individuals. Group-oriented societies have as a consequence the consuming of freedom of the individual for the sake of social capital, but people are always protected, surrounded and supported by others.

5.2.5 The In-Group

Relationships within the family are permanent and stable and caring for family members is an obligation. Everyone in the family has to fulfill the needs of the others without any clear expectation of receiving something back in return. Filial piety and unconditional love for one's parents is the most important form of reciprocity. A child does everything for its parents, always and everywhere, whatever happens. This is the child's duty.

The Chinese will give part of their wages to their parents, even if they live abroad. In relation to their children we can also see the group-orientation of Chinese families. A child is brought up as a member of the family, part of the group. Westerners sometimes find it strange that the Chinese who live in the West for many years will leave their child behind in China. It is even possible that when a Chinese couple has a baby in the West, they will send it back to China to be raised there. Sometimes this is due to economic circumstances. Today many people from the countryside in China work in the city; they don't necessarily have the means or possibility to keep their child with them. So when they have a baby in the city, after a few months they will bring it to the family in the countryside, after which they might only see it once a year, around Chinese New Year.

The relationship with friends is not a family tie, but they can be part of one's close network. Reciprocity dominates these relationships. The closer the ties people have, the higher the expectation of reciprocity. Each relationship is built on mutual exchange. Friends can be close or less close to an individual. When you are really close, friends will use the familial terms of address for you, like older sister, younger brother, aunty, and so on. The closer the tie, the higher the loyalty will be.

5.2.6 Establishing a Relationship

Establishing a relationship can be done by way of an intermediary who introduces both parties. An introduction by an acquaintance implies that the people being introduced are trustworthy. The intermediary is a kind of guarantee. *Guanxi* are at stake again: people who have a relationship will not want to harm this relationship by introducing someone who is not trustworthy. In fact this means that relationships, or *guanxi*, can be passed on. When no one is available on the spot, people will tend to search for a common acquaintance. Once such person is found, communication will loosen up and become more open.

When starting to work with the Chinese in any area, it is important to establish acquaintance by way of an introduction. If you have Chinese acquaintances you can ask for their help. If you don't know anyone you can look for a Sinologist to help you, or you can try via an official organization, for instance, economic representatives of your country in China.

Starting up business with China through the Internet is not an ideal situation because there is no personal relationship. When things go wrong there is no one you can turn to. You will be an outsider and no one will feel obliged to help you or to take any responsibility.

If you decide to start your cooperation with China via a trade fair, check if the person you first deal with is really what he claims to be. It may turn out to be a very good cooperation, but it can turn out very differently if the agent does not have the backup he claims to have.

In cooperation at any level with the Chinese, it is always important to set up a good relationship and to cherish that relationship. Only commitment will result in fruitful cooperation.

When people meet for the first time, they will try to establish an image of each other. The same questions reoccur: about both professional (function, position, title) and private life (marital status, children).

When an official delegation goes to China, the first meeting will always be informal, to establish the relationship. At the next meeting, business can be done, or policy can be discussed.

In e-mail correspondence, the Chinese will often start with an introduction during which the relationship is established. 'How nice to hear from you', 'How is your family?' 'I hope you are OK', and so on. Sometimes when twenty e-mails go back and forth, a Chinese person might continue to make use of an introductory sentence in every mail.

5.2.7 Regional Chinese Differences and Intercultural Communication

While indirect communication patterns are familiar to all Chinese, the goal being to maintain harmony and avoid losing face, and direct communication patterns are familiar to all Westerners, intercultural communication between Westerners and the Chinese will be influenced by the specific personal and regional and cultural background of the people involved. Some Westerners tend to communicate more indirectly than others, and some Chinese are more direct than others.

When comparing regions in Mainland China, different aspects and features will prevail in Beijing, Shanghai, Guangdong and Sichuan. Beijing is usually perceived as the most traditional and also the most Communist area. Shanghai has the longest tradition of international interaction, which is clearly reflected in a more open attitude that leans towards a more Western and direct way of communication. People from Guangdong tend to be very much focused on doing business and money, resulting in a more pragmatic style of communication. Sichuan is usually considered as easy-going. Life and business culture here tend to be more relaxed in comparison with other regions.

Hong Kong and Taiwan are regions with their own specific historical background. Both regions tend to be more adapted to doing business in a Western manner, while both have cultures that are strongly influenced by Confucian and family traditions. In general, Westerners experience cooperation with overseas Chinese from Hong Kong, Taiwan, Singapore or other areas as easier than working with Mainland Chinese. For this reason, overseas Chinese sometimes end up in managerial positions in the PRC. It is important to keep in mind the rivalries between different Chinese regions when appointing people to a certain position.

5.3 Face

5.3.1 The Concept of Face

The concept of face can be interpreted literally: the facial features of a person. To communicate people use language, body language and culture-specific communication patterns. The face of a person is one of the most important aspects in body language. The eyes of a person sometimes reveal what is left unspoken in words. Western people tend to have difficulty reading Chinese faces, claiming that the Chinese are less facially expressive than Westerners. From their side, the Chinese claim that Westerners often put themselves in weak positions by voicing what is on their mind and by showing their emotions. In the indirect communication environment, Chinese people learn to keep their emotions hidden.

On the other hand, the Chinese attach a lot of importance to physical facial features, like the shape of the eyes and eyebrows, length and size of the nose, shape of the ear, mouth and chin, shape of the forehead, shape and number of wrinkles, the location of moles on the face, etc. Inspired by holistic thinking, you could say that physical features reveal the character of a person. Even in today's China, there are books and CD-Roms for sale that teach about the aspects of *mianxiang*: 'Find Out Your Lifelong Luck'.[10] The science of 'Face' (*mianxiang*) can be decisive even in today's business environments. The CD-Rom mentioned above targets Chinese business people. The Chinese depicted are dressed in business suits, and carry mobile phones and portable computers at meetings located in modern office buildings.

The term face (*mianzi*) also refers to a more abstract idea, the public and social image of a person. Face refers to an individual's claimed sense of positive image in a relational and network context.[11] Face, in essence, is a projected image of one's self in a relational situation. It is an identity that is defined conjointly by the participants in a setting.[12]

In analyzing cultures, a distinction is made between so-called shame-cultures and guilt-cultures. In collectivist cultures the honor of the group is the most important aspect in human interaction. To avoid losing the honor of the group, people's behavior will be dominated by the avoidance of losing face in any given situation. In individualist cultures, which are sometimes called guilt cultures, people develop an inner conscious dominating behavior. When a person transgresses the prescribed social rules he will experience feelings of guilt. In individualist cultures, face is associated mostly with self-worth, self-presentation, and self-value, whereas in collectivist cultures, face is concerned more about what others think of one's worth, especially in the context of one's in-group.

Mianzi or face has several aspects.[13] First of all there is *qingmian*, the 'face of the feelings', connected to reciprocity in human relationships. One should always respect the concept of reciprocity. Not observing your social obligations leads to loss of face.

A second aspect of face is *changmian*, the 'face of the place where people gather', the 'public face'. This is connected to the way a person presents himself in public, linked to outward image. It is linked to hierarchical position in society. One should always behave according to his societal position. This aspect is responsible for the fact that the Chinese tend to overstate their image (exaggerated curriculum vitae, exaggerated size of a company or organization, exaggerated titles on a business card). This is related to power. Powerful people in China tend to organize huge banquets or big celebration parties to show off their power.

A third aspect of face is *timian*, the 'face of the body'. This is linked to dignity, correctness, decency. People should display dignity in all situations. This aspect is often used to describe family pedigree and well-educated behavior; it means 'face', 'appearances', or social respect for a family or an individual.

Ting-Toomey identifies three face concerns: self-face, other face, and mutual face. She argues that people in collectivist cultures are more concerned with other face compared with those in individualist cultures.[14]

Gao Ge and Ting-Toomey (1998) make the distinction between *lian* and *mianzi*, which can both be translated as face.[15] The concept of *lian* is associated with personal integrity and moral character of a person. It refers to an inner moral dimension. *Mianzi* is connected to prestige, to what a person has realized in life. *Mianzi* thus has a more outward connotation. The terms *lian* and *mianzi* are interchanged in literature. The conceptualization of face includes the following aspects:
- A sense of one's social self-worth or others' assessment of our social 'worthiness' or both.

- A vulnerable resource in social interactions given that it can be threatened, attacked, maintained, and enhanced.[16]

In China gaining and losing face is connected with social pride, honor, dignity, insult, shame, disgrace, trust, mistrust, respect, and prestige.[17] Face should be respected in all situations. In any interaction, giving face and avoiding loss of face should establish harmony. This can be done by observance of etiquette rules, respect for social position, respect for *guanxi*, and indirect communication strategies. Etiquette rules in China go a lot deeper than just being about good manners.

It is not only a person who has face; an organization, company, or a country also has face. An introduction about your company shows the face of your company. It is always a good idea to refer to the history of your company, to the history of its cooperation with China, to refer to all the important people who have any connection with your company, to refer to international activity and radiance. All these things will add up to the face of your company and will put it as high up as possible in the hierarchy.

5.3.2 Face and Guanxi

Face is connected to *guanxi*. The more *guanxi* with important people one has and the better one succeeds in building a network, the more face one will build up. It is the building of social capital in a Chinese sense that adds up to your face. The more high connections one has, the higher one's status becomes. The social status of a person is reflected in rank and titles and is linked to obligations.

This is the reason why a business card is so important in the Chinese context: it is a mirror of one's social position. This is also the reason why the Chinese like to have pictures of themselves with important people. To be on a picture with someone important lifts you to a higher position.

5.3.3 Reciprocity and Trading Face

Face can be employed as an influencing tactic in interpersonal relationships. Chinese face can be saved or lost; it can also be 'traded'.[18] A person who has been given face is expected to give face in return. In negotiations face is used as a means to exploit or to convince the other. For instance during negotiations between two people, a Chinese person might try to convince the opposite party to give into a certain bargain by claiming that he will lose face towards his superiors if he does not gain something from the negotiations.

5.4 Communication Patterns

5.4.1 Communication Patterns in Diffuse and Specific Cultures

by Fons Trompenaars[19]

Cultural theorist Fons Trompenaars makes a distinction between diffuse and specific cultures.[20] Involvement between people can be specific or diffuse. A person can allow other people to become involved in specific (limited) areas of his life and specific aspects of his personality. Or a person can allow other people into various domains of his life and different aspects of his personality. In cultures that are mainly specific, a manager will restrict his relationship with his subordinate to the business sphere and keep private matters distinct. Business and personal life are separated and this is usually the case in Western countries. In diffuse cultures all aspects of life are intertwined. The director is a director in authority wherever you meet him. His ideas are more important than the ideas of his subordinates. In these terms Chinese culture can be called diffuse.

The difference between diffuse and specific contexts leads to different communication patterns. In a specific culture communication follows the pattern on the right hand side of the picture above. Communication starts from a direct point of view. People start with the core of the message and then explain it.

In a diffuse culture the pattern on the left hand side is used. Communication circles around the subject and reaches the core issue at the end of the conversation.

Chinese people often use the communication pattern on the left. This pattern is used in collectivist cultures where losing face is to be avoided. By circling around the subject you go through a process where you build up a relationship, where you get to know what the other party's ideas are and what he really thinks.

In intercultural communication it is crucial to gain insight into communication patterns used by different parties. For people coming from a specific cultural background, circling around the subject may be experienced as indirect, apparently inefficient, and a waste of time, while for people coming from a diffuse cultural background, direct communication might be experienced as too direct and arrogant.

5.4.2 Group Dynamics

Group dynamics in China are dominated by the concepts of face, *guanxi*, hierarchy, and harmony. In any situation all members of a group need to be respected in their hierarchical position. To keep harmony means to respect the hierarchy between all group members. In principle, the one highest up in the hierarchy is in authority. He is the authority who has the knowledge, who speaks, who decides, whose words have to be obeyed. The others need to follow him. All group members have to make sure that no one loses face. Communication will be limited to the recognition of the authority of the leader (if the highest person is in a very high position the other people will often knod their head in appreciation of the words spoken by the person in authority). All the others will be superficial, to keep the harmony in the group. When a group of people is not familiar with each other and it is not very clear who is the highest in position, no one will take the lead, or take initiatives. To speak up when the possibility exists that one of the others present is higher in position than you would imply an insult to that person.

5.4.3 Indirect Communication and Indirect Actions in China

To avoid losing face and to avoid other people from losing face, the Chinese have developed a way of communication called 'indirect communication', and linked to this way of communication 'indirect actions' are taken. Ting-Toomey calls it Facework[21] or face-directed communication strategies[22]. Facework involves communicative strategies that are used to enact self-face and to uphold, support, or challenge the other's face. Face-directed communication strategies involve non-confrontation, compliance strategies, provisional responses, using intermediaries, and gossip (*yi lun*).

Non-confrontational strategies in communication are used because conflict is regarded as undesirable. Criticism belongs to the domain of conflict and needs to be approached in an indirect manner. The issues at stake in disagreements or arguments cannot be dealt with in public, especially when a superior is present. Chinese tend to comply in public, to preserve face, and to deal with disagreement in private. Assertiveness is not appreciated in Chinese culture. Instead of using affirmative or negative answers like yes or no, the Chinese use provisional responses like 'we will look into it' (*yanjiu yanjiu*), 'we will reflect on it' (*kaolu kaolu*), 'not convenient' (*bu fangbian*), or 'a bit difficult' (*you dian kunnan*). To avoid direct confrontation a third party (*di san fang*) or intermediary (*zhongjian ren*) is used. Through mediation by a third party direct confrontation is avoided and both parties preserve face.

Michael Bond sees gossip as another strategy in face-directed communication.[23] The superficiality of public conversations where individual opinions are yielded to protect face and to observe status differences is compensated by engagement in gossip in private conversations where true feelings can be outspoken. The fear of gossip and the spread of face-threatening information makes people limit the disclosure of personal information to the people they trust.

5.4.4 Communication Layers and Underlying Messages

Communication between the Chinese has multiple layers. The words that are spoken are the superficial layer. The symbols that are used in communication refer to something else. The real message has to be detected underneath the surface. For Westerners this kind of communication is confusing and misunderstandings arise. The Chinese however understand each other when they use indirect messages towards one another, because they are used to taking the whole picture into consideration and they have a clear view of hierarchical structures and the consequent desired behavior. When words are spoken one always has to be aware of the hierarchical position of the person speaking. Depending on his position, his words can have another meaning.

5.4.5 Avoidance of Responsibility

Lack of efficiency during the planned economy resulted in an attitude where people sometimes refuse to take responsibility. Chinese use several terms to avoid responsibility. When you need to see a person you might get 'bu zai', 'not here' as an answer. This may mean the person is not there, or that he may not want to see you, or that he does not work there. The answer 'bu zhidao', 'I don't know', creates an even stronger barrier. If people don't want to help you for some reason, you get this answer. Another common one is 'wo ye mei you banfa', 'it is beyond my control'. It blocks all possibility of further communication.[24]

5.4.6 Guanxi and Requests

Making a request and the way this is done is connected to the relationship between the people involved. When people have a relationship and reciprocity needs to be kept, it will be very easy to make a request. The more renqing or the stronger the reciprocity, the easier it becomes to request something.

Making a request to someone with whom you have no relationship will be a lot more difficult. The ideal situation would be to set up a relationship first, make sure the person you need 'owes' you something. However, it is not always possible to build relationships first. A request from someone you don't have a relationship with will often be very indirect. Something might be promised first, before the request is done. Or a story is told where the request is underlying the surface of the story.

When a request is made, a Chinese person will never reply with a 'no'. This would imply that the relationship is being damaged. Saying 'no' to a request is just not done. The consequence is that people reply with formulas like 'I will do my best', 'I will look into it', things that a Westerner might interpret as a 'yes', but which don't mean 'yes'.

5.4.7 Non Confrontational Criticizing

Chinese people can criticize each other by referring to historical events, or by referring to something else. To a Westerner who is used to direct communication patterns, the real message is often not understood. Confrontational criticism harms the harmony between people and is thus avoided in Chinese culture. The use of an intermediary means that loss of face and direct confrontation is avoided. The message will be understood, but the relationship between the people is not harmed. This is called indirect action.

In business and other professional situations in the Chinese context, criticism is best done in a non-confrontational way. A meeting can be held during which general remarks about problems can be discussed. But when a certain person is involved in a problem, it is not a good idea to confront him in the group. The chance is very high that he will deny his responsibility. This approach to criticism is too confrontational and people will have no choice but to do everything possible not to lose face. A confrontational approach will be contra productive. Not only the person who is openly criticized will be disturbed, the other people in the group may also become frustrated because confrontation disturbs harmony and everyone is supposed to know that this is not done, even a Westerner.

One-to-one meetings can be more open. Loss of face will still come into play, depending on the hierarchy between the people involved and depending on the situation. Losing face has to be avoided at all costs. When a boss calls someone into his office to criticize him, the others in the company will know and this implies loss of face. When the boss passes by the desk of an employee and asks them very informally and casually about a problematic situation, it will be less confrontational. These issues have to be kept in mind in corporate cultures with intercultural employee groups.

Westerners also use double layer communication that is confusing to the Chinese. In criticizing each other they sometimes use a kind of sarcastic humor. For instance, when a colleague has made a real mess of something, a Westerner might tease him by joking with a paradox: "I understand you were rewarded for your excellence in this job?" The Chinese do not usually understand or appreciate this kind of sarcasm.

5.4.8 Long Distance Cooperation

Due to the characteristics of communication in Chinese culture, long distance cooperation is problematic. If long distance cooperation is the format of cooperation your company chooses, make sure that some physical presence in China is assured. Having a contact person in China and one in the West to coordinate the cooperation process will limit misunderstandings and will result in more efficiency.

Long distance cooperation implies a lot of e-mail, and telecommunication. Generally speaking the Chinese prefer to use the telephone rather than e-mail communication, being reluctant to write e-mails or leave behind traces of written material. Some organizations even have policies to discourage written communication. In comparison to the West, the telephone is used a lot more in China than e-mail.

Conference calls may not always be the most efficient way to work either. Group dynamics with strategies to avoid loss of face, like they occur in real situations will be transplanted to group dynamics in conference calls.

[1] Smith P., Bond M. H., Kagitcibasi C., *Understanding Social Psychology Across Cultures. Living and Working in a Changing World*, Sage Publications, London, Thousand Oaks, New Delhi, 2006, p 7

[2] Peng Shiyong, (2003) *Culture and Conflict Management in Foreign-invested Enterprises in China. An Intercultural Communication Perspective.* Peter Lang, European University Studies, Vol. 369, p 73

[3] Wiedenhof Jeroen, *Grammatica van het Mandarijn*, Bulaaq, Amsterdam, 2004, p 7

[4] Bond, 1991, p 84

[5] Gao Ge, Ting-Toomey, 1998, p 29

[6] Tu Wei-ming, *The Living Tree. The Changing Meaning of Being Chinese Today*, Stanford University Press, 1994, p 121

[7] Haley George, Haley Usha, Tan Chin Tiong, *The Chinese Tao of Business. The Logic of Successful Business Strategy*, 2004, John Wiley & Sons (Asia) Pte Ltd, p 11–12

[8] Tu Wei-ming, *The Living Tree. The Changing Meaning of Being Chinese Today*, 1994, p 113

[9] Haley George, Haley Usha, Tan Chin Tiong, *The Chinese Tao of Business. The Logic of Successful Business Strategy*, 2004, John Wiley & Sons (Asia) Pte Ltd, p 12

[10] *Mianxiang. Toushi ni yi sheng de xingfu*, Beijing Zhongti Yinxiang Chuban Zhongxin Chuban Faxing

[11] Gao Ge, Ting-Toomey, 1998, p 53

[12] Gudykunst William, Ting-Toomey Stella, 1988, *Culture and Interpersonal communication*, Sage Publications, Newbury Park, London, New Delhi, p 85

[13] Three aspects of face often referred to by Huang Jinrong, an influential Shanghainese mafia godfather in 1930–'40s Shanghai. See: Shen Ji, *Shanghai Godfathers* (Shanghai Daheng), Xue Lin Chubanshe, Shanghai, 2001

[14] Gao Ge, Ting-Toomey, 1998, p 62

[15] Ibid pp 55–56

[16] Ibid p 56

[17] Ibid p 54

[18] Fang Tony, *Chinese Business Negotiating Style*, International Business Series, Sage Publications, Thousand Oaks, London, New Delhi, 1998, p 146

[19] Trompenaars, Fons, Hanpden-Turner Charles, *Over de grenzen van cultuur en management*. Contact, Amsterdam, Antwerpen, 1998, p 115

[20] Ibid p 105

[21] Gao Ge, Ting-Toomey, 1998, p 53

[22] Ibid p 60

[23] Bond, M.H., *Beyond the Chinese Face. Insights from Psychology*. Oxford University Press, Hong Kong, 1991, in Gao Ge, Ting-Toomey, p 67

[24] Michael Harris Bond points out that Chinese societies are intolerant of aggressive behavior but there might be less obvious ways of being hostile towards others: "Passive resistance is rarely labeled as 'aggressive' and hence not punished, although it may be equally effective in undermining the pressure of superiors.", Bond, p 16

6 Corporate China

6 Corporate China

6.1 From Planned Economy to Market Economy

Critics of planned economy claim that the sustained development of an economy can only be achieved through market forces. Pro-planned economists claim that sustained periods of development in centrally planned economies were also achieved. Whatever may be the case, in 1978 China decided to evolve from a Soviet inspired planned economy towards a market-oriented economy. The government loosened its grip on the management of State Owned Enterprises, gradually allowing foreign capital to enter China, and allowing more freedom for private initiatives. The result is an enormous growth of the economy, faster than anyone could have expected a few decades ago. The move from a planned economy towards a market economy has turned China into another country and it has global impact.

6.2 De-collectivization of the Communes and Decline of the Work Unit System

The move away from a planned economy and the subsequent privatization in society started with a rural reform: de-collectivization of the communes. The Chinese government imposed collective ownership after 1949. The reform brought a revival of household agriculture and a raise of productivity. Many family businesses were set up. Following the success of the rural reform, similar reforms took place all over China and enterprises started to change in nature from State Owned Enterprise to more and more privately owned.

The privatization of companies brought privatization of housing. More and more people in China buy their house today. Families, sometimes friends invest their private money in real estate. Real estate is now a big thing in China and a lot of money can be made. Many people engage in buying and selling real estate. The ground remains state property, but the buildings are privately owned. Many Chinese who own real estate, own not one house, but several. Because more people have private possessions, the government changed the constitution in 2007 to protect private property.

The work unit as it existed in pre-1978 Communist China was slowly but surely dismantled. Before the reforms, the work unit not only completely controlled the lives of all citizens; social security and basic needs were also taken care of. The architectural structures and infrastructure of the work unit still exists today in many cases, but the housing that used to be free, now has to be paid for. Health insurance that used to be free now has to be paid for. Schools that used to be free, cost a lot in the new China. The all-encompassing function of the work unit in former Communist times doesn't exist anymore. In spite of the fact that changes in the system of the work unit already started in 1978, some changes reducing the impact of the work unit on the life of an individual are quite recent. The dismantling of the work unit is not an overnight event; it is an evolution developing over decennia. Work units have lost their relevance in today's fast changing China. The end of the work unit system, and the changes in the Chinese social security system connected to it, are having an enormous impact on Chinese society.

Taiwan and Hong Kong never introduced the Communist work unit system. This means that traditional family structures have survived. This explains why many companies there are still family businesses.

6.3 Towards a Diversification of Ownership

In October 1984, the Chinese People's Republic decided to decentralize and privatize ownership. The economic reforms and privatization took place under central control, leading to a state-led growth or 'local state corporatism' as Oi calls it.[1] Some key elements of the Communist state were retained, while control and administration were decentralized to a point. De-collectivization in the countryside and fiscal reform were incentives to encourage local governments to become entrepreneurial. State Owned Enterprises are now responsible for their own management and operate more or less as private enterprises, because they have to compete in the market economy. The state no longer subsidizes badly performing enterprises; it now gives loans.

Initially the reforms knew a certain amount of success. In 1988 an economic crisis arose because too many State Owned Enterprises appeared to be making losses. Productivity of many companies was very low while they employed far too many personnel, to whom they not only had to pay wages, but also take care of their pension, health care, and housing.

In 1989 the State Owned Enterprise Bankruptcy Law was passed and enterprises could be declared bankrupt. A consequence of the closing down of many enterprises was that thousands of people became unemployed in a country where hardly any social security existed.

Solutions were sought in the restructuring of enterprises, in the selling of shares to employees and others, or in looking for financial support from abroad. As a consequence, privatization and decentralization were enforced and a diversification of ownership came into being.

Employee Shared Ownership (ESO) emerged in the beginning of the eighties when small and medium-size enterprises asked their employees to invest their savings in the company to relieve the company's financial difficulties. ESO was first formalized in the beginning of the nineties. ESO was followed by Township and Village Enterprises as other forms of ownership.[2]

After the reform various forms of enterprises now coexist side by side in China. The main forms of enterprise are:[3]
• State Owned Enterprises (SOE)
• Domestic Privately Owned Enterprise and Self Employed Businesses
• Listed Companies[4]
• Township and Village Enterprises (TVE)
• Foreign Owned Enterprises (FOE):
  • Joint Ventures (JV)
  • Wholly Foreign Owned Enterprises (WHOE).

6.3.1 State Owned Enterprise (SOE)

The State Owned Enterprise is fully owned by the Chinese government. During the planned economy, the management was formalized and standardized, and highly centralized by the state. Since the reforms of 1984, each SOE is responsible for its own management. Different measures are taken to improve efficiency. In the middle of the nineties new reforms were implemented: fixed duration and collective labor contracts instead of jobs-for-life; new remuneration systems to reflect performance, post and skill levels; and new welfare schemes in which all employers and employees are required by law to make contributions to five separate funds: pension, industrial accident, maternity, unemployment, and medical insurance.[5]

6.3.2 Domestic Privately Owned Enterprise and Self Employed Businesses

Many different forms of privately owned enterprises exist. They can be family owned, or owned by a group of independent people. This sector has been growing and expanding rapidly and steadily. The majority of businesses are involved in labor-intensive light manufacturing and commercial services. They operate in gaps and niches and are highly profit driven. Their organizational structure is becoming increasingly formalized with limited liability and share-holding entities are becoming the mainstay of private businesses.[6]

6.3.3 Listed Companies

Since the establishment of stock markets in Shenzhen and Shanghai in the early 1990s, the number of listed companies in China has increased. Although the capitalization of China's stock markets has grown enormously, the number of listed companies is only a small fraction of all the enterprises in China. Many of the major listed companies are former state owned enterprises in which the state retains a controlling share, with only a small proportion of the shares traded publicly. As a result, there is often little to show that stock market listing has fundamentally changed their management or performance.

6.3.4 Township and Village Enterprises (TVE)

To combat the stagnating agricultural economy in the mid-eighties, the government stimulated non-agricultural production within de-collectivized communes. Rising from the remnants of these de-collectivized communes were the so-called Township and Village Enterprises. The workforce was readily available. Most of the TVE are collectively owned by local citizens or privately owned. Local townships and village governments often control them in order to gain access to resources. A great diversity of TVE exist in terms of geographical location, size of enterprise, ownership patterns and governance structure.

6.3.5 Foreign Invested Enterprises (FIE)

Since China's opening up, foreign companies are attracted to invest there. The main incentives for foreign enterprises to do this are the investment incentives offered by the Chinese government, the availability of cheap labor, and a huge domestic market.

6.3.5.1 Joint Venture (JV)

Joint Ventures were mainly established during the eighties and nineties. In the first twenty years after the opening up of China, when most companies were state owned and strongly protected by government, most foreign companies entering China set up JVs with state owned enterprises.

There were two main ways of forming a JV. The SOE converted their existing factory and production buildings, equipment and land into shares in the JV, while the foreign partners invested capital, technology or equipment. A second possibility was that the SOE restructured itself into first a share-holding company, and then transferred part of the shares to the foreign investor.[7]

On establishment of a JV, local government appointed a local management team to maintain equilibrium with the foreign management. Local representatives were responsible for assuring the advantages on the Chinese side. At a later stage, foreign companies also set up JVs with the privately owned companies in China that were established after the reforms.

Generally speaking foreign investment in a Chinese company cannot be less than 25%. The form of the investment by the different partners can be money, tangible or intangible assets. Central government regularly publishes new guidelines for foreign investment. These guidelines outline which industries foreign investors can have more than 50%, or even 100% shareholding in.

For some sectors, a JV is the only legal option. For other activities one might need a specific partner. The advantage of a JV is that it offers a link with China from the very beginning. The Chinese partner already has a *guanxi* network (with government, customers, suppliers) that the foreign partner can make use of. Establishing a relationship with government will be go more smoothly than in the case of a Wholly Foreign Owned Enterprise, where this aspect might require a lot of time and effort.

Problems arising in a JV are often due to a conflict of interests. The Chinese want to make as much money as possible in the shortest time, while the foreign partner might want to develop a long-term strategy. It is crucial to subject the Chinese partner to an extensive and diligent appraisal before taking the step towards a JV. To correctly assess your future partner, to align your goals from the start, to strive for the same ethical standards and to set up an intercultural climate in which good relations can blossom will avoid many unpleasant surprises.

In terms of corporate culture, a JV will be a mixture of Chinese and Western corporate culture. Western companies tend to impose their corporate culture, but often find that adaptation to the Chinese partner and the Chinese environment is necessary.

6.3.5.2 Wholly Foreign Owned Enterprise (WFOE)

The first official regulations concerning a Wholly Foreign Owned Enterprise date from 1986, although the phenomenon already existed before that time. The WFOE is now the most common form of foreign investment. Just like a Joint Venture, a WFOE has pros and cons. The foreign enterprise has everything under control and there is no conflict of interest with a Chinese partner. The disadvantage is that there is no direct contact with China and a relationship with the government needs to be established, which can be a lengthy process.

However, there is no government control inside the enterprise, although the Chinese government does invite WFOEs to take on a representative of the Chinese Union, the ACFTU (All China Federation of Trade Unions), which is under control of the

CCP. WFOEs are not appreciated in certain areas. They can experience problems with, for instance, energy supply. Sometimes the situation is so difficult that a WFOE decides to set up a JV instead. In a WFOE, the top management is often Western but the majority of the personnel are Chinese. In the field of corporate culture, the same features and problems as a JV prevail.

6.4 Attracting Foreign Investment

6.4.1 Special Economic Zones (SEZ)

When in 1978 the Chinese government decided to attract foreign companies to invest in China, a number of areas were selected to receive these companies: the Special Economic Zones. The admittance of Western companies into China only happened under strict control of the Chinese government. The SEZ received a separate statute for national planning and had authority over economic management at provincial level. The local government of the SEZ also received legislative authority.

In the SEZ, Chinese-foreign Joint Ventures, partnerships and Wholly Foreign Owned Enterprises were established. Production was in the first place directed towards export.

In 1980, five SEZ were designated. Shenzhen, the area bordering Hong Kong, was the first in May 1980. In August of the same year SEZ in Zhuhai, Xiamen, Shantou and Hainan were established, all in the South of China.

All kinds of advantages were offered. The different SEZ competed with each other to attract foreign enterprises. They used their competence to approve special tax tariffs and support measures like advantages related to infrastructure. Today the five SEZ have existed for almost three decades. In the meantime, evolution has taken place with, amongst others, marked improvements in the law system and in management. This explains why these zones are better adapted to international needs and requirements than most other cities in China. Due to competition between the different zones, the advantages they offer respectively have almost reached the same level.

In 1984, apart from the SEZ, fourteen coastal cities were also opened to foreign enterprises: Dalian, Qinhuangdao, Tianjin, Yantai, Qingdao, Lianyungang, Nantong, Shanghai, Ningbo, Wenzhou, Fuzhou, Guangzhou, Zhanjian, and Beihai. In 1985 the coastal SEZ were extended so that the economic zone stretched along the Yangzi River Delta and along the Pearl River.

In 1990, the Chinese government decided to open a new SEZ in Pudong, Shanghai and other cities along the Yangzi River. Pudong was called the 'Dragon's Head', because it was one of the largest and most comprehensive development zones located in one of China's largest cities. From 1992 onwards still more areas were opened up.

Special advantages offered in Pudong included the lowering of custom and income taxes, and the admittance of foreign banks to perform transactions in RMB (*Renminbi*). Six branches of industry were set up: automotive industry, microelectronics and computers, electronic household goods, bio-medical, optical, mechanical and electronic products.

Sometimes the government decides to stimulate development. In October 2007, it announced that a twin-city SEZ in Sichuan province would be established between Chongqing and Chengdu to stimulate the economic development of the area.[8]

6.4.2 Industrial Parks

Industrial Parks were set up to facilitate all the material and infrastructure for investing foreign companies. The Industrial Park is like a 'walled' complex with guarded entrance gates. Everyone entering or leaving is controlled. The files on workers active in the Industrial Park are kept by the Park's central administration. The government retains control over human resources. The difference between an Industrial Park and a Communist work unit in terms of the social system is that a Park does not always provide logistics. Workers live outside and schools and health care are organized outside. However, in large Industrial Parks it is possible that schools, hospitals and housing are still organized within the walls, but the costs will no longer be paid for by the government.

6.4.3 Representative Office

The simplest form of establishing a presence in China is a Representative Office (Rep Office). The establishment and registration of a Rep Office is a relatively simple procedure. A Rep Office has no independent legal status. No commercial activities are allowed. Invoices must be issued abroad, which can result in problems with RMB transactions. The Rep Office is under the strict control of the government. Government even allocates the location for the Rep Office, usually in expensive office buildings. Government offices recruit the Chinese personnel for the Rep Office. If in practice this happens in some other way, the recruit has to be registered at the Labor Service Bureau upon recruitment.

6.5 Stages in Regional Economic Development and Development of Infrastructure

From the very beginning of the reforms, the Chinese government decided on a gradual development of the economy in the different regions of China. As Deng Xiaoping put it, some people had to be allowed to get rich first, before the others. The coastal cities and coastal areas were to be developed first, followed by the interior regions and cities, followed by the less developed interior and the West of China. The development of coastal areas is well on the way and many regions have reached a high level of development.

The rapid economic development of the last decennia has required the development of transport and communication systems throughout China. When China opened its doors in 1978, roads, railroads, aircraft, and harbors were in terrible shape. Since that time, China has gone through an infrastructural revolution. Numerous airports have been built and new flight connections established. Gigantic new railways stations have been built with the most modern trains. The South station in Beijing is the largest station in Asia. Brand new subway systems serve several cities and are under continuous expansion. In Shanghai the world's fastest train, the Maglev, connects Pudong Airport with the center of the city. China's harbors have also undergone a metamorphosis. The Hangzhou Bay Bridge, the longest cable-stayed bridge in the world, connects Shanghai with Ningbo. Thousands of kilometers of railroad have been built connecting cities and within the cities themselves, drastic structural changes have been implemented. More and more people own a car, making a fast adaptation of the road system indispensable.

This new infrastructure was first developed in the fastest economically growing areas. The Chinese government is very much aware of the inequalities in this respect between the different regions in China and therefore has a policy to extend economic development to the West of China. In 2000, the 'development of the West' (*xi bu da kaifa*) policy was implemented. By developing transport and infrastructure, economic developments are being stimulated. A railroad network has been built linking all of China's strategic places and connecting China to neighboring countries. In 2006, the railroad connecting Beijing with Lhasa, running over the Tibetan High Plateau, was opened. In fact a railroad network now stretches from Singapore to Uzbekistan. New roads have been built between China and Laos, Nepal, Kazakhstan, and Pakistan.

The rapid development of the transport network in the West of China has met with criticism. The economic opening up of the Western regions will stimulate the influx of Han-Chinese into the Autonomous Regions of Tibet and Xinjiang. Critics claim that roads are being built solely for the exploitation of natural resources and mineral reserves found there.

Despite the enormous efforts being made in the development of transport infrastructure, there are still many problems, such as constant traffic jams in cities and on main roads.

The CCP's 'development of the West' is not limited to infrastructure development: graduated students, teachers, engineers, agronomists, administrators and doctors, are being encouraged by the Communist Party Youth League to go and work in the West of China, (Tibet, Xinjiang, Yunnan) for a few years. In each of the past five years, the Communist Party Youth League has selected 10,000 volunteers to help people in China's least developed, and often ethnically strained regions.[9]

Corporate China

6.6 Understanding Cultures and Corporate Cultures

6.6.1 Culture and Work-Related Culture

Before we go any deeper into corporate culture in China, we will focus on the impact of general culture on corporate culture. All too often, what happens inside companies is seen as disconnected from the general culture of a country or an area. Corporate culture is part of a larger social context and is related to general cultural norms and values. The culture inside a company is largely influenced by the culture of the people who work in it and the culture of the country where a company is active.

Cultural theorist Fons Trompenaars explains how people in a culture where face and loss of face are crucial take time to get to know each other before they talk about doing business.[10] Doing business with these kind of cultures is time-consuming, precisely because you have to go a long way before you can build up trust. In China, the concept of face influences all human interaction. You need to build a good relationship before you can do good business or expect efficient cooperation. To build up the relationship, business people will have to participate in banquets and karaoke singing, or in tourist outings. In the eyes of many Western business people this is a waste of time. In the eyes of the Chinese it is necessary, because a good relationship is crucial. It is necessary to think in the long-term when working with the Chinese. Once a relationship is good, doing business in a good way will automatically follow.

Geert Hofstede provides a framework for the study of cultures and work-related values.[11] He began his research in 1972 when working at IBM, a multinational corporation active in over 50 countries worldwide. By surveying more than 100,000 IBM employees and by statistical analysis of the survey data, he arrived at his theory of the five dimensions. According to Hofstede, all cultures score to a greater or lesser extent in all five dimensions.

For Geert Hofstede, the human being is mentally programmed. Hofstede sees a universal, a collective and an individual level in that programming. What people of the same culture share, belongs to the collective level. His analysis focuses on the collective level of cultures. In that collective level Hofstede distinguishes five dimensions: power distance, uncertainty avoidance, individual versus collective, masculine versus feminine, and long-term versus short-term orientation.

In the next paragraph we will go into the specific features of each of the dimensions as described by Hofstede because they provide an overall framework through which we can look at cultural differences between China and the West (Europe and the US). Some of the dimensions are less important (masculine-feminine) than others when we talk about China. But the general framework offers a good view on, for example, the differences between power distance, or individual or group-orientation in China and the West. We could almost say that the differences between China and the West occupy opposite positions for some dimensions. But this is of course only true if we speak in very general terms. We always deal with individual people who might be completely different from the so-called general framework they belong to. This is an interesting framework, but it is no more than that. It is certainly not a working tool for intercultural communication. The working tool should always be an open attitude without prejudices.

6.6.2 Geert Hofstede: Five Dimensions in Cultures

Power distance is related to the different solutions cultures give to the basic problem of human inequality.[12] Power distance is the degree of inequality in power between a less powerful individual and a more powerful one, both belonging to the same social system. Answers to questions dealing with hierarchical relationships differ systematically across countries. This has influence on, for example, leadership styles or on how social position in society, in education or in a company is regarded.

In societies with low power distance, parents treat their children as equals; children learn to respect the rules and to be competent and independent at a young age. At school, teachers see their students as equals; students treat their teachers as equals. Students can initiate communication in class and the quality of learning depends on two-way communication. At work level, low power distance results in decentralized decision-making structures, less concentration on authority, flat organization structures, and a low proportion of supervisory personnel. Managers rely on personal experience and on their subordinates. Subordinates expect to be consulted. Hierarchy in organizations is functional. Consultative leadership leads to satisfaction, performance, and productivity. Sweden is a good example of a culture with very low power distance.

In a society with high power distance, parents teach their children to obey. Respect for parents and older relatives are a basic virtue. Children are not seen as competent until they reach a certain age. At school, the students depend on teachers. They treat their teacher with respect, even outside the classroom. In teacher-oriented education, the teacher initiates all the communication in class. In work situations, these cultures have a centralized decision-making structure with much concentration on authority. In tall organization pyramids with a high proportion of supervisory personnel, managers rely on formal rules. Subordinates expect to be told what they have to do. The ideal boss is a good father who sees himself as a benevolent decision maker. Authoritative leadership and close supervision lead to satisfaction, performance and productivity.

Uncertainty avoidance is related to the level of stress in a society in the face of an uncertain future.[13] Uncertainty creates anxiety. Human society has developed ways (technology, law, and religion) to cope with the inherent uncertainty of living and an uncertain future. Uncertainty avoidance refers to the extent to which the members of a culture feel threatened by uncertain or unknown situations.

In low uncertainty avoidance cultures, parents control their emotions, a higher satisfaction of home life is experienced and lenient rules exist about what is dirty and taboo. Few rules exist and if children cannot obey these rules, the rules should be changed. In interaction, undifferentiated and informal forms of address are used, and non-traditional gender roles are accepted. At school, students expect open-ended learning situations and good discussions. Teachers are allowed to say they don't know something. Self-efficacy and independence are important. In work situations there is weak loyalty to the employer, a short average duration of employment, preference for smaller organizations but little self-employment. Innovators feel independent of rules.

In high uncertainty avoidance cultures, parents behave emotionally, and a lower satisfaction of home life exists. There are tight, explicit rules on what is dirty and taboo. Many rules exist and if children cannot obey these rules, they are sinners who should repent. Strictly differentiated forms of address are used and traditional gender roles are preferred. At school, students expect structured learning situations and seek the right answers. Teachers are supposed to have all the answers. Students attribute achievement to effort, context and luck. Self-efficacy is low. Parents are seen as an extension of the teachers. Traditional role models are preferred. In work situations, strong loyalty to the employer and long average durations of employment exists. There is a preference for larger organizations but at the same time much self-employment. Innovators feel constrained by rules. According to Geert Hofstede, in higher uncertainty avoidance cultures, innovation is more difficult to bring about.

The dimension of individual versus collective describes the relationship between the individual and the collectivity that prevails in a given society.[14] It is reflected in the way people live together, and it has implications for values and behavior. In some cultures, individualism is seen as a blessing and a source of well being, while in others, it is seen as alienating.

In cultures with low individualist tendency, people live with or close to relatives or clan members. Others are classified as in-group or out-group. The family provides protection in exchange for lifelong loyalty. Strong family ties exist with frequent contact. Children learn to think in terms of 'we'. Unrelated persons can be adopted into the family. Care for aged relatives and worship of ancestors is important and a marriage without children is incomplete. Nobody is ever alone. Harmony should always be maintained and direct confrontation avoided. Opinions are pre-determined by the in-group. Financial and ritual obligations to relatives exist. The in-groups determine friendship. Trespassing leads to shame and loss of face for the self and the in-group. The individual has low public self-consciousness and is other-directed.

Managers in low individualist or collectivist cultures stress conformity and orderliness. Activities are dictated by role and context. At school, individual initiatives are discouraged and students associate according to preexisting in-group ties. Students expect preferential treatment by teachers from their in-group. Harmony, face, and shame predict behavior. Diplomas provide an entry to higher-status groups and are thus valued highly.

In work situations, employees live up to the interest of their in-group. Relatives of the employer and employees are preferred when hiring. The employee's commitment to the organization is low. Employees perform best in in-groups. Training is most effective when it is focused at group level. Treating friends better than others is normal and ethical. In business, personal relationships prevail over tasks and the company.

Collective decisions are seen as better. The individual has less control over their job and working conditions. Management is the management of groups. Incentives are given to in-groups. Direct appraisal of performance is a threat to harmony.

In cultures where individualism scores high, people live in nuclear or one-parent families. Others are classified as individuals. Children are supposed to take care of themselves as soon as possible. Weak family ties with rare contacts are common. The children learn to think in terms of 'I'. Aged relatives should care for themselves. Ancestors are unknown and irrelevant. Privacy is normal. Speaking one's mind is a characteristic of an honest person. Personal opinions are expected. There is financial independence from relatives. There is a need for specific friendships. Lasting relationships are difficult to achieve. Trespassing leads to guilt and loss of self-respect. Marriage is supposed to be love-based. 'Individualistic' is important as a personality characteristic. People have high public self-consciousness and exhibit extravert and acted behavior.

At school, teachers are dealing with individual pupils. Pupils' individual initiatives are encouraged. Students associate according to tasks and current needs. In-group membership is no reason to expect preferential treatment. Students' selves are to be respected. Students are expected to speak up in class or large groups. The purpose of education is learning how to learn.

In work situations, employees are supposed to act 'economically'. Hiring and promotion is based on skills and rules. Family relationships are seen as a disadvantage in hiring. The employer-employee relationship is a business deal in a labor market. Poor performance is a reason for dismissal. Employees perform best at individual level. Relationships with colleagues do not depend on their group identity. Treating friends better than others is nepotism and unethical. In business, tasks and the company prevail over personal relationships. A belief in individual decisions dominates. People have more control over their job and working conditions. Management is the management of individuals. Employees can be seen as individuals. Incentives are given to individuals. Direct appraisal of performance improves productivity.

The dimension of masculine versus feminine is related to the division of emotional roles between men and women.[15] The duality of the sexes is a fundamental fact that different societies cope with in different ways.

In societies with low masculinity, there is weak gender differentiation in the socialization of children. In the family, both fathers and mothers deal with facts and feelings. At work, the focus lies on equality, solidarity, and the quality of working life. Managers are employees like others. Managers are expected to use their intuition, deal with feelings and seek consensus. More women have management jobs. A smaller wage gap exists between men and women. Career ambitions are an option for both man and women.

In societies with high masculinity, a strong differentiation in the socialization of children exists. Fathers and mothers have different role models: fathers deal with facts, mothers with feelings. In work situations, people live in order to work. Managers are expected to be decisive, firm, assertive, aggressive, competitive, and just. Fewer women have management jobs. There is a larger wage gap between men and women. Conflicts are resolved through denial or fighting until the best one wins.

Long-term versus short-term orientation is related to the choice of focus for people's efforts: the future or the present.[16] When Geert Hofstede first formulated his theory, he described only four dimensions. After studying South-East Asian cultures he formulated the fifth dimension of long-term versus short-term thinking.

Although different Western countries score very differently in Hofstede's dimensions, in comparison to strongly group-oriented societies like in Far Eastern, or North African countries, European and American societies have an overall tendency towards a low power distance, a low uncertainty avoidance, and tend to be highly individual oriented, feminine and short-term thinking.

In Chinese culture, influenced by Confucian hierarchy and Communist centralist structures, power distance scores very high. Uncertainty avoidance also scores high resulting in many rules and high formality in dealing with unknown situations. Individualism scores low. China is highly group-oriented and collectivist. The masculine-feminine dimension is less important. Due to Communism, the traditionally low position of women has changed and an emancipation movement took place resulting in a far less explicitly masculine society than existed before communism.

China scores high in long-term thinking. Long-term thinking prevails in relationships and efforts don't need to be rewarded immediately. People can spend a lifetime trying to make things better. At the same time, due to economic developments at the professional level, a very short-term thinking has emerged, resulting in continuous job-hopping.

Peng Shiyong who analyzes culture and conflict management in foreign-invested companies in China, compares the US, France and China in his study. He comes to the conclusion that although distinct differences exist between France and the US, in contrast with China they show a similarity in their cultural values. Working together in the intercultural environment of foreign-invested enterprises, cultural adaptation to Chinese society by Americans and the French, as well as Chinese adaptation to the Western corporate environment, becomes obvious in aspects like conflict management and leadership styles on which we will elaborate later.[17]

6.6.3 Mixtures of Corporate Cultures

In China many different corporate cultures occur depending on the kind of organization or company in question. Chinese State Owned Enterprises have other features than Joint Ventures, which by their very nature implicitly have a mixed corporate culture. This mixed corporate culture will depend on the nations involved. A Chinese-Korean or Chinese-Japanese Joint Venture will be organized differently from a Chinese-US or Chinese-European Joint Venture. In Joint Ventures, the percentage of ownership will be decisive in the level of imposition of one or other corporate culture.

Chinese Privately Owned Enterprises will differ from Wholly Foreign Owned Enterprises. Multinational companies implement global strategies, and in China they might adapt to some extent, but global corporate culture will be used in China as well. Privately Owned Chinese companies may be a mixture of overseas Chinese and Mainland Chinese, who have very different backgrounds. To understand corporate cultures it is important to analyze the background of a specific company as well as to analyze the different cultural backgrounds of the people working in it.

6.6.4 Western Culture Influencing Western Corporate Culture

Before we focus on corporate culture in China, we want to look into some core issues of Western culture and corporate culture. We stated earlier that to understand China today, a look into history is illuminating. The same counts for Western culture. Western corporate culture is influenced by Western cultural traditions. The West inherited the Greek, Roman, and Christian traditions. The West had the Renaissance and the Enlightenment.

The way the West deals with knowledge and information in everyday life can be traced back to Greek and Roman traditions. Western children learn to argue their case. In education they learn to choose a topic, to make a statement, and to argue that statement. It is important to have your own opinion and to defend your ideas with rhetoric and arguments. Corporate culture in the West consequently attaches a lot of importance to talking, discussing, arguing, brainstorming, giving feedback; input from all people can be valuable. Each employee in a company is expected to give input and to participate actively in a discussion. Not so much the hierarchy between people decides group dynamics in discussions, it is more the democratic idea that all voices need to be heard and that each person's ideas can be equally valuable and will be respected. Each person can come with new ideas. This is experienced as most natural and evident. Western companies moving to China might be confronted with the fact that open discussions and being open about what one thinks are not natural to all cultures. As we've already seen, face and hierarchy influence group dynamics in China.

The Christian code of conduct that influences Western culture in general, prescribes that people should not lie or cheat. There is no insider-outsider concept; the concept of 'neighborly love' means people should be good to everyone. Honesty and trustworthiness are crucial. Cheating is never allowed, not with people you know, nor with people you don't know. In contrast, cheating is accepted to a certain extent in China. Loyalty exists towards the in-group, not necessarily towards the out-group. If you sign an exclusivity contract in the West, and then work with your partner's competitors behind his back, this will be interpreted as a fraud. In China this is not uncommon in business. Loyalty exists mainly to the in-group.

The West introduced the separation of power centuries ago. A great deal of importance is attached to law and justice. Laws, regulations and contracts are taken seriously and have authority. As we will see in the section on Copyright Law, the position of law in Chinese society is different from the West. Western law is built on the basis of cultural core issues, like equal rights for all, or respect for the individual and private life. These principles are less predominant in the Chinese juridical system. Intercultural cooperation should always be inspired by the idea that one's own values are not necessarily universal and shared by all cultures.

6.6.5 Chinese Culture Influencing Chinese Corporate Culture

Corporate culture in the People's Republic of China is influenced by communism and by the traditional, hierarchical Confucian organization model. The most striking feature of purely Chinese corporate cultures practiced in state owned enterprises but also in privately owned Chinese enterprises, is top-down management, and little if any participation from the base. There is little interaction between different levels in the company or the organization. Everyone follows orders from above.

Analyzing evolutions in corporate culture in the People's Republic of China, the scholar Fang Lee Cooke makes a distinction between three periods:
- During the first period between 1949 and 1978, corporate culture was dominated by the setting and following of behavioral norms, whereby much importance was attached to 'role-model' organizations. The values promoted at the time were honesty, diligence, endurance of hardship, and thrift.
- During the second period, from 1978 until the middle of the 1990s, there was increasing freedom to pursue material wealth and entrepreneurship was encouraged. This new freedom often led to striving for personal gain at the cost of the organization.
- From the middle of the 1990s onwards, a new corporate culture arose under the influence of the increased presence of multinationals and Joint Ventures acting as role models. Corporate culture as a management technique was imported.[18]

It is not always evident for a Chinese person who grew up in the Chinese Confucian and socialist system, to understand exactly what the foreign colleague means or expects. Vice versa, it is not always easy for the foreign colleague to find out where exactly a problem lies and how the Chinese look at it. As in other areas, it is crucial to establish optimal communication, to look at a situation from all sides, to gain insight into the culture of the people you work with and to be aware of and to explain your own cultural background. By gaining insight into each other's backgrounds and communication patterns, cultural differences can be overcome and an optimal cooperation climate can be created.

6.6.6 Western Corporate Culture in Chinese Companies

The Chinese use a lot of slogans in society: to maintain good order in society, to impose ethics and etiquette rules, to spread ideological messages. The use of slogans also occurs in companies to implement policy on attitude (responsibility, dealing with mistakes, order in the company, hygiene). In the use of slogans Western companies should make sure that the slogan is a real Chinese message and not merely a translation of an English slogan.

Multinationals usually impose their global strategy. Western companies can publish corporate rules to enforce Western corporate models. They should provide clear guidelines and regularly repeat their core values with integrity and respect. The most efficient way of implementing Western management concepts and establishing efficient cooperation is to provide training, to Chinese employees as well as to Western expats working in China, and even to Western people working at a distance with China, or Chinese working at a distance with the West.

Multinational companies such as Motorola, Ericsson, Siemens, and Procter & Gamble have even established their own internal 'universities', 'business schools' or management training centers in China, where courses on standard business topics such as effective supervision, marketing, financial management, business strategy, and human resources management are offered.[19]

6.6.7 The Perception of the Chinese Global Citizen

Perceptions of the Chinese global citizen exist both in the West and in China. Western people working in multinationals in China often tend to think that, especially young Chinese, are becoming westernized and that cultural differences are fading. On their side, the Chinese also perceive themselves as being 'globalized', 'there is no difference anymore between China and the West'. These perceptions should be handled carefully because they ignore cultural backgrounds. Chinese people are very pragmatic. They learn how to adapt to multinational or international environments, but this does not mean that Chinese hierarchical thinking, or Chinese work ethics have suddenly disappeared. All parties in intercultural environments should be careful in ascribing values to each other. It is certainly a mistake to think that China is adopting everything Western.

6.7 Working in China

6.7.1 China's Workforce

Since the reforms, government at every level has implemented active employment policies to increase job opportunities in China. In 2005, the total number of employed people was 758.25 million, increasing by 6.25 million by the end of 2004. Among these, the number of urban employed was 273.31 million, an increase of 9.7 million and a net increase of 8.55 million. From 2006 to 2010, China plans to continue to promote employment and reemployment.[20]

6.7.2 Recruitment and Employment

Recruitment of new workers in China is executed in different ways:
- Due to the *guanxi* system, recruitment is sometimes done via family and friends.
- Today more transparent recruitment methods are used, like job fairs organized by universities or local government.
- People look for work via the Internet.

The image of a company is influential in attracting new work forces and in retention.

In terms of gender equality, there is still a difference between the State Owned Enterprise (SOE) and the Wholly Foreign Owned Enterprise (WFOE). In the SOE, traditional corporate culture strongly influences human resources management policy. There is a clear preference for men in recruitment. Focus is put more on gender than on competence. In a Joint Ventures or WFOE, a higher percentage of the employees is female.

China often uses collective contracts. This is a written agreement between employers and employees. A collective council where both parties are represented agrees upon the requirements and conditions. Both parties sign the contract. The original is kept in the government Labor Bureau. Collective contracts can be established within a company or within a region.

6.7.3 Remuneration

Remuneration in China today consists of several parts. A monthly wage is paid. Minimum wages are stipulated by law and differ in different regions. Apart from a wage, Chinese companies work with bonus systems. Chinese New Year is the one supreme moment of the year when all people working in China receive an annual bonus. In addition, other bonuses are given based on behavior, or production quota. Sometimes a punishment system is used. If workers do not succeed in reaching a quota or if they talk to each other during work, they will lose part of their wages.

Social security is also part of the remuneration: pension, health insurance and housing funds. Slowly but surely China is developing a social security system to replace the former work unit system. A national reform of social security started in 1998. A new kind of health insurance was set up in which more individual contribution is required. In September 2004 the government announced profound reforms in medical health care. It wanted to create a medical care system for the whole Chinese population. Also in 2004, a pension system based on a Western model was introduced, whereby individual pension savings systems are stimulated. The reforms in the social security system imply that the company or enterprise contributes part of the social security costs. Some contributions for the company are obligatory, others can be offered as incentives.

As well as this, employees have an individual social security. Due to these reforms, private insurance companies are a booming business in China and most of the international insurance companies have found a way into China.

6.7.4 Work Attitude and Position in Hierarchy

Confucian influence is responsible for the fact that people attach extreme importance to position in society and consequently to their professional position in a company or organization. Position in the hierarchy is associated with clearly outlined assignments and responsibilities. Promotion implies that as you climb up, you are no longer involved in 'lower' tasks. This may lead to situations that appear strange in Western companies, where tasks are often not clearly defined.

A company might have to recruit someone for tasks like collecting and opening letters and packages, because the employee with an administrative function thinks this task too low for him or her.

In a technical team, when the Western management decides to promote the employee with the best skills to manage the rest of the team, this might have unexpected consequences. Once promoted to manager, this employee may not want to be involved in 'lower' technical tasks; consequently his skills will be lost.

The Chinese usually take their well-described task to heart and will perform it with dedication, but they do not easily take any initiative to do something outside this. A Chinese person doesn't like to take responsibility for an assignment he is not clearly empowered to undertake. People prefer to do nothing rather than doing something wrong and being punished for it. Before taking on any task outside of their outlined responsibility, they will first consult a superior.

In multinationals with less hierarchical structures the same person executes 'different level tasks', unrelated to hierarchical position. Chinese employees might, in some cases, feel uncomfortable with the expectations of a multinational company. If an employee is asked by his boss to perform a task that he perceives too low for his level, he might obey and accomplish the task, but he may well perceive this as a loss of face.

6.7.5 Status, Uniforms, Titles

Uniforms symbolize the importance of status and position in Chinese society. In restaurants, for example, different 'levels' wear different uniforms: the people who clear tables, the people who take orders and serve tables, the person supervising, the person in charge of payments.

Multinationals in China often have no dress code; all personnel address each other on first name terms, regardless of hierarchical position. The outward signs of a distinction between statuses are thus removed. This aspect of Western corporate culture goes against Chinese tradition.

Lining up to get instructions

6.7.6 Teamwork and Loyalty

Lin Yutang analyzes the Chinese individual and society in 'My Country and My People'.[21] According to Lin Yutang, the age-old family system is responsible for the way Chinese behave and think and how they relate to each other:[22]

- Indifference as a social attitude, related to the lack of legal protection.

- Roguery, which Lin Yutang links to Daoism. "We are great enough to draw up an imperial code, based on the conception of essential justice, but we are also great enough to distrust lawyers and law courts. Ninety-five per cent of legal disputes are settled out of court. We are great enough to make elaborate rules of ceremony, but we are also great enough to treat them as part of the great joke of life."

- Pacifism, the Chinese focus their attention on life on earth, a life full of pain and sorrow, but a life they try to live happily.

- Contentment, the one who is content, is happy.

- Humor is for the Chinese a way of looking at life, it is the product of contentment. Humor is linked to defeatism. According to Lin Yutang, the Chinese are cool-minded, sober defeatists. Life is a joke and people are pawns in the game.

- Conservatism. "Behind all the outward changes ... the Chinese retains a sneering smile for the hot-headed young man who wears a foreign coat or who speaks English too well."

Loyalty is in the first place directed towards the interests of the family and friends, the *guanxi*. Teambuilding in a company in China is difficult. In their working environment people will be pragmatic in their relationships.

6.7.7 Different Generations

Inside China, a generational gap exists between those born after the opening up and those born before. The people who experienced pre-1978 Communist times have a different work attitude than the younger generation. The older generation has a different educational background. Pre-1978 education was very much focused on the Communist ideology, rather than on specialization.

The younger generation is more open-minded towards international cooperation. Their English language skills are much higher and they are far more ambitious. Young people start to learn English at the age of twelve. English language skills are highly valued in China. The better one's English language skills, the easier one can build a good professional career. Young people are very aware of this. If their English is good, they will use this fact when applying for a new job to state their pay demands.

Young Chinese people are also very eager to learn about foreign management styles. Universities in China are starting to teach 'discussion techniques' because this is one of the requirements for working in an international environment. Many of the young Chinese working in international companies have studied in the West, or have been to the West for training. The cultural gap between Westerners and the younger generation is therefore much smaller than with the older generation.

Today, young Chinese people adopt an English name for the convenience of working in international environments because it is difficult for Westerners to remember Chinese names. Traditionally, name giving in China has always been an important issue; a name should be carefully chosen to bring the individual in harmony with nature. In Maoist times people had names like Red, or Protect the East. The English names young people adopt today reflect their aspirations: Legend, Tiger, Tech (from technology), or Sisi (perceived as typically European).

6.7.8 Returnees

Since the opening up in 1978, China has been sending students abroad to study. In the eighties and early nineties only students already holding a university degree were sent abroad to specialize and obtain a Ph.D degree. The prevailing trend was for Chinese students to remain in America, Canada or Europe after graduation.

During the last decades, more and more cooperation projects have been set up between Western and Chinese universities. Eighteen-year olds go abroad, learn the language of the country they study in, attend university and then return to China. For a long time these people were highly in demand because they usually had specific language and communication skills, and understood about life in the West. They functioned as a kind of cultural buffer or cultural communicator. After studying abroad, these people were known as the 'golden collars'. They had high expectations and requirements, for example, in terms of remuneration.

In the meantime masses of Chinese have returned home and the exceptional position enjoyed by the so-called 'golden collars' has largely disappeared. More and more companies are sending their employees to the West for training (for weeks or even months), while they remain employed by the company. Chinese people who have lived and studied in the West help to bridge the gap between China and the West.

6.7.9 Leadership

6.7.9.1 Leadership and Management in China

"If a king adorns himself with the highest virtue,
All the states will show him their obedience" [23]

Leadership in China originates in other qualities than in the West. Moral quality prevails. If a leader displays virtuous behavior, people will follow him and be loyal to him.

In the meritocracy that China is, the best are stimulated and pushed forward and upwards. This system automatically creates its own rulers on the basis of attitude and knowledge. Virtually all the Chinese learn to obey and to follow and they also learn to take up leadership if a situation requires it. In a system where the best are stimulated, it will be those who best fit the system that will be promoted.

6.7.9.2 Chinese Leadership Styles

Sheh Seow Wah who links leadership in China today with China's tradition, makes the distinction between the 'rulership' of the Emperors in Imperial China and the 'leadership' of today's leaders. [24] In Chinese leadership he sees the influence of four traditions, each resulting in a certain approach to leadership: the Humanistic or Confucian Approach, the Legalistic Approach, the Naturalistic or Daoist Approach, and the Strategic Approach, inspired by Sunzi.

Confucian humanistic leadership demands an effective leader to have moral character, proper conduct, humanity (*ren*), to engage in life-long learning, and to maintain a balance (*zhongyong*). In the chapter on Confucianism we described the aspects related to virtuous Confucian behavior.

The legalistic leadership approach is based on the writings of Han Feizi who lived in the 3rd century BC during the time of the Warring States. Han Feizi believed that human nature is evil. Therefore strict rules and severe punishments were needed. Emphasis lay on penal code instead of moral conduct. Han Feizi made significant contributions to the Penal Code of Law and the legalist school that emerged in the 6th century BC. An efficient leader should not display his own talents but should be able to attract talented and capable people to work for him (delegation of power). A wise leader is careful in assigning or delegating tasks to his subordinates without revealing his true motives. If accomplishment of the delegated task answers requirements, rewards will be handed out. If not, the subordinate will not receive any reward, which is already a punishment. The best way to prevent crime is to have harsh laws and heavy punishments for any form of violation: "We need to punish the one in order to warn the hundreds". [25] A good leader is a disciplinarian; he is able to balance compassion and benevolence with strict and harsh laws.

The third kind of Chinese leadership style is the naturalistic approach based on Daoist principles. The opposite forces of *yin* and *yang* should be in harmony. Good leadership comprises both. Western management style emphasizes 'rights and responsibilities' (*yang* component), Asian style leadership relies more on 'relationship and values' (*yin* component).[26] Both are equally important. Western management styles, which consider courage, charisma, outspokenness, and risk-taking (*yang*) as good leadership qualities, should be complemented with wisdom, patience, tolerance, and perseverance (*yin*). Like the transparency of water, a true leader is almost invisible. The principle of *wu wei*, 'non-interference' or 'doing nothing' leads to the 'principle of least action'. Effective leadership comes from balancing different components, different types of people into a united entity, from the ability to combine the basic elements in accordance to the situation. A leader should apply the principle of impartiality. The source of human problems begins when people start to distinguish right from wrong, good from bad. The apparent distinction exists in the human mind. Making distinctions will lead to judgmental thinking. The wise leader always sees things from a holistic viewpoint, he holds two or more contrasting views at the same time without discriminating against them; all things are equal. In dealing with paradoxes, a leader should have a probing mind, and look at a problem from different angles. A wise leader understands that reality is relative. He subscribes to the principle of moderation or middle path.

The strategic approach to leadership is based on Sunzi's Art of War. A good leader should have moral influence. He has to refine his own character through practice; he needs to establish his character before he seeks to lead and establish the characters around him. He needs to have the ability to command, which according to Sunzi demands wisdom (in thought and actions), trustworthiness (full commitment in long-term relationships), benevolence (kindhearted, treating all men equally), courage (righteous, without fear, brave, decisive, prepared to take calculated risks), and firmness (authority, administering of laws), enforcing discipline (responsible and impartial). A leader should always assess all the elements before taking action. To Sunzi warfare is a game of deception, attacking by stratagem where the enemy least expects it, with a strategy that remains undetected until the last moment. Besides acting as a strategist, an effective leader should be a good organizer. He should have a clear and efficient organization structure with properly defined authority and responsibility, reporting relationships and communication structure. A leader should be flexible, use different leadership styles depending on the task at hand, the followers, and the environment. Sun Pin, a descendent of Sunzi, stressed the importance of continuous training and education.

Although Sheh Seow Wah analyzes four traditions in Chinese leadership, in reality a Chinese leader will have influences from all four. The legacies of Confucianism,

Daoism, legalism, and strategic thinking are interwoven in every aspect of Chinese culture and corporate culture of which leadership is one.

In the middle of the eighties, Xu Liancang at the Institute of Psychology in Beijing identified another factor of leadership behavior in the PRC, which was labeled as 'moral character'. It included such characteristics as commitment to abide by the law and avoid corrupt practices; a positive attitude towards the Party and willingness to follow the Party dictates even when in conflict with one's personal views; fairness to all employees; a positive attitude towards political workshops held during working hours; receptiveness to suggestions from workers. This dimension is not found outside the PRC. It reflects the intense politicization of corporate culture in China.[27] The conditions for corporate culture in the PRC have thoroughly changed since then. We can presume that this kind of leadership behavior is mainly found in SOE.

Another influential factor in leadership in China today is the presence of foreign companies. Even state owned companies are starting to attract foreign management. This implies an intercultural exchange. Chinese companies are eager to implement efficient management systems and by doing so, they adopt Western influences. This will automatically result in new aspects or new emphasis in leadership. Depending on the kind of company, and the composition of the management team, the number of foreigners and so on, leadership will differ.

6.7.10 Unemployment and Job Security

The reforms and downsizing of SOEs in the eighties resulted in massive unemployment. A nationwide redeployment plan was set up including skills training, internal redeployment in existing businesses, and providing employment information about the external labor market in coordination with local employment agencies.[28]

The Chinese term for 'unemployed' is 'daiye', which means 'waiting for employment'. To appoint unemployment, different expressions are used. The genuine rate of unemployment is in fact unknown. In official unemployment rates, temporary non-active workers are not included, (about twenty million), nor are rural people leaving their hometown to look for work the city (about one hundred million).

A job for life is not even guaranteed anymore for those working in civil service. In 2003 the government decided to implement a system of temporary contracts and renewal would be based on an evaluation exam.

Until a few years ago unemployment was only high amongst workers and unskilled workers. During the last few years, more and more university students can't find a job after graduation.

Surviving on scrap collection 2007

The Chinese government is well aware of the necessity to create enough jobs to maintain social stability. In 2004 premier Wen Jiabao pointed out in his government report that job creation was a priority for the government. This has to be achieved by promoting labor-intensive industries, small and medium-sized enterprises and the private economy, as well as by encouraging flexible employment and self-employment.[29]

6.7.11 Loyalty and Job-Hopping

There is a huge shortage of managers in China, partly due to discrepancies in the education system and the market in China, but also to the absence of management and middle management systems during the planned economy. Many Chinese today are not familiar with the idea that they can grow into management positions through their experience within a company. Climbing up in society is a priority. People will stay in a job as long as they have the perception that they are developing, but whenever a better chance comes along they will grab it. With the fast growing economy, new high-level jobs and new opportunities are created continuously. The problem is greatest in the developing areas. Because demand is much higher than supply, it is difficult to retain people.

The loyalty of a Chinese worker towards a Western company is usually very low. One of the severe problems companies have to deal with in China is the phenomenon of job-hopping. Chinese workers change to another employer the moment they see an advantage in doing so. This often happens without any prior communication, often to the utmost frustration of the Western employer. This phenomenon not only occurs at worker level, but at all levels.

The motivation behind changing job can be that a person will earn more money in the new place, or just that the new company is bigger and more famous, which adds to one's prestige. If a very famous company restructures and decentralizes and the famous name is replaced by a new company name, the chance is high that many employees will resign. The prestige of a famous company affects the prestige of the employees.

Chinese New Year is the one moment of the year with the highest job turnover. Companies pay a yearly bonus to their employees and everyone returns home, sometimes thousands of kilometers away from the job. Many don't return.

Companies try to keep employees by offering all kinds of privileges or fringe benefits, like travel or training abroad, housing or social security. In some cases the social security is even extended to include the whole of the family. Training, and especially training abroad, is valued very high by Chinese employees as it offers the possibility to develop. Training can be used as a tool for retention. A good long-term strategy for retention is to create opportunities for employees for advancement within the company.

When training involves specific technological knowledge, it might be a good idea to make a contract stating that they have to stay in the company for a certain number of years.

The problem of job-hopping is much lower in big multinationals than in small or medium-sized companies. Multinationals offer better long-term prospects and possibilities than smaller companies.

6.7.12 Trade Unions

The role of the national union in China (All-China Federation of Trade Unions) is stipulated in two laws: the Union law, formulated in 1950 and adapted in 2001, and the Labor Law of 1995. The national union coordinates all trade unions in China. While a kind of equilibrium existed between leaders and workers in the socialist system, the last decennia has seen more and more conflicts arise as a result of contractual agreements that change the relationship between the two parties.

The traditional task of the union is to organize social events, the welfare of workers, to support management in implementing operational decisions and to coordinate the relationship between management and workers. Today this task remains largely unchanged although the economy has changed dramatically. In theory the union has to ensure that what is stipulated in Labor Law is put into practice. In reality the union is mainly an organ for the flow of information from the government to the workers. Defending the rights and interests of workers is not necessarily at stake. Thus the concept of trade union has another meaning in China compared to the West and the national union falls under the control of the CCP.

The union is represented in all SOEs and Joint Ventures in China. Usually foreign companies have a negative attitude towards union representation in their company because it is viewed as a control organ of the state.

The establishment of independent unions, outside of the national union is illegal. However, research shows that workers are not just passive victims. Chen Meei-shia and Anita Chan claim that workers in China do have a voice to a certain extent via the Staff and Workers' Representative Congresses (*zhigong daibiao dahui*).[30]

Peter VERSTRAETEN, CEO United Fashion

Peter Verstraeten started to work in China in 1995, after several years of experience in other Asian countries. Each country has its own specific characteristics. Working in the PRC is different from other Asian areas like Hong Kong, Malaysia, Singapore, or India. As the CEO of a medium-sized textile company, Peter Verstraeten believes in exercising strict control over the whole business process. He continuously travels around Asia and to the West in order to do this.

In China, he has built up good relationships with his partners and he's happy to work there. Thanks to his many years of experience, he's able to clearly see 'points for attention' specific to China, to anticipate them, and to work as efficiently and harmoniously as possible. In spite of the fact that he enjoys good cooperation with suppliers, a number of issues related to working in China today demand continuous follow-up.

'Leadership and Face
One of the most sensitive things about working in China is the concept of face. An employee will do anything to avoid losing face. I have learned to take this into account. When things go wrong in the West, I sometimes choose open confrontation. In China, however, I try to deal with mistakes in a more indirect and thoughtful manner. We have meetings during which the general outlines are discussed. I never criticize anyone in the meeting. When problems occur I try to give my employees face by informally passing by his or her desk and checking on things in a rather informal way. I understand that the Chinese don't like to be called to my office for an interrogation In an intercultural environment, I try to choose the best and most suitable way to manage.

Lack of Loyalty and Job-hopping

One of the main problems of working in China as a medium-sized company is lack of loyalty and the problem of job-hopping. It takes a lot of energy to select and recruit the right people, and it's an even bigger struggle to keep them in the job. In developing areas like Ningbo where we are located, people don't stay long enough in the company to grow into their job and climb up. They switch jobs continuously. The result is that it is virtually impossible to find experienced managers. Selection and recruitment on the basis of curriculum vitae is not always reliable. Some people claim to have a very high level of English language skills whereas in reality their knowledge of English is rather low. On the basis of a CV you can see how many companies a person has already worked in. If someone changes jobs frequently, this is an indicator of the fact that they will not stay in your company for long. We try to select the right people and try to keep them in the job by offering incentives like housing or other extras. To limit the consequences of job-hopping we try to put two people on a certain project to build in a kind of backup. But not even this is a complete guarantee because people don't always share information with each other.

Low Quality and Quality Control

Another problem in China is the quality of textile products. In almost 100% of production, something goes wrong. Quality control is constantly required. Control has to be exerted at all stages of production. To obtain the right quality we try to anticipate the Chinese reality in our order. This means we order a higher quality than required so that we get the right thing. Recently a shipment could not leave. When I checked this it appeared that my employee did not understand the color codes. But she didn't ask anyone to help her. This is an example of how something very small can have huge consequences. Due to the fact I follow up everything closely I can detect little problems like that. This avoids a lot of undesirable consequences. Through constant follow-up we try to improve the situation day by day.

Change of Mentality in the West

Nowadays many low quality products come onto the Western market and I can see a shift of attitude in the West. Many Western people get used to low quality. They buy cheap products, and when they break they buy new ones. There is an interaction between the mass production of bad quality products and the buying behavior of customers. Low quality products certainly don't come from China alone, but also in China I think we still have some way to go before Chinese textile production delivers wide scale good quality products. The lesson I learnt is that good relationships in China create a more reliable environment and continuous control of the whole cooperation process makes working in China worthwhile.'

6.8 Time and Time Management

6.8.1 Traditional Time Concept: Cycles in Cycles

"The cyclical nature of the Universe shows us that the only constant is change. However, if we probe deeper, all changes in Nature will go back to their original states. Thus, in the broader perspective, nothing really changes. The rotating and revolving characteristics of Nature have created day and night and the four seasons. But these are never ending in the large scheme of things. What we always perceive as change in the actual physical sense is just a matter of cycle or rotation."[31]

The way a culture deals with time obviously has consequences for ways of thinking and acting. Or vice versa: actions in a culture are a reflection of how time is experienced.

Fons Trompenaars makes a distinction between cultures that experience time as a straight line, in which a range of events sequentially take place in minutes, hours, days, months and years, into eternity, and cultures that experience time as a rotating circle in which minutes are repeated every hour, hours every day, days every month, months every year. Time can be a chronological concept or a concept in which events are synchronic and take place at the same moment.[32]

Westerners have a chronological time concept. Time is presented as a straight line. A timeline runs from left to right and has a chronological development, whereby the present is experienced as the point we find ourselves now. A year planning is based on a chronological time concept. For Western people it is normal to fix a meeting months or even longer ahead in the future. Every single person has a diary and life is like a laid out plan. Westerners tend to plan everything, even when they visit their family.

The Chinese look at time in a more cyclical way. Chinese history is presented as cycles following each other. Time is submitted to the cyclical movement of the seasons, the order of nature, and human life is part of this cycle. A complete cycle of the moon calendar is sixty years. A cycle of twelve months repeats itself five times. Everything is in movement and repeats itself, everything comes and goes and comes back again.

6.8.2 Professional and Private Time

Apart from a difference in the concept of time, there is also a difference in the division between professional and private time in China and the West. During the planned economy when everyone worked and lived in work units or in communes, work and life was not divided. Privacy was totally absent. Private time and private space did not exist. There was no distinction between professional and private. At that time, the concept of 'noon' referred to a period of a number of hours. In Communist times, people tended to rise very early, at five or six o'clock, and take a long break at noon to cook, eat and take a nap.

Today the Labor Law stipulates limited working hours. Eight hours a day, and a maximum of 44 hours a week. Although this is not yet a reality in all of China, more and more companies use a system of limited working hours. This implies that time spent at work should be used in an efficient and productive way.

Multinationals might have time management systems in China. Like other developing areas of management in China, time management will exist in some cases, but more often than not it will not be implemented yet.

Today the distinction between professional and private time is still not always clear in China. Receiving a weekend assignment in the West is considered as 'overtime' and has to be paid for as such or compensated at a convenient moment. In China, working hours are in many situations not yet clearly demarcated. When a boss needs employees or workers at the weekend, people won't necessarily associate the weekend as being 'private time'. Usually people find it normal to be available most of the time, especially in SOEs or in private Chinese companies. Activities never stop and many people work every day and only take the official holidays, and sometimes not even that. The situation is changing, especially for people who work in offices or multinationals with limited working hours.

The Chinese concept of time has an impact on a number of aspects of corporate culture. Western business people sometimes complain that it is difficult to implement long-term planning. The Chinese seldom use an agenda. Appointments are not written down but memorized and reconfirmed by telephone. It's always possible something unexpected will turn up meaning the appointments need to be changed. Flexibility is necessary in Chinese society because everything changes continuously.

It may also be difficult to implement a year planning, but this does not mean that the Chinese don't think long-term. They certainly think long-term when it comes to relationships. And the government also works with a five-year planning. Within the larger planned timeframe, however, more flexibility usually exists in China than in the West. In China, time is a more dynamic term than in the West. Chinese are often perplexed when confronted with the way Westerners deal with time and planning. Sometimes the Chinese tend to experience the strictly limited working hours in the West as being 'slow', 'inefficient', or as the total lack of flexibility, or even as a lack of commitment. If an urgent situation arises, the Chinese will not understand if you tell them they have to wait because you'll be on holiday for a few weeks. This might be interpreted as a total lack of commitment and lack of interest from the Western side. The Chinese have a strongly pragmatic attitude. They treat time in terms of what the situation at hand requires, with high flexibility and changeability.

6.8.3 Time Management: Time Is Money

Time management in Western corporate culture is linked to the idea that time is money. Time for Westerners is divided into professional and private time. In the West, the concept of time management is associated with the use of tools and techniques to plan and schedule to increase efficiency as the ultimate goal. People make 'to do' and priority lists, and implement these in goal management. The idea of time management is normal in Western corporate culture. Employees should be as efficient as possible during working hours.

The concept of 'time is money' does not exist everywhere in China, although it may exist more in Guangdong and Shanghai. But efficient work is often linked to relations. This means that apart from working, time needs to be spent on building relationships.

Western people, used to a clear demarcation between professional and private time and their concept of professional time management, often get frustrated in China at the beginning where they encounter a different reality. They will have to spend considerable time eating and drinking to build relationships. Their feeling of 'inefficiency' will disappear as soon as they discover that good relationships can lead to extremely efficient work and problem solving.

Appointments in China can be subject to hierarchy. An appointment with someone higher in the hierarchy will get priority. If person X has an appointment with person Y at a certain moment, but person Z, very high up in the hierarchy wants to see person Y, than this appointment gets priority. This explains the high need for flexibility in Chinese society.

6.8.4 Process-oriented versus Result-oriented

Dealing with time in China is focused on the process rather than on the result. It is the path to a certain goal that is important, rather than the result in itself. Chinese employers tend to attach considerable weight to their employees' work attitude and the effort they have made in their work, often disregarding the outcomes.[33] Because the process is important in China, Western management concepts are used more by multinationals than by Chinese companies.

Westerners tend to work step by step, in a sequential way. Time evolves chronologically; the evolution in a process also evolves chronologically. The Chinese tend to work synchronically. This means that they do different things at the same time.

6.9 Conflict Management

6.9.1 Conflict and Culture

"Since different cultures have different perceptions of the nature of conflict and the expected outcomes of conflict management, what is thought to be constructive conflict management by members of one culture will not always be so interpreted or understood by members of another culture." [34]
Peng Shiyong

The perception of what a conflict is and how to deal with it is culture-specific. Some cultures experience conflict as something negative, so they will try to avoid it; other cultures see conflicts as something that can be constructive.

In intercultural communication between Westerners and the Chinese, a distinction can be made between Chinese among themselves, between Chinese and Westerners, and between Westerners among themselves in a Chinese context. Western people tend to deal with conflicts in a direct confrontational way, while Chinese tend to avoid conflict. Conflict management in China should go hand in hand with intercultural understanding. Avoidance of conflict in China is related to face and societal harmony.

6.9.2 Instrumental versus Expressive Conflict

Ting-Toomey borrows the concepts of instrumental and expressive conflicts that Olsen had formulated in 1978.[35] Instrumental conflict is characterized by 'opposing practices or goals', and expressive conflict is characterized by 'desires for tension release from hostile feelings'. Members of individualist cultures tend to view a conflict as instrumental, and are able to separate the conflict from the individuals involved in it. They tend to adopt direct and confrontational styles to manage conflicts.

Members of collectivist cultures tend to view conflicts as expressive, and are not able to separate the conflict from the individuals involved in it. They tend to adopt indirect, non-confrontational, and passive styles. Confrontational management styles tend to be taken very personally.

6.9.3 Chinese Cultural Aspects Influencing Conflict Management

"The Chinese avoidance of conflict and the need for harmony is a product of the Confucian notion of zhongyong (moderation, compromise, harmonization)."[36]
Tony Fang

Studies of conflict management from a native Chinese cultural perspective, examine how conflict is perceived and managed by Chinese people in a Chinese cultural context. They show that the major factors determining how conflict is managed in Chinese society are *guanxi*, face, interpersonal harmony, and favor.[37] Taiwanese scholar Hwang argues that Chinese people are not always non-confrontational and don't always avoid interpersonal conflicts.[38] They may choose different conflict management styles, including confrontation, endurance, severance, private defiance, or compromise depending on how the other conflicting party is categorized and what one's concerns are.[39]

Kozan proposed a framework of three distinctive models of conflict management: the harmony model, the confrontational model, and the regulative model.[40]

In the harmony model, conflict management starts with efforts to 'prevent or to fail to acknowledge them rather then to actually resolve any conflict'. Cooperative behavior is emphasized in order to handle conflict. Face-saving is the criteria used to judge the effectiveness of conflict resolution.

In the confrontational model, conflict is openly acknowledged, and some level of conflict in the organization is considered desirable. To resolve conflict, confrontation and compromise are employed.

In the regulative model, bureaucratic means are generally used to manage conflict. This model focuses on avoidance and authoritative command.

Although Kozan emphasizes that the coexistence of these models in any particular culture can occur, in reality we detect that the Chinese tend to use the harmony conflict model. Face saving is a major concern. Intermediaries are very often used in everyday life in China to resolve difficult or conflict situations. And the Chinese tend to ignore conflict. When something goes wrong, ignoring it seems to be the best way to handle the situation.

In Joint Ventures or Wholly Foreign Owned Enterprises in China, campaigns are being started to stimulate Chinese people to be open about mistakes. On the other hand, Western managers, who might use confrontational conflict management in their own culture, will have to adapt to the Chinese situation.

Mike COOPER, Vice President, Asia, Rogers Corporation

'**Harmony.** That single word epitomizes what China seeks to achieve while it enjoys the fastest growth and expansion of wealth that this planet has ever seen. It is archaic as well as futuristic. When conducting business, decisions are made daily, to change, modify, and improve. The loose definition of a 'decision' is that somebody will not agree with the proposed action, otherwise it is not a decision. However, the principal of harmony dictates that all must agree with an action, no decision is required or needed since everybody agrees.

Harmony drives inefficiency, lack of innovation, no cross currents, low productivity, non-transparent financial management and unclear time management; in other words, no change.

We are currently implementing the new Employee Contract Labor Law in China. The primary requirement of this new law is a Union that has a primary goal of harmony between the company and its employees. What we understand is that the new Labor Law requires harmony and there is no possibility of doing anything disruptive (no strikes or work stoppages). All employees, senior management, management, and labor are part of the 'Union'. They all have to agree. If they can't agree, nothing will change. So now we are in the trap of increasing productivity, implementing change, and making decisions without disrupting the harmony of the company. Humans by nature are adverse to change so it is an interesting concept to juxtapose harmony with change. China is driven to improve and excel in the global market. Yet it clings to its past while trying to make more changes and improvements in a just few decades than it has in several centuries. As a society, they embrace the concept of harmony – regardless of the apparent futility of it. As individuals, they are focused on driving change, improving processes, and creating wealth.

Daily, I observe several obstacles to China achieving its goals. There are two primary impediments to success – the education infrastructure and the legal infrastructure. I can train my employees and they can achieve 100% mastery of the knowledge I impart to them but they are unable to apply that knowledge to real life challenges. It takes a significant amount of effort and many very small steps to get them over the threshold of attempting to make change or innovate a solution to a problem. Once they 'get it' they are very good at applying their knowledge. Out of the 1000 employees that I have, about 2% achieve the velocity of change and innovation required to break the cycle of learning by rote. Until the basis of the education process in China is changed, the desired rate of change and the sustaining of foreign-implemented processes in China will fall short of expectations. Although intelligence tests may show a great gain in knowledge in China, the aptitude to apply that knowledge is not gained within China. It comes from education and experiences in the Western cultures of Europe and the US. This is the greatest challenge I face on a daily basis – giving smart people the courage to attempt to apply their knowledge against the status quo.

An indirect impact of the education process in China is the over-staffing required to run a production line in China. Although we have had success with yield and quality, the staffing levels are between 125–135% of what is required to do the same thing in the US and Europe. Most of this deals with the fact of longer tenure (better trained operators and supervisors) in the US and Europe compared to Asia. However, I believe that all the world will shift to a shorter tenure and the turmoil caused by turnover will cause production lines to increase all over the world. Some unintended consequences might be lower wages for more employees since they will never achieve a level of 'senior' or 'master' in their position. I have no data to support this.

There is no easy way to sum up the impact of a poor legal infrastructure. The current environment is dominated by the theme of 'harmony'. Settle out of court, agree to a consensus, and avoid adjudication (or decision). I have recent experience that shows me that although the Chinese are quick to rattle the saber of court and lawsuits, few are inclined to take it past the threat stage. If I have no compelling reason to settle the issue, then I will win based on patience and refusal to compromise. Many meetings, many attempts to negotiate, and consistent social pressure to reduce friction (opt for harmony), are the tools of negotiation and if I refuse to play that game, I ultimately will win. Unless I deal directly with central government; they still hold the trump card. They will not negotiate and they will use harmony as the reason I must quit fighting. I find it strange that harmony is a one-way street.

Guanxi is the root of success and failure. I have an employee who recommends an outside company to provide a service for my company. But they ask for a kickback from the outside company since they got my company to agree to use the outside company for the service. The outside company comes to me and complains about the kickback. I want to fire the employee and need a statement from the outside company. Because of *guanxi*, the outside company won't make a formal complaint. Relationships are a normal part of all cultures but here it gets in the way of good business by encouraging or protecting bad behaviors.

We are a Wholly Owned Foreign Enterprise in China. The benefits of a WFOE are well defined and supported. However, new tax laws are starting to erode those benefits. Tax benefits will cease and everybody will pay 25%. If I can convince the government that I am high-tech, my tax will be 15%. I can buy that through appropriate use of *guanxi*. Three years ago I was enticed to establish a regional Headquarters License in China and I was promised all the benefits of a WFOE plus other perquisites. I went through the process of creating the proper legal entity, registered capital, licensing, etc. I later learned I got no benefits – now it will take almost two years to undo that license and get my capital investment out of China. This is just an example of the unstable and unpredictable process that foreign investment enterprises can be subjected to.

Most of the threat to my company in China deals with reacting to the rules and regulations that China will implement along the way to correcting trade imbalances and currency appreciation. Once China becomes the consumer of manufactured goods as well as the producer, it will be economical to continue to manufacture and sell in China. Today most of what we produce is consumed outside of China. That is changing but won't hit critical mass (more consumed than exported) for several years. Until we get there, we can expect many changes such as the HS[41] code changes in summer of 2007. In late June 2007, several HS codes were identified as being subject to lower VAT rebate (8% less rebate). This change was implemented in July and companies had little time to react. The ultimate solution was to modify the HS code to intended application instead of product content. This could have been very costly and similar changes will be implemented in the future. We can't predict what will happen or when but it will be oriented around trade imbalance and currency appreciation.'

[1] Oi, J.C. (1995), *The role of local state in China's transitional economy*. The China Quarterly, pp. 1132–1149, p 1132

[2] Fang Lee Cooke, 2005, p 83

[3] Ibid p 23

[4] Fang Lee Cooke does not mention China's Listed companies in his overview. We added this category.

[5] Ibid p 20

6 Ibid pp 25–26

7 Ibid p 24

8 http://www.atimes.com/atimes/China_Business/IJ31Cb02.html

9 http://www.washingtonpost.com/wp-dyn/content/article/2007/06/14/AR2007061401 892.
html

10 Hampden-Turner, C.,Trompenaars, F., *Riding the Waves of Culture: Understanding Diversity
in Global Business*, Mc Graw-Hill, 1998

11 Hofstede Geert, *Cultures Consequences, Comparing Values, Behaviors, Institutions and
Organizations Across Nations*, Sage Publications, Thousand Oaks, London, New Delhi, 2001

12 Ibid, p 79

13 Ibid, p 145

14 Ibid, p 209

15 Ibid, p 279

16 Ibid, p 351

17 Peng Shiyong, (2003) *Culture and Conflict Management in Foreign-invested Enterprises
in China. An Intercultural Communication Perspective.* Peter Lang, European University
Studies, Vol. 369

18 Fang Lee Cooke, *HRM, Work and Employment in China*, Routledge, London, New York,
2005, p 180

19 Fang Lee Cooke, 2005, p 106

20 http://www.china.org.cn

21 Lin Yutang, *My Country and My People, Wu Guo yu Wu Min*, Foreign Language Teaching
and Research Press, Beijing, 1998. His book was republished in 2000: Lin Yutang,
Zhongguo Ren, Xue Lin Chubanshe, Shanghai, 2000

22 Lin Yutang, 1998, pp 46–75

23 Form *Book of Songs*, quoted in: Fu Genqing, Liu Ruixiang, Lin Zhihe, The Classical of Filial
Piety, Shandong Friendship Press, 1998, p 15

24 Sheh Seow Wah, *Chinese Leadership. Moving from Classical to Contemporary.* Times
Editions, Singapore, 2003, pp 40–112

25 Ibid, p 71

26 Ibid, p 75

27 Bond, Michael Harris, 1991, p 78

28 Fang Lee Cooke, pp 4748

29 Ibid, p 196

[30] Chen Meei-shia, Chan Anita, "Employee and union inputs into occupational health and safety measures in Chinese factories", Social Science & Medicine 58, 2004, pp 1231–1245 Anita Chan has been studying labor conditions in China for a few decennia. More research conducted by Anita Chan on: http://rspas.anu.edu.au/ccc/pubs/chan_a.php

[31] Sheh Seow Wah, 2003, p 77

[32] Trompenaars, Fons, Hanpden-Turner Charles, 1998, *Over de grenzen van cultuur en management*. Contact, Amsterdam, Antwerpen, p 23

[33] Fang Lee Cooke, 2005, p 70

[34] Peng Shiyong, 2003, p 30

[35] Ting-Toomey Stella, "Toward a theory of conflict and culture" in: Gudykunst W.B. and Ting-Toomey S. Eds, *Communication culture and organizational processes* (pp 71–86), Beverly Hills, CA, Sage Publications, 1985

[36] Fang Tony, 1998, p 139

[37] Peng Shiyong, 2003, p 65

[38] Hwang, K.K. (1997–8), Guanxi and Mientze: Conflict resolution in Chinese society. Intercultural Communication Studies, 7 (1), pp. 17–42

[39] Peng Shiyong, 2003, p 66

[40] Kozan, M.K. (1997), "Culture and Conflict Management: A Theoretical framework". *The International Journal of Conflict Management*, 8 (4). 338–360, Quoted in: Peng Shiyong, 2003, pp 60–61

[41] Harmonized System: commodity classification system

7 Commercial China

7 Commercial China

"Although the Chinese market is progressing towards a market economy, it is still deeply rooted in its own cultural values of harmony and relationship building." [1]
Zhu Yunxia

7.1 China and the WTO

At the end of 2001, after 15 years of negotiating, China became a member of the World Trade Organization (WTO). This accession to the WTO was an important symbolic event: China is making a clear choice for the international free market economy and engages in integration into a world economy with prescribed rules. This implies diminishing high import taxes for foreign products and not putting foreign companies at a disadvantage. Apart from the fact that greater transparency of laws and procedures is required, a harmonization of procedures and rules at national level must also be implemented. Corruption must be fought, the bank sector has to be reorganized, and the trade in stocks better organized. Before reality meets these requirements, hundreds of laws need to be adapted. Some people voice doubts that China will ever meet and respect all the agreements of the WTO. Respect of the agreements cannot be imposed by the WTO itself. This can only be done by individual member states.

7.2 Laws and Regulations

7.2.1 Copyright Law in Context

"Twenty years ago, China did not recognize property, let alone intellectual property. Today, China has a reasonably respectable property system covering trademark, patent and to a lesser degree copyright." [2]
H.J.H Wheare

China's society has been dominated by Confucian thinking that focused on the right public behavior to bring harmony, rather than on imposed laws. According to Confucianism, people's behavior cannot be regulated by way of law. Harmony has to come from virtue and ritual, from the right public behavior of all people in society according to their position. The age-old Chinese pragmatism plays a decisive role in the Chinese attitude towards law and regulations. It is crucial to understand that the Chinese traditionally have another attitude towards law than Westerners, who have a history of centuries of the separation of power or *trias politica*, as coined by the French political thinker, Montesquieu.

Ecoffee: the Chinese Starbucks

The development of a performing law system in China that complies with international standards and expectations today is a complex issue. The law system in China is on the one hand linked with Chinese traditions influenced by Confucianism, on the other hand by communism, and today it is under continuous international pressure. Adaptation of the Chinese law system to meet the requirements set by WTO standards and implementation in Chinese reality is complex and difficult.[3]

The problem with many laws in China is that in reality they are not observed. China tends to draft laws and regulations as very general outlines. These general outlines are interpreted to suit the situation at hand. This is difficult for Western companies and organizations that are used to totally relying on a regulation system that ensures objectiveness and credibility to a large extent. More often than not, Chinese laws contain gaps and ambiguities.

We have seen in the chapter on contemporary history that Chinese society went through many changes at the beginning of the twentieth century. Fundamental changes in the law system were part of the wider society reform at the time. The first peak of legal reform in Chinese history, that took place at the beginning of the twentieth century, led to the establishment of a set of legal codes which were mechanically imported from the West. The second peak of legal reform followed in the eighties.[4] We will look into the complexity of this topic of law in China on the basis of the development of copyright law in China. This is one of the hottest and most controversial international law issues when dealing with business in China.

Heated discussions are held between China and the West for the infringement of copyright. The concept of copyright is in fact a purely Western concept that is imposed onto the rest of the world. In group-oriented state-controlled China, knowledge is collective. Westerners take it for granted that everyone in the world is familiar with the Western concept of copyright. This is not always the case, not in China and not in India and not in many other places around the globe.

Other issues are equally controversial, for instance environmental regulations, or human rights. We limit our focus on the issue of copyright as an example of the complexity of the elements at play in the development of a law system in China to match international standards, largely decided on and imposed by the West.

Qu Sanqiang has conducted extensive research on the development of copyright in China. In the context of this book where we try to comprehend contemporary China from an historical and cultural point of view, Qu's publications are illuminating. A look into the history of copyright in China and the development of a performing copyright law explains to a great extent why it remains such a difficult issue. Qu Sanqiang's analysis:

- There was no copyright norm in Chinese feudal history. Copyright originated in the West and was a purely Western concept introduced into China at the beginning of the 20th century under pressure by Western powers.
- The modern notion of copyright, in essence, is in contradiction to Chinese cultural tradition.
- Copyright, as a sort of monopolized right over intellectual creation, is basically inconsistent with Marxist and socialist ideology.
- Copyright in Chinese law, to a large extent remains a means to an end, rather than an end in itself.
- The system of acknowledging the rights of authors prior to the economic reform of the 1980s was only a product of the planned economy, incomplete in the sense of a modern copyright system.
- In dealing with liability for infringement of copyright, Chinese law emphasizes the interests of society over the interests of individuals.
- In adjustment of the copyright relationship, Chinese law is more inclined to resort to administrative or criminal liability to deal with this rather than to employ civil liability.[5]

In traditional Confucian culture, natural order and social order react constantly upon one another. Confucius advocates the concept of *li*, ceremony/rituals/rules to bring social order and universal harmony. Confucius resists the notion of equality and individuality. Everyone has to occupy the right position in the hierarchy of society and live according to that. 'A king is a king, a subject is a subject, a father is a father, a son is a son'. Individuality is to be eliminated. 'The heavenly ethical principle needs to be observed, individual desire needs to be destroyed' (*cun tianli, mie renyu*). Intellectual knowledge is seen as the common heritage of all Chinese people, rather than ascribed to private individuals. Law in a Western sense does not exist.

In the 19th century, Western economic involvement in China expanded and at the same time infringement of intellectual property, such as the use of foreign trade names and trademarks, began to occur. Actions were taken at international level to protect intellectual property: in 1883 the Paris Convention dealing with patents and trademarks was adopted, and in 1886 the Berne Convention dealing with copyright followed. Westerners expected their rights to be respected in China.

With the collapse of the Qing dynasty China began to take the first formal legal steps to protect technological and artistic creation. A law reform took place at the beginning of the 20th century, including the establishment of a copyright system. Commercial agreements were concluded with the US, the UK, and Japan. In reality China did not provide any legal protection for copyrights until 1910 when an experimental copyright act, the Law of Authorship of Daqing Dynasty entered into force. But adoption of the law at that time was merely a passive response to pressure from the West. Empress Dowager Cixi, who ruled from 1861 until 1908 saw law reform as a kind of a short-term expedient necessary to appease the treaty powers.

When Chiang Kai-shek and the Guomindang (Nationalists) gained control of China in 1928, a thorough transformation of the Chinese government took place. The Guomindang developed and promulgated a formal legal structure with legal advisors, many of whom had studied abroad. The first Copyright Law was passed in 1928, borrowing extensively from the German model and Japanese adaptations. The law system failed to achieve its stated objectives because it presumed a legal structure and a legal conscience, neither of which existed in China at the time. Courts were inaccessible, judges incompetent, and there was interference by authorities other than the judiciary in the administration of justice. A separation of power was never introduced in China.

After 1949, China adopted the concept of historical determinism. A legislative break with the past took place with a repeal of the Nationalist law system. The CCP invalidated the entire corpus of law the Nationalists had used. Policy became the legitimate source of legal norms in Communist China. Mass campaigns, propaganda and ideological indoctrination were means of social control. The policy of the CCP was considered superior to the law. The CCP advocated class struggle, leading to the isolation and destruction of class enemies. All copyright laws and agreements were abolished, along with the rest of the Nationalist legal system. Following the example of the Soviet Union some regulations were adopted stating that authors were entitled to a basic remuneration, but rights could only be enjoyed after approval by the state, which was in total control. The state freely reproduced anything written. Intellectualism was looked down upon. All attempts that had been made to formulate laws and regulations to protect copyright before in China were destroyed.

The law and justice system as it existed in pre-1978 Communist times underwent thorough changes after opening up. The impact of the reforms and internationalization signaled a move away from the strict authoritarian Communist system pre-1978 towards a more decentralized policy.

After 1978 China wanted to restore its legal system and set up a framework for the regulation of copyright. Traditional ideas about the notion of copyright remained largely unchanged in the first years after the opening up and China even proclaimed that 'all fruits of intellectual creation were the common heritage of humankind'[6]. But China wanted and needed to obtain foreign scientific technology so it had to adapt to international standards. Foreign companies were reluctant to invest as long as China did not create a performing system for copyright protection. China realized it needed to install a reliable legal system. Foreign pressure became one of the major reasons for legal reform in China during the last decades.

Preparation for the drafting of a copyright law started in 1979. China signed bilateral Sino-American treaties about cooperation in scientific technology. It was obliged to protect foreigners' copyrights for the first time since the establishment of the CCP. Between 1979 and 1985, a number of administrative regulations were drafted. In 1985 the State Council emphasized the need to adhere to international copyright conventions, the Berne Convention and the Universal Copyright Convention.

In 1986 the concept of 'copyright' was used for the first time in a legal document in the PRC. At the end of 1986, China sent a document entitled Ten Main Points of Copyright Law to the World Intellectual Property Organization (WIPO). In 1990 the Copyright Law of the PRC was passed. In 1992 the PRC ratified the Berne Convention and the Universal Copyright Convention. In 1993 China passed the Unfair Competition Law to protect business secrets, unregistered trademarks and product packaging.

Accession to the WTO in 2001 has put pressure on China's law system and led to review and amendments. Today China has a Trademark Law, Patent Law and Copyright Law. This does not mean, however, that protection of intellectual copyright is no longer problematic in China. The laws exist, but implementation or enforcement is difficult.

But constant improvements are apparent, especially in the attitude of the government. This is being shown in the issuing of awards to companies respecting Intellectual Property. By doing this, they create role models for other companies.

Kong Xiangjun, Lawyer at Dahwa Law Firm Shanghai

'Copyright Protection in China today

Copyright Law in China was first promulgated in 1990, but in order to reflect the requirements of the WTO (especially the principles and rules provided in the TRIPS Agreement[7] of the WTO), Chinese Copyright Law and its Implementation Regulations were revised in 2001 and 2002 respectively. They are the fundament of the current Chinese Copyright Law system.

Concerning the protection of copyright, the rights enjoyed by the copyright owner can be generally sorted into two categories: personality rights and property rights. In order to clearly address which right or what protection could be available for the copyright owner, the 2001 Copyright Law provided a defined classification for all of the 17 types of rights under Article 10 of this law. Within these 17 different rights, the first four are now recognized as personality rights (right of publication, authorship, alteration and integrity), and the other 13 as property rights (right of reproduction, distribution, rental, exhibition, performance, showing, broadcast, communication of information on networks, making cinematographic work, adaptation, translation, complication and any other rights a copyright owner is entitled to enjoy by law).

According to the current Chinese Copyright Law, a publisher has the right to permit or prohibit any other person from using the typographical arrangement of books or periodicals already published; and the rights of performers have been extended. There is no distinction between published works and unpublished works, and it is mandatory to obtain prior consent from the copyright owners before using any sound/video works.

The collective administrative system in China has now been clearly defined in Article 8 of Chinese Copyright Law. Copyright owners may authorize the collective administrative organization to exercise their rights to collect the royalties or to represent them in disputes regarding rates.

In Chapter V of the 2001 Copyright Law, the legal liabilities and enforcement measures were defined. In Article 46, anyone who commits any of the 11 acts of infringement shall bear civil liabilities, such as publishing a work without the permission of the copyright owner; publishing a work of joint authorship as a work created solely by oneself without the permission of the other co-authors; having one's name mentioned in connection with a work created by another in order to seek personal fame and gain when one has not taken part in the creation of the work; distorting or mutilating a work created by another, plagiarizing the work of another person; and so on. Serious copyright offenses will also incur criminal punishment.

There are other innovations of this new Copyright Law. For the first time, copyright protection in China has been extended to the works created by stateless persons. The protection of acrobatic performances, architectural designs, model works and literary and artistic works published via the Internet is newly introduced in China as well.'

Copyright Licensed DVD shop

7.2.2 Chinese Characteristics of Law and Judicial Practice

In comparison to Western jurisdictions, Chinese law has its own specific characteristics and chooses its own focuses. Qu Sanqiang summarizes:

- When dealing with the relationship between individuals and the state, both Chinese law and judicial practice place more stress on the 'public interests' of society than on the 'private interests' of the individual copyright holder.
- When assessing whether infringement of copyright is established, both Chinese law and judicial practice emphasize the moral blameworthiness of the subjective aspect rather than the factual damages of the objective aspect.
- In judicial practice the courts most often apply administrative liability rather than civil liability when dealing with this kind of infringement.
- When dealing with the relationship between infringements of economic rights and infringement of moral rights, both Chinese law and judicial practice give priority to the former over the latter.[8]

7.2.3 Implementation of Laws

"Although the introduction of Western notions and norms has considerably improved the copyright system of China, it cannot change the attitudes of instrumentalism and state-centralism towards copyright which are inherently rooted in Chinese culture."
Qu Sanqiang[9]

The Chinese proverb 'A policy is imposed from above; A counter policy is executed from below'[10] is often quoted when referring to the traditional attitude towards law and regulations in China. This attitude is comparable with ancient times: central government sets the rules, but they are interpreted to suit the local situation in a very pragmatic way. But change is on the way. Slowly but surely China is adapting to international standards. It may take a while, however, before China can completely live up to international standards.

The contribution by Kong Xiangjun above shows that law and regulations are well defined in China today.

7.3 Evolutions in Business Communication

Zhu Yunxia researches the changes in business communication and sales genres in China after the establishment of the People's Republic of China until the present day.[11] He distinguishes two periods: the first from 1949 to 1978, a period when China exercised a policy of de-linking from the market economy and implemented a planned economy, and the second after 1978, when the country re-linked with the market economy. He argues that a change in business communication accompanies a change in economic structure and changes in the social context. In each period, business communication is conducted by means of very different sales genres. In the planned economy before 1978, business communication followed the hierarchical line top-down, while in the emerging market economy after 1978, business communication runs along a horizontal axis, between people in an equal position. Zhu's study is exemplary for understanding the many changes in the move from planned to market economy.

7.3.1 1949–1978

After the establishment of the PRC, market mechanisms were only accepted to a limited extent and were gradually replaced by a planned economy. The Communist Party implemented a system of public ownership of production. The CCP controlled production and the market. Commodity exchange was practiced and controlled by public ownership at different levels. All enterprises were state owned and could not make independent decisions in relation to buying and selling. Products were sold and distributed along a top-down trajectory. At the top, the headquarters of the

Central Commercial Ministry resided over the lower levels: provincial, district, town and grass roots. The Ministry made all the decisions about selling products. The lower levels only received what the higher levels distributed to them.

There was no need to use promotion to facilitate selling, because everything was already planned and decided on by the different levels. Business communication was not used to promote products. It was used only to implement the nationally planned sales policy. Sales documents reflected the hierarchy of the centralist planned economy and public ownership; they also reflected the relationship between the people using them.

Three types of Official Sales Letters (*gongwen*) were used in the planned economy:
- The one used by subordinate levels towards the top (*shangxing*) to make a request;
- The one used by superiors towards the bottom (*xiaxing*) to express approval;
- The one used between people at an equal level (*pingxing*).

In the planned economy, the sale of products was conducted between superior and subordinate organizations. This hierarchical business communication reflected the hierarchy between the people. Top-down letters contained phrases like 'After discussions', referring to the fact that approval was agreed upon by a number of people, by a group of decision makers. The superior had control over the (national or local) stock supply. Approval of a request could be granted but would not necessarily meet the customers' need. Shortages could occur as a consequence. Companies or products did not compete against each other.

Advertising Girl

7.3.2 1978–Today

With the open door policy, the Chinese economy started to work on the basis of an equal and mutually beneficial cooperation with other countries and by adopting the world's advanced technologies.

A re-linking to the market economy was initiated and consequently business communication changed. In the market economy, sales are carried out between companies or organizations at an equal level, without a superior-subordinate relationship. Competitiveness between enterprises prevails. Today business communication is used to promote products. Instead of business communication forms that reflect the hierarchical relationship between different levels in the planned economy, they now focus on an equal level of communication whereby the other has to be motivated and stimulated to buy a certain product.

Zhu Yunxia remarks that promotion in China differs from other countries. In China where relationships and *guanxi* are prevalent in business and throughout society, the establishment of a relationship is important even in sales and business communications. Greetings in business communications indicate politeness, and serve to build a friendly relationship with the reader. Establishing a relationship will help to promote a product in China. Harmony and politeness are important in China and because of this, business letters tend 'to include personal information at the beginning, and use it as a politeness strategy for relationship building with the reader'.[12]

In further analysis, Zhu Yunxia shows that sales letters in China today fit in well with the AIDA model of attention, interest, desire, and action, reflecting the basic communication mode in market economy.

7.4 Promotion and Advertising in China

7.4.1 From Ideological Slogan to Commercial Advertising

Before 1978 the only color visible in the street was the red of political propaganda. Slogans reflected CCP policies like: 'Never lose track of the class struggle', or 'Bring the Cultural Revolution to a thorough end'. Commercial advertising was obsolete. No competition, no promotion, no reason to strive for quality. All products had socialist brand names like East Wind, Red Flag, and Liberation.

The earliest sign of changing China was the appearance of advertising in the street, and a little later on television. In 1986 the first foreign television commercials were shown: Colgate, Nescafe, and Tide. The commercials preceded a program they sponsored, the first foreign series, called 'One World', which was made for a Chinese audience. The series was produced by an overseas Chinese who lived in the US and offered topics as diverse as Egyptian pyramids, Iowa farmers, microwave cooking, and an episode about New York with people looking for food in garbage cans, the 'proof that life is not all roses in the ultimate capitalist metropolis'.[13]

At the beginning of the nineties, billboards were still painted by hand. Several people worked on them for weeks at a time. Today Chinese cities are dominated by advertisements. Virtually every space is filled: Western slogans alternate with Chinese characters; Western beauties compete with Chinese; colorful billboards alternate with flashing LCD screens; Chinese products compete with Western products.

Hand Painted Billboards. Shanghai 1994

7.4.2 Politically Controlled Commercial Advertising

Corporate and commercial culture in China is intertwined with politics. Even today the government stipulates rules concerning advertising. During the eighties, commercial advertisements continued to have ideological messages and were in fact a kind of a mixture of socialist and capitalist propaganda. In 1982 the Central Administration for Industry and Commerce declared that advertising could be used to "promote productions, invigorate the economy, increase consumer convenience and promote moral standards".

In 1984 Deng Xiaoping issued a directive stating: "Western cultures and ideas should be adopted only if they fit *guo qing* (national characteristics). Good ideas applicable in China should be promoted; corrupt and inapplicable ideas should be discarded." [14]

Methods and ideas imposed by foreign companies will meet with resistance. Therefore, to successfully appeal to the Chinese consumer, Western companies should take Chinese characteristics into account.

In 1987 Wan Li, Premier of the State Council stated: "advertising is an indispensable element in the promotion of economic prosperity". In 1995 the Chinese government imposed a set of descriptive and strict regulations applying to all forms of Chinese advertising. With these policies, the PRC granted more freedom and at the same time imposed more restrictions on China's advertising. The government put great emphasis on honesty, reverence, and positive representation. [15]

7.4.3 The Focus in Advertising in China

How do the Chinese advertise? Which elements influence the Chinese consumer? Are Western companies aware of Chinese consumer behavior? Why is one product extremely popular and the other totally neglected?

The forces influencing Chinese society as a whole are also at work in the area of promotion and advertising: Confucian traditions, the link with the family, the shift from planned economy to market economy, and interaction with the West.

Good products need to have a history. Therefore, references to the history of a product are important. Dates reflect sound and reliable products. In many cases the link with traditional China plays a crucial role: the Chinese Wall, Imperial architecture, antique Chinese coins, traditional clothing, traditional symbols like the Chinese knot, lions, dragons, the abacus, calligraphy, ink painting, and so on. Many Chinese advertisements make use of traditional symbols, numbers, and colors, on which we will elaborate later.

In some advertisements, the link with pre-1978 Communist times prevails. A fine example is the advertisement of China Mobile Telecommunications, which is almost a mirror image of a Cultural Revolution Propaganda poster.

Some products are linked to Chinese achievements or topics that can boost the image of China, like for instance space travel, or the Olympic Games in Beijing. In preparation for the Beijing Olympics, many advertisements use the same visual language as in pre-1978 times: healthy bodies with strong resolute faces looking up towards the future.

1970s Cultural Revolution Propaganda Poster "Involve a whole life in Revolution; Study a whole life the Thoughts of Mao Zedong"

Western brands symbolize quality. In advertising for Western brands, a luxurious Western lifestyle is promoted: Italian clothing, Swiss watches, and French wines. Western brands and trademarks are very much appreciated.

Some messages are clearly directed at the changes taking place in Chinese society and at the new generation of young Chinese, who have different expectations than their parents. While group-orientation still prevails, we see advertisements referring to individualism of young people: 'I am different from the masses'. 'Young people have no limits'.

7.4.4 Promotion Campaigns and Popular Culture

In China today, a new kind of popular culture has come into being in huge promotion campaigns: a mixture of popular music, songs, dance, and martial arts performances. Some campaigns last a full day. In the shopping streets and squares, stages and tents are set up, and a group of Chinese dress up in the same color to match the promoted product. Green, yellow, red, silver, blue latex or other flashy suits, or traditional Chinese clothing is worn. As soon as the show starts, interaction with the public is sought. People are invited to participate in the act of cooking, quizzing, game playing, or whatever is happening on the stage. Incentives and promotional material of all kinds are handed out to the winners or to the people participating.

China Mobile Telecommunications Advertisement, Chengdu 2006

Thermos Promotion Campaign, Shanghai 2007

7.5 Brands and Logos

7.5.1 Brand Names

The Chinese are extremely sensitive to brand names in this era, especially the newly rich. Despite the fact that big brands are copied and fake products flood international markets, consumers who have enough money attach a lot of importance to quality instead of price. All the big Western brands are available in China. More and more high quality Chinese products are being produced. 'Made in China' is losing its negative connotations. In the meantime, there are already a number of Chinese brands with an established international reputation, like Lenovo and Haier.

7.5.2 Translation of Brands and Corporate Names

The Chinese attach a lot of importance to the translation of company names or brand names. A company name or brand name in Chinese will sound phonetically like the original Western name. But apart from sound and pronunciation, one should try to have a translation with a lucky, prosperous meaning and a favorable connotation. In the translation of beauty products, the name will often refer to beauty. In drinks and food the character 'happy' or 'healthy' often appears. For instance Coca Cola, *Ke kou ke le*, could be translated as 'a joyful taste and happiness'; Lays crisps are called *Le shi* or 'Happy case'. A BMW car is called *Bao ma*, 'Treasure Horse', Carrefour is called *Jia Le Fu*, 'Happy and Rich Family'.

The name Revlon is linked to a famous poem describing the love between a Tang Dynasty ruler and one of the four most beautiful women in Chinese history. Revlon is translated as *luhua nong*, meaning 'the fragrance of flowers that are covered with morning dew'.[16]

7.5.3 Symbolism in Advertisements and Brands

Holistic thinking in China leads to an extensive use of symbols in Chinese society. One of the areas dominated by symbolism is advertising and branding. All sorts of double or multiple layers in language and symbolism are used: numbers, colors, animals, Chinese characters, and so on.

Even numbers are *yin*; odd numbers are *yang*. Imperial symbols only use odd numbers. In the Forbidden City, the most important buildings are situated on terraces comprising three levels. In front of the Forbidden City there are five bridges to enter the city. On the emperor's robes the dragon has five claws. Nine is the highest odd number. At the entrance to the imperial palace the doors are decorated with nine times nine golden knobs. In the architecture of the Temple of Heaven the number nine is evident: stairs with nine steps, nine times nine tiles on the terrace.

The number four is a phonetic reminder of death because *si* can mean 'four' but it can also mean 'death'. The number four is avoided in every possible way in China. Buildings in China often don't have a fourth floor. People will never buy four items of a product. The number four is avoided in telephone numbers.

The number eight, that phonetically sounds like 'wealth', is by far the most favored lucky number. Financial transactions, or the start up of a production line preferably take place on the eight of the month, or better still on the eighth of August. The Beijing Olympics will start at eight o'clock, on the eighth of August 2008. All license plates and telephone numbers preferably contain the number eight, several eights or a combination with six and eight is also considered propitious.

One hundred is a term for 'many'. The hundred names (*lao bai xing*) refer to the population. In a bookshop one finds books such as 'One hundred Famous Chinese' or 'A Hundred Poems from the Tang Dynasty'. To have a hundred sons used to be the marriage wish for newly weds.

The 'ten thousand things' refers to the whole universe. Ten thousand is the highest number. The slogan *Mao Zedong wan sui*, 'Long live Mao Zedong', literally means 'Ten thousand years for Mao Zedong'. Chinese count with ten thousand as a standard. Instead of saying a 'hundred thousand', they say 'ten ten thousand'.

Yellow is the emperor's color because the word for both emperor and yellow is *huang* and is thus a good color. The roof of the Forbidden City is yellow. The emperor's robe is yellow. Green is the color of youth. The Confucian temple roofs, where the Confucian schools were organized in old China, are green. Red is the color of good luck. The color red is very popular in China. Traditionally, a bride's dress is red. At Chinese New Year, children are given *hong bao* or 'red envelopes' containing money.

A dragon (*yang*), symbol for the emperor, represents masculine power and vitality. A phoenix (*yin*) is pictured in the company of the dragon. A bat, *fu*, is the phonetic symbol for 'luck'. Fish, *yu*, are phonetic symbols for 'abundance, wealth'. A crane represents long life.[17]

7.5.4 Mottos and Corporate Spirit

Organizations or companies in China often use mottos reflecting the corporate spirit, implying a kind of moral property. Dahwa Law Firm in Shanghai uses the motto of 'Wisdom, Honesty, Ambition and Excellence' in their publicity. Henan Tourism Group Co. Ltd. claims that their outstanding achievements are greatly owed to the corporate spirit of 'Unity, Advancing, Truth and Dedication'. Just like in education, the moral quality of people is also important in corporate culture.

Fresh Food in the Supermarket

7.6 Chinese Consumers

7.6.1 Consumer Behavior

Part of the consuming game is 'just looking'. The Chinese proverb 'Never make a purchase until you have compared three shops' shows a disinclination for impulse buying.[18] Now that China is flooded with new things, the Chinese enjoy window-shopping as a pastime. Group dynamics dominate buying behavior. If one person – even more so if he is a person in authority – decides that a certain product is the best, the whole group will follow him. A product will sell better when it is already known, tested, and approved of. The Chinese will always buy something they already know rather than something they have never heard off. The Chinese tend to buy many of the same products.

The way products are displayed influences buying behavior. The most important thing when buying food is that everything should be fresh. Supermarkets in China understand this. Fish, meat and vegetables will not be pre-packaged like in the West, but will be displayed on stalls as if the supermarket were an open-air fresh food market.

Advertisements on TV present things as if they were within the grasp of everyone: huge villas with beautiful women and expensive cars, golf clubs next to the desk. Over the past decennia, a new class has come into being in Chinese society: the rich. But it is the new middle class that is the primary target of most advertising. They are the ones striving for a better quality of life (as depicted in advertisements). They are the ones with an IKEA interior, who drink coffee instead of tea.

Fresh fish in the market with a string through the top fin, ready to be carried away

Westerners should be aware that products must be adapted to the Chinese market. Beauty products, for example, are for whitening the skin, as the Chinese beauty ideal is a pale skin, or the fact that some products are just not wanted by the Chinese, like a paper agenda.

Chinese customers are very demanding; they always want the best product for the lowest price. They are even more demanding of foreign products. These are associated with the cliché 'perfect quality'.

7.6.2 Customer Service

In the centrally planned economy, after-sales care or customer services hardly existed. The relationship between supplier and customer was largely neglected. Today commercial interests motivate better customer services. However, in many cases it is still difficult to get the Chinese to pay for these services.

Sourcing in China requires strict control and follow-up. Only strict control will assure that the right amount of the right product is shipped on time. Thorough control before the export of products will save you a lot of problems afterwards. If you have reliable relationships in China, problems can be limited. For example, don't count on after-sales services in China when things go wrong internationally if you don't have someone to rely on in China. Once the wrong products or bad quality products have been shipped, it will be very difficult to solve the problem. The best scenario is that you will receive some kind of compensation on the next shipment.

7.7 Trading Ethics

Insider–outsider ethics are responsible for the fact that promises are not always kept. 'Treating friends better than others is normal and ethical' implies that if you are not a 'friend' the relationship is utilitarian, dominated by purely commercial motives.

Trading companies are usually reliable if you have established a good relationship with them. Negotiation is necessary when a supplier does not keep his word and raises his initial price, which means the trader loses his share. In this case, negotiating tactics and strategies, on which we elaborate later, are useful. The Chinese are shrewd and cunning negotiators. China is a negotiating and haggling society; from childhood on, people learn how to negotiate.

A Chinese company will always keep an eye on its clients' competitors and suppliers, even after an exclusivity agreement. If a competitor offers a better deal, the Chinese company might neglect the agreement.

Bart DAUWE, Business Manager ChinAdvice

'Trading Ethics in China

With the existence of international agreements such as incoterms[19] and payment conditions stated in the L/C[20] one would be entitled to think that an ethical trading climate has the same meaning globally and is not open for interpretation, and that in principle unethical trading cannot exist.

But unfortunately there are exceptions like, for instance, in the flax sector. It used to be common to pay 95 to 98% of the value by L/C with the agreement that the rest would be paid upon delivery after quality control. As flax is a natural product, it is very difficult to guarantee consistent quality and in each shipment there may be a few fibers of lower quality than the rest. The Chinese often take the few bad fibers claiming that the quality is not perfect and consequently the rest of the money is not paid. As a consequence of this, the flexible attitude on the European side tightened, and nowadays the whole sum is paid by L/C.

I went through the experience when, after signing a contract, more and more 'obscurities' appeared as the date for payment approached. Initially we agreed that the commission was a proportion of the total value of the offer, thus a part of the total CIF price.[21] The initial deal was changed into a commission on the FOB price[22], and a few days later it became clear that the commission would only be part of the ex-works price.[23] All of a sudden, the person I had made the agreements with did not seem to work for the supplier anymore so there was no one I could turn to. On top of all this, the Chinese company did not want to pay me in USD, but in Renminbi. The initial agreed commission was decimated in the space of a few days. I paid my learning money on this case.

Amongst each other, trading companies usually have a pretty good fellowship. Traders attach a lot of importance to their reputation in the sector. Very often trading is not about one shot deals, but about long-term co-operations. Traders thus like to think long-term.

A Chinese firm operating as an intermediary might have difficulties because payment can take a long time. Sometimes the commission is partially based on the 'tax refund after export'. Since 1985 China adopted tax rebates for exporting enterprises. That means that central government pays back a certain proportion of the consumption taxes and value added tax (VAT) to the enterprises after they have paid taxes for exported goods. The tax refund – and thus the related commission – takes a long time to arrive, and sometimes the commission is not paid at all.

European ethics are described in China as *yi shi yi, er shi er* (1 = 1, 2 = 2). This means that a given word is binding. An example of this is a price quotation. A quotation in Western business is binding. In China an offer is accepted, followed immediately by negotiations about the price. The European side prefers CIF offers[24] with long-term validity. But in China product and freight prices change very fast; it is difficult to set a long-term standing price. On top of this, the Chinese government can change policies about, for instance, revaluation of the RMB, tax refunds, export taxes and implement them very fast. European demand to guarantee long-term fixed prices is difficult to deal with in a fast-changing China.

What is crucial in trading, like in other areas of doing business with China, is to cherish relationships and *guanxi*. A few months ago we received a Chinese delegation from a Chinese paper plant. We offered *laozong*, the boss, a pricy Antwerp diamond, and gifts of famous brands to the rest of the delegation. About one month later we shipped 500 tons of old paper to China. Upon arrival of the shipment, the Chinese discovered that the paper from our Belgian supplier had been sprinkled with water to make the weight heavier. The bottom of the container was wet and rotten. Thanks to our relationship the incident was dealt with in serenity and the money was paid.

It is impossible to give a complete picture of trading ethics in China; I stick to the saying 'There's no business like China business': it is always true and keeps business exciting.'

7.8 Dealing with Money

7.8.1 Chinese and Money: Private Saving and Investing

When the Chinese need money, they will first turn to the family, rather than to an official bank. A phenomenon occurring in China and in overseas Chinese areas is the use of *hui*. A number of people or families put their money together and invest it in a common project, like for instance real estate. Usually the *hui* is purely based on an oral agreement. No contract is involved.

Tony Fang analyses the Chinese way of dealing with money from a Confucian point of view.[25] He ascribes the Chinese obsession with money to the lack of legal institutions and the dominance of families in Confucian society through the ages. He sees the obsession with money as an essential by-product of the Confucian family system. Families got stronger if they gathered more wealth. A Chinese family was a kind of insurance company for all its members.

Chinese rank among the highest in saving rates in the world. Private domestic saving in China is 39 percent of the GNDI (Gross National Disposable Income).[26] Money is saved and invested.

7.8.2 Corruption

A consequence of the system of *guanxi* and relationship building in China is the exchange of services and gifts. A Westerner who is not used to dealing with *guanxi* may be surprised in the beginning. Those who gain insight into the working of *guanxi* will learn how to deal with it.

Sometimes the dividing line between gift and bribery is thin. Especially with the intertwined interests between government, Communist Party and business world in China, corruption is a huge problem. Being a member of the Communist Party results in favors. Business people need all kinds of permissions from officials. Bribery is more often than not involved.

Corruption is not only about money. A bigger problem is the production of fake products. This becomes problematic when it comes to fake medicine or food products.

The Chinese government is involved in the fight against corruption, but it is almost impossible to extinguish it, exactly due to the intermingling of parties and the absence of a separation of power. At the time premier Zhu Rongji pleaded for anti-corruption actions in 1999 and 2000, Jiang Zemin launched a national campaign against corruption. In 2006 president Hu Jintao dismissed the mayor of Shanghai for reasons of corruption.

The fight against corruption, even with anti-bribery laws, is however very complicated, as Luo Yadong points out: "In China, there are both legal and informal social aspects to the concept of the bribe. The difference between acceptable gifts and improper bribes depends on arbitrary, delicately poised cultural conventions, which, moreover, vary according to context. This makes the enforcement of anti-bribery laws very difficult in China. What is acceptable reciprocity at one place or time may be viewed as corruption at another place or time."[27]

7.9 Negotiating with China

7.9.1 Stages in the Negotiation Process

In the West negotiations between opposite parties usually have a clear starting and ending point. When the parties involved in negotiations have come to an agreement and the contract is signed, the negotiations have come to an end. The agreements as they have been put down on paper have to be respected by all parties. In the Chinese context, negotiations are usually not as clearly defined. Negotiations never come to a real end. The stages in a negotiation process in China can be divided into the pre-, actual, and post-negotiations.

The pre-negotiation period is used to set up the relationship and to set the general framework. The actual negotiations will go through the process of technical, financial, legal, and other aspects, depending on the situation. When the parties have come to an agreement and the contract is signed, Westerners tend to see this as an ending point. For the Chinese, however, the contract is more a stage in the cooperation; it is a kind of commitment to cooperate. A contract in China should always be seen as open to renegotiation and adjustment to changing circumstances.[28]

7.9.2 Decision-Making Process

One of the difficulties about working in China is how to gain insight into organizational structures. Westerners are not used to governmental involvement in organizations, in negotiation and decision-making processes. To understand the involvement of government, at different levels, and to understand the mixture of organizational forms, Huang Quanyu, Leonard Joseph and Chen Tong's book 'Business Decision Making in China' is illuminating.[29] They describe manufacturing organizations, service organizations, governmental organizations, state owned, joint venture, foreign owned, and so on, and they provide schemes of all these different kinds of organizations to show how business and political interests are interwoven. In the state owned enterprises, not only the Party might be involved, but sometimes also the military. The authors describe the mixtures and interconnections between all parties and the complexity this brings in business decision-making. They also analyze the influence of concepts like *yin* and *yang*, or the influence of Sunzi and strategic thinking in the process of decision-making.

They see two general models of decision-making in China.[30] In the first, higher authorities make decisions. This was the method of decision-making used during the planned economy, decisions run along the centralist pyramid. Today this decision-making model is still used in Chinese organizations and companies. The second model is used in independent companies where decisions are based on the interest of the enterprise or on market analysis instead of being based on higher authority. But even in the second model there is very often some kind of government involvement.

At the negotiation table this means that different parties can be involved. The Chinese side will not give insight into the interests of their side. These interests may even be conflicting. Very often the people at the negotiating table have limited or no decision-making power. They have clear outlined assignments they have to obey and justify to a higher level.

7.9.3 Chinese Strategic Thinking

In the 5th century BC Sunzi (Sun Tzu) wrote 'The Art of War'. During the Ming Dynasty an anonymous writer formulated the 'Thirty Six Strategies'. Sunzi's work and the 'Thirty-Six Strategies' have been extremely influential through the ages. Both treatises have been translated into many languages, and have been interpreted many times. Today they are applied to business and to negotiating styles. An example in English is 'The Art of War for Managers'.[31] Negotiations in China are influenced by political, economical, legal, technological, and cultural conditions, by Confucianism and Daoism, but certainly also by Chinese strategic thinking.

Many of the contemporary books on negotiating with the Chinese are written by Westerners. Tony Fang researches Chinese business negotiating styles from a specific Chinese cultural background. He focuses not only on the tactics used in Chinese negotiations; he argues that the most important strategic component, the crucial factor of Chinese business culture is the concept of *ji*, which he translates as 'stratagem'.[32] He traces the secrets of Chinese negotiation back to this concept. The Chinese character *ji* is a combination of two other characters: *yan*, 'to speak, say, tell', and *shi*, 'ten'. Put together they mean 'speak to ten', 'count to ten', 'count from A to Z', or 'Think through the whole situation'.[33] When you have an overview of the whole situation and prepare in detail, you will win. Chinese managers are trained to make use of 'The Art of War' and the 'Thirty-Six Strategies' to deal with foreign business people.[34]

The Chinese have multiple moral standards in dealing with people and they believe that "principles which are correct for one set of circumstances may not be appropriate for another at all, but the principles in each case are equally honorable".[35] Consequently, Chinese people use different ethics in different circumstances. They also follow different teachings (Confucianism, Daoism, Buddhism) at the same time. All these factors together are the key to understanding the complexity of the Chinese business negotiating style.

7.9.4 Chinese Business Negotiating Style

The Chinese tend to negotiate in large teams. For Westerners this is often a confusing factor. During the negotiations, people come and go, new people arrive and others leave. People from different backgrounds can take part in the negotiations: business, political, and even military background, as we mentioned in the previous paragraph on decision-making. Changing levels or specialist negotiators from different bureaus can be involved. This is the consequence of compartmentalization and the tradition of narrow specialization, the separation of financial and technical decision-making.[36]

There may be some technical people at the table, or people with specific knowledge of the subject under discussion. The opposite negotiating party is not informed of this. Negotiators should try to find out whom they are talking to, which parties are involved and who is at the table. Sometimes people bluff about their power and competence. The interests of the different members of the team at the negotiation table will not be made explicit. Interests will be masked. When the Chinese side is happy about a proposal they will not necessarily show it.

Negotiations take place in Chinese, with an interpreter, but it's very possible that the Chinese team has someone with very good English language skills who only listens; the opposite negotiating party is not informed of this. The Western party in the negotiations should make sure they bring their own interpreter, a person they have a relationship with, so that advice and information about communication 'between the lines' can be provided afterwards. Chinese interpreters sometimes filter what Western people say, often to avoid loss of face. If the Chinese side brings an interpreter, a lot of information will be lost for the Western side.

Indirect ways of communication will be used. Body language should be observed attentively. The Chinese have learnt to control and hide their emotions since childhood. They control their facial expression, but sometimes show their nervousness with their hands. Chinese people sometimes take their time to think in silence.

Chinese teams always respect the principle of 'speaking with one voice' at the table. The result is a lack of transparency about the backgrounds of the people involved and the interests of the different parties involved in the negotiations. Westerners should use the same tactic in China, making agreements with colleagues and thorough preparations beforehand so as to be able to speak as one voice at the table. Preparations beforehand include being informed about the Chinese side and having decided what goal must be reached at the negotiation table. The Chinese interpret discussions between people from the same party as losing face. Therefore, any discussion should take place away from the table.

During negotiations, the parties will check each other's strengths and weaknesses. Each side should be prepared to go through a period of 'mental struggle'. It might be interesting to keep in mind Trompenaars' picture of communication patterns: going from general to specific; checking each other along the communication process, and coming to a conclusion at the very end. Issues on the negotiation table will only be settled and decided at the very end. Persistence is a good attitude.

During the process, closed items will be reopened and renegotiated. Aspects already agreed upon will be brought back into the discussion. Repetitive questioning and meticulous note taking is done in order to learn about Western technology and business practices. Don't expect an item per item sequential process. Parties should be careful with information sharing, especially with technological know-how.

Insider-outsider ethics will be used involving all kinds of tactics to put the opposite party in the position of the outsider: shaming techniques, claiming you don't understand China, claiming false authority, using friendliness and anger alternatively to influence your emotions. Sometimes an anti-foreign attitude will be displayed. Psychological pressure might be used, exaggerating Chinese concessions and minimizing yours. If you as the opposite party are perceived as an insider the reciprocity concept will be played upon: friends have obligations towards each other and you should observe your obligations.

Competitors are played off against each other to increase pressure for conditions. To undermine confidence, the Chinese may create artificial competition with a focus on prices, to gain technological knowledge, or just to check out of fear of exploitation. Time pressure is also used. When the Chinese know the opposite party will only be in China for three days, they will wait until the very last moment before making any decision.

Changing location or changing people at the table can be used as a tactic to exhaust the opposite party. The Chinese side will always push to find the bottom line. It may be useful in some situations to show anger or frustration as part of the game. Patience and awareness of the use of tactics will help.

No matter how hard negotiations become, make sure that when they are over, all parties can walk out the door with their relationship intact. Banquets, sightseeing, and karaoke can also belong to the testing method, an opportunity to create an informal forum, or a way to compensate for low payment.

The contract is not the final point in the process; post-negotiations follow.

When a Chinese version and an English version of the contract are provided, both versions should be compared before signing. In many cases, only the Chinese version has legal power. The English version is often only a resume or a draft of the full Chinese version.

[1] http://immi.se/intercultural/nr3/zhu.htm

[2] Wheare, quoted in: Qu Sanqiang, 2002, p 51

[3] An overview of all the laws adapted since the opening up, as well as all the documents and agreements on the accession of China to the WTO, in English and in Chinese, can be found at: www.lawinfochina.com/

[4] Qu Sanqiang, 2002, pp 50–51

[5] Ibid, p iii

[6] Pendleton, quoted in: Ibid, p 39

[7] Agreement On Trade-related Aspects of Intellectual Property Right

[8] Ibid, p 257

[9] Ibid, p 397

[10] Shang you zheng ce, xia you dui ce

[11] http://immi.se/intercultural/nr3/zhu.htm

[12] Ibid

[13] Pan Lynn, 1987, *The New Chinese Revolution*, Hamish Hamilton, London, 1987, p 132

[14] Yan Rick, "To Reach China's Consumers, Adapt to Guo Qing", *Harvard Business Review on Doing Business in China*, Harvard Business School Press, 2004, p 126

[15] Li Xiaodong, *Dancing Dragons. Chinese Aesthetics since 1979*, Drills Publishing, Utrecht, 2000, pp 73–88

[16] Yan Rick, 2004, p 131

[17] More information on symbolism in China: Eberhard Woltram, *A Dictionary of Chinese Symbols*, Routledge, London, NY 1986

[18] Yan Rick, 2004, p 130

[19] International Commerce Terms devised and published by the International Chamber of Commerce

[20] Letter of Credit, issued mostly by a financial institution

[21] CIF includes transport and insurance

[22] Free On Board, exclusive freight and insurance

[23] The seller makes the goods available at his premises, all charges are to be paid for by the consignee

[24] Price to the harbor of destination

[25] Fang Tony, 1998, *Chinese Business Negotiating Style*, IBS, Thousand Oaks, London, New Delhi, p 132

[26] Perkins, Radelet, Snodgrass, Gillis, Roemer, *Economics of Development*, W.W. Norton & Company, 2001, p 395

[27] Luo Yadong, *Guanxi and Business*, World Scientific, Asia-Pacific Business Series – Vol 1, p 30

[28] Carolyn Blackman describes the stages in the negotiating process, the cultural and societal inspired underlying patterns of Chinese negotiations, as well as offering valuable case studies that highlight many aspects of negotiating with the Chinese in a very clear and recognizable way: Blackman Carolyn, *Negotiating China. Case Studies and Strategies*. Allan & Unwin, 1997, pp XV–XViii

[29] Huang Quanyu, Leonard Joseph, Chen Tong, *Business Decision Making in China*, International Business Press, New York, London, 1997

[30] Ibid, pp 75–79

[31] Sun Tzu, Michaelson Gerald, *Sun Tzu: The Art of War for Managers; 50 Strategic Rules*. Adams Media Corporation, Avon, Massachusetts, 2001

[32] Fang Tony, *Chinese Business Negotiating Style*, International Business Series, Sage Publications, Thousand Oaks, London, New Delhi, 1998, pp 152–153

[33] Ibid, p 153

[34] Ibid, pp 175–181

[35] Ibid p 27

[36] Blackman Carolyn, 1997, xvii

8 Conformist China

8 Conformist China

Confucius said: "For teaching to love one another, nothing is better than filial piety; for teaching people to be gentle and obedient, nothing is better than fraternal duty; for changing social customs and manners, nothing is better than music; for securing tranquility for the ruler and peace for the people, nothing is better than etiquette. Etiquette is nothing but reverence. If the father is revered, his sons will be happy; if the elder brother is revered, the younger brother will be happy; if a ruler is revered, all his subjects will be happy. To revere the one man – the son of heaven – will please thousands upon thousands of his people. Reverence for just a few makes many feel happy – this is what is called an important rule of conduct."[1]

8.1 Ritual, Etiquette, Reverence

In ancient China the 'Ministry of Rites' was extremely important. All rites, rituals and ceremonies needed to be administered correctly to preserve harmony in the universe. To avoid disturbing the natural order, all things had to be approached and carried out correctly, according to the prescriptions. For this reason, etiquette has a much deeper significance in China than in the West. Etiquette and rituals are more than manners or politeness alone. These ancient rules are to some extent still applied in today's new China. Chinese etiquette rules are mainly connected to hierarchy and social position. It is amazing to see how many of the rules of etiquette described in 1878 by John Henry Gray still survive today[2].

Bernard PIERRE, Ambassador of Belgium in Beijing

'Protocol Used for Official Delegations in China

Delegations from governments, parliaments... can only be called 'official' on the basis of an official invitation: without that, the visit will be considered as totally private, which implies no official contacts (and no banquet, for that matter), but also no logistic support of any kind, for example, at the airport (Prince Laurent had to register his bags all by himself last year!).

Once that official invitation is obtained, the authority from which it stems will grant support for the organization of the program and will take responsibility for part or all of the 'official' program and contacts (also note that there is a difference between official invitations received without asking and those which result from our insistence: the key word here seems to be the national interests of China in granting such an invitation).

Who makes the official invitation is an indication of the level ascribed to the delegation by the Chinese authorities: Minister President Leterme (Minister President of the Flemish Region in Belgium in 2006) was invited by a Vice Minister of MofCom[3], Belgian Prince Philippe by Vice Premier Wu Yi and President De Croo (President of the Belgian Parliament in 2006) by President Wu Bangguo (President of the National People's Congress).

The first meeting is *always* formal: it looks like two 'chief mandarins' who only greet each other, congratulate each other, and set the framework for the 'technical work' that will obviously be done by lower level collaborators. Questions of substance are therefore seldom discussed (the exception to this rule being Minister Bo Xilai, but that is probably a consequence of his character).

The composition of delegations should be as perfectly matched as possible (meaning not 10 people on one side and 35 on the other). It is exceptional that persons other than the heads of delegations do the talking.

The delegation exists only because it has a leader: if the head of the foreign delegation decides not to attend a meeting, this would mean that the delegation no longer actually exists. This is valid for the attendance of journalists: their presence and participation is accepted (tolerated) only because of the presence of that particular delegation. No journalist should arrive before the delegation or be allowed to stay once it has left.

Even if agreements are to be signed during or after this meeting, they should be seen as the beginning of something, and not its conclusion.

It is very bad manners to try to discuss matters that have not been agreed upon beforehand: never put your interlocutors in a corner by raising themes without previous notification.'

8.2 Host and Guest

"With the set up of rites, the hierarchical order between the noble and the humble is well defined; with the popularization of music, both the superior and the inferior are on good terms; and with the standardization of people's likes and dislikes, the worthy and the unworthy are clearly distinguished."[4]

When receiving a guest, the hierarchical position of the host and the guest need to correspond, to maintain equilibrium and harmony. When a guest arrives he is received (*qing*) and welcomed by someone of the same social position, so that harmony can exist. When the guest leaves the host will accompany him (*song*) and see him on his way so that he leaves in harmony.

The correspondence of social positions between host and guest is taken very seriously: a minister is received by a minister, a vice-minister by a vice-minister, a PhD student by a PhD student, and a manager by a manager.

In situations where hierarchical position is unclear, or where a Chinese version of the hierarchical position of the guest does not exist, discussions take place as to who the right person is to receive the guest.

If a person is appointed to receive a guest and for some reason he cannot be present at the time of his/her arrival, problems may occur because no one of the right level is available.

If a Western delegation comes with two people both in high positions, one of them has to be chosen as the highest so that equilibrium between host and guest can be obtained and the necessary rituals can be performed.

The observance of hierarchical positions between guest and host not only plays a part in governmental delegations. It can occur in academic, business, and all other kinds of situations as well.

It is the responsibility of the host to look after his guests in every possible way. Everything a guest might possibly need is thought of and provided for, even before the guest might even feel the need.

8.3 Ritual and Official Delegations

Hierarchical centralist thinking is equally reflected in the structure of a delegation. A delegation – business, governmental or any other delegation – always has a pyramid structure. The leader of the delegation on top of the pyramid is the person in power. He speaks for the group; he decides everything, his wish is their command. The whole group obeys and submits to the authority of the leader. *Ting Dajia de* means 'We obey authority'. If a program is planned and the leader falls sick, the whole delegation will stay in the hotel and the program will be cancelled.

8.4 Banquets

8.4.1 Banquets and Harmony

"When the prince of the state raises his cup and proposes a toast to his guests or subjects, all the guests or subjects are to descend the hall and *kowtow* to express their gratitude and then ascend the hall again, thus finishing the rite. This is done to show the proper decorum on the part of the subject. On the other hand, the prince is to answer the salutes, as it is stipulated in the ritual law that 'Every salute must be returned without exception'... the Rite of Banqueting is meant to

Phoenix Claw

confirm the fundamental principle for the proper relations between the prince and his subjects." [5]

The Book of Rites prescribes the Rite of Banqueting as the 'fundamental principle for the proper relations'. In China the banqueting ritual is still observed. Not to the same extent as in the old days when all the guests needed to *kowtow* after the host proposed a toast, but status is always made explicit by seating positions at the table or by the position of the glass when toasting.

The host sits farthest away from the door looking over his guests in the same way that a ruler surveys his empire. The most important guest sits on the right hand side of the host. The second host sits across the table from the first host. The importance of hierarchy continues along the line of the guests around the table.

The favorite way to build relationships in China is by organizing banquets: eating and drinking and spending time in harmony. A banquet is a perfect example of the quest for harmony between *yin* and *yang*. Traditional philosophy is fundamental in Chinese cooking. There has to be balance in the food as well as in the actions at the table that contribute to, or even define, the harmony of the people and the harmony in the interaction between them. The building up and cementing of human relationships is also coupled with banquets that are constituted according to the *yin yang* principle and etiquette, *li*.

Not only the food at the table is significant, but also the way it is prepared. Colors and flavors have to be varied and balanced. The five flavors sweet, sour, salty, bitter and hot must be in balance as well as the five colors. The combination of dishes includes different preparation methods such as warm and cold, roasted, steamed and boiled. A balanced meal includes fish, chicken and meat combined with all kinds of vegetables and other ingredients. Numbers are symbolic: there will never be four cold dishes, always three or five. The names of the dishes are symbolic. Some dishes also have symbolic meaning: the chicken foot, or Phoenix Claw in Chinese, is auspicious.

The host at the head of the table starts and controls the proceedings. He dictates when to eat or drink. He ensures that harmony is maintained at the table. If two people get into a discussion he will mediate and make sure that tranquility and harmony is preserved. Everything should be peaceful, pleasant, light-hearted and harmonious.

A Chinese banquet usually starts around 6pm. All the guests are seated at one or several round tables of 10 to 12 people. In the middle of each table, a round turning disc is used to put all the dishes on. It turns around continuously during the banquet. The dishes will be served facing the guest: a duck, chicken, or fish head will always point towards the guest. The sequence of the dishes is as follows: a number of cold dishes, followed by a number of hot dishes, followed by a whole fish (symbol of abundance) at the end, followed by soup, and only after that rice or other 'staple food' (*zhu shi*) will be served. It is not polite to eat a lot of rice at the end of the banquet because that means the food was insufficient or not nice.

8.4.2 Hierarchy: Toasting and Speeches

"If your feelings are deep, finish the wine in one swallow,
If your feelings are shallow, just take a lick."

Toasting is an integral part of Chinese banqueting and like everything else at the table, connected to ritual. 'To propose a toast', *(jing jiu)*, contains the characters *jing* 'to esteem' and *jiu*, 'wine', in other words, 'to show your esteem with wine'.

It is possible that the host first proposes three toasts, each with a small speech. Following the first three toasts, the second host will propose three toasts. And after that, the guest is supposed to propose three toasts, each with a small speech.

The host proposes the first toast and directs a small speech towards his guest, in which he welcomes his guest, praises the friendship, the harmonious cooperation, the good relationship between the two countries if the guest is a foreigner, and the intention to work together for a long time in the future. He finishes his speech with the word *ganbei*, which means 'ad fundum' or 'bottoms up'. At the moment of *ganbei* they touch glasses. The guest makes sure his glass is in a lower position than that of the host. This shows his respect for the host. After emptying their glasses, people might show each other that their glasses really are completely empty stressing the respect they want to show. If the host stands up, the guest should also stand up. After the initial toast by the host, a number of toasts follow according to a fixed ritual, as described by Zhang Xiaojia below.

The guest has to return the same number of toasts that the host has proposed to him, observing the prescribed rule of 'Every salute must be returned without exception'. His small speech should have almost the same structure, content and length as the host's, to maintain harmony and equilibrium.

When several tables of guests are present, the host will go to every table to propose his toast in the course of the banquet. When the boss of a company makes a toast this means he gives a lot of honor. Women can also propose a toast if they would like to do so, especially if they are in a high position, but even women in lower positions can propose a toast. Any people in lower positions, men or women, may propose a toast if they want to, but they are not obliged to.

The ritual of toasting depends on the situation. When a manager has proposed a toast during a business dinner and one of the employees proposes a toast to him, then all the employees need to propose one. If a person in higher position proposes a toast to people in lower positions they have to finish their glass. If a person in a lower position proposes a toast to someone in a higher position, the one higher up is not obliged to finish his glass. If an assistant notices his boss cannot drink anymore, he should take over, pretending he wants to drink himself. In this way he gives face to his boss.

Trendy Guangzhou

More often than not, the guest gets very drunk. This is interpreted as a sign of real friendship. A person who is very drunk shows his real self, he is open and cannot 'pretend' anymore, and that glorifies the friendship.

ZHANG Xiaojia, Student of Economics, Peking University

'Although at university we don't follow any course purely on etiquette, the topic is part of various classes. I learnt most of the business etiquette in Shandong Province, while doing social science research with the director of our department at Peking University, where we had dinners with the mayor, the vice-mayor and other officials who had been students at Peking University.

1. Seating Position at the Dinner Table
In formal situations, Chinese people have dinner at a round table. The circle is the symbol of 'union'. Usually there are two hosts at each table. The first host (either the man with the highest position or the host of a family) sits facing the door. This is the most honorable seat at the table. In ancient China, wars occurred frequently. A seat facing the door enables the host to overlook the situation; when an attack occurs he can get away quickly. The second host (usually the host with a lower position or the hostess of a family) sits with his/her back to the door. This place is called *xia shou* in Chinese, *xia* meaning

Fish is served facing the guest

'lower', referring to the least honorable seat at the table. If there are other hosts (usually, the number of hosts is either two or four because the Chinese prefer even numbers to keep equilibrium), they will sit in the middle of the first and second hosts.

As for the guests, the one with the highest position should sit to the right of the first host. The right hand side confers respect. The one with the second highest position sits to the right of the 'first guest', and so on. However, in most cases, only the host's and the first guest's position are really fixed, the other guests usually sit randomly. Sometimes, if the host really wants to please the first guest who might be in a higher position, the host can even let the guest sit at his place (the most honorable seat). In very formal situations, such as a dinner with a mayor, depending on position and gender, everybody's seat is arranged beforehand, and there will be a small card with your name in front of your seat. In informal situations, it can sometimes be difficult to decide who is the most important guest. It usually takes a lot of time for other guests to 'push' or 'pull' the one with the comparatively highest position to the 'first guest seat'. Due to modesty, people usually appear unwilling to sit there!

2. The Order of Actions

If you have dinner with Chinese people, remember to respect the following order: old people (or the people in high positions) always act first. They sit down on their seats first; they taste the dishes first, and so on.

The order of toasts is complex. The first host proposes the first toast. Usually he will stand up and make a speech about how happy he is to have you all as his guests. This speech can sometimes be very long, all the people at the table should look at him, keep quiet and stop eating. After the host's speech, people should stand up and toast with him. Usually the host will toast with the first guest first, and then one by one with those around him (either clockwise or anticlockwise). For those seated far away from him, he will just raise his glass in their direction and look into their eyes. After that, everyone should tap their glasses on the round turning disc (by doing so, it is like you have toasted everyone at the table) and then drink the wine. When two people toast, the one in a lower position should hold his/her glass lowest. After that, the second host begins his toast, followed by a toast of the first host again, then the second host again, finally followed by the third toast of the first host again. The main goal of a formal dinner is not eating; it's purely about etiquette and ritual. In this process the hosts will say something each time when proposing the toast, but it will be much shorter than the speech the first host makes when he proposes the first toast. After all this is finished, the first guest should then propose a toast to the hosts. He or she will make a speech as well, thanking the host for the wonderful meal. As for the other guests, if they want, they can toast with the hosts too after that; they are free to choose.

Wine plays a very important role in Chinese etiquette. At the first toast, everyone should finish the wine in his/her glass. As the old Chinese saying goes, "If your feelings are deep, finish the wine in one swallow, if your feelings are shallow, just take a lick"[6]. You are supposed to finish the wine very quickly without pausing.

Sometimes, if you can't empty your glass, the toaster will try to persuade you, saying things like: "They say you can finish all the wine in another county, but you refuse to drink with me. Does this mean you were happy over there but unhappy in our county?" or "I'm a farmer. If you don't drink with me, it means you look down upon us farmers." Usually guests in high positions can drink according to their wishes, but guests in low positions should always be persuaded to finish their wine. Sometimes, they should even drink for guests in high positions (if they are their leaders), and pretend that it is not because the leaders can't drink, but because they like to drink a lot themselves. Most Chinese look down on a man who can't drink a lot of wine. This is why some Chinese companies on their recruitment application forms ask people "Can you drink wine?" Women and teenagers don't have to drink too much wine, and in most cases people won't force them like they will 'force' men.

The wine the Chinese drink in formal situations is very strong distilled spirits. Sometimes men eagerly await each other's drunkenness. But I think most Chinese won't 'force' foreign guests to drink too much.'

8.5 Hierarchy, Business Cards, Addressing People

Business cards in China mean much more than business cards in the Western context. A business card in China mirrors social status and is therefore to be treated with respect.

Title(s) should be mentioned on it. Sometimes the Chinese use high quality paper, traditional Chinese characters in gold, red, or embossed. The business card of a person high up in society will be a listing of all his or her titles, a description of his or her position.

Westerners should make sure they have bilingual business cards. People working with the Chinese regularly can use a Chinese name, and not solely a translation of their name based on pronunciation. The Chinese name will have three characters. The character chosen as a surname will be a real Chinese surname. The characters of the first name will tell something about the person, associated with specific features related to his personality, character, occupation, or position. In Chinese names, the surname comes first, because the family is more important than the individual.

A business card is offered with both hands, and received with both hands. Upon receiving a business card one should pay attention to it, read the name and titles as a sign of respect. You should always make sure you have enough business cards with you because usually more people show up than one expects and they should all receive a card.

In professional situations, people often address each other by their professional title followed by their surname: President Li, Director Wang, Manager Huang, Guide Zhang, Driver Chen. In this way the position of each person in the hierarchy is reconfirmed.

Business card of Huang Yongnian. Top: name and profession 'professor'; above the line: titles; below the line: address

8.6 Hierarchy, Guanxi, Status and Gift Giving

"Whenever people meet for the first time, the emperor will bring wine, the princes will bring an elongated pointed tablet of Jade, high government officials give lambs, scholars bring geese, ordinary people bring ducks, children put gifts on the floor and then quietly depart, field officers do not have gifts to offer so they must give ribbons, leather belts and arrows." [7]

From the quotation above we understand that the giving of gifts is also connected to hierarchy. In today's China, gift giving may not be as clearly prescribed as in the old days, but it is still connected to hierarchy. The highest in rank receives the largest present.

Gift giving is an integral part of the building up of relationships or *guanxi*. The Chinese exchange a lot more gifts than in Western cultures, even in business environments. Symbolism needs to be respected: don't use white or black wrapping paper, use red or gold instead. Don't give a clock as this refers to death. To maintain equilibrium, the Chinese like to give even numbers of gifts, but avoid giving four gifts because the number four brings bad luck.

Typical things from your country are always appreciated: French or Italian wines, Belgian chocolates, or Swiss knives.

A gift should be offered with both hands and received with both hands. The Chinese don't open the gift the moment they receive it. It will be left unopened until the guest has left. Westerners who are not aware of this sometimes get frustrated thinking they did something wrong. From their side, the Chinese think it is strange when the person who receives a gift immediately 'checks' what is inside.

[1] Fu Genqing, Liu Ruixiang, Lin Zhihe, *The Classical of Filial Piety*, Shandong Friendship Press, 1998, p 23

[2] Gray John Henry, China. *A History of the Laws, Manners and Customs of the People*, Dover Publications, Inc. Minneola, New York, 2002 (first printed in 1878 by Macmillan London)

[3] Mofcom is the Ministry of Foreign Affairs

[4] Xu Chao, Lao An, *Liji, Book of Rites*, Shandong Friendship Press, 1999, pp 176–177

[5] From the chapter "The Significance of the Rite of Banqueting" in: Xu Chao, Lao An, *Li Ji, Book of Rites*, Shandong Friendship Press, 1999, pp 412–415

[6] Ganqing shen, yi kou men; ganqing qian, tian yi tian

[7] Quotation from the *Liji: zhengyi*, in The Thirteen Classics, 3 vols, quoted in: Dutton Michael, 1998, p 39

Conclusion

I n this book we have tried to bring insight into many aspects of China. We think Westerners will benefit from this overall picture and as a result, will to be able to work more efficiently in China. Going to China is easy, working there can be more difficult than people first expect. Westerners going to China with the best intentions sometimes end up surprised and discouraged. Their enthusiasm can quickly turn into utter frustration. This is why people need to gain a better understanding of China and Chinese culture.

We started this book with the main philosophical and ideological trends influencing Chinese culture today: Confucianism, Daoism and Communism. Having explored these ideologies we subsequently focused on a number of aspects of Chinese society: contemporary history, politics, media and information, education, people and society, and even calendar use. We think each of these topics helps to paint an overall picture of the complexities of Chinese society today, one in which people have to work or do business. Once you understand the Chinese way of thinking and how Chinese society is organized, it will be easier to understand issues relating to communication, corporate culture, and Chinese commerce.

In the final chapter we focused on ritual and etiquette, which mean a lot more than just having polite manners in China. Ritual and etiquette are central to establishing good relationships and cooperation. The Chinese think holistically: etiquette and ritual are key to maintaining harmony between people, in society, and with the universe.

As a Westerner it may take many years before one fully understands the impact and extent of hierarchy in Chinese society. The better one understands centralist hierarchical thinking and the holistic aspects of Chinese culture, the better one is able to perceive what is at stake and the easier it becomes to cooperate with China.

Gaining insight into each other's cultures will also help to build good relationships. This is a two-sided process. Being aware of and explaining one's own cultural background, which influences the actions one takes and the expectations one has, should go hand in hand with gaining insight into the other culture. The better you understand the other person, the better you understand yourself. Intercultural communication is like looking into a mirror. An open attitude is required at all times by all parties. There is no good or bad; there is no right or wrong. Every culture has strong aspects and we can all learn from each other.

In China, the legacy of the planned economy is still strongly apparent. But China is evolving and in due course, quality standards will improve and management systems will become more internationalized. The presence of many Western companies in China today and the internationally directed attitude displayed by China is resulting in constant interaction. China is becoming more and more part of the global economy.

The splendid 5000 year-old Chinese culture is well on its way to another revival, again in a new form. We can see Chinese culture resurrecting slowly but surely, shaking off the dust of former difficult times and getting ready for another glorious period. It is so exciting to be part of these developments and to see what the country has realized over the past few decades.

Working in China or with the Chinese can be fruitful and harmonious. Gaining insight into Chinese culture and building long-term relationships will make your cooperation a success story. Only when you become an insider will you be taken seriously. Only when you show commitment will you reap rewards. Reciprocity means that the more you give, the more you get: a win-win situation. We hope this book will be a guide for you, that it will help you to build lasting relationships in China and to work there efficiently, so that all parties will benefit and that this intercultural cooperation will be an enriching experience for all.

Selection of Official Websites
from the People's Republic of China

Central People's Government: http://www.gov.cn/

Ministry of Foreign Affairs: http://www.fmprc.gov.cn/chn/

Ministry of Education: http://www.moe.edu.cn/

Ministry of Science and Technology: http://www.most.gov.cn/

Ministry of Civil Affairs: http://www.mca.gov.cn/

Ministry of Finance: http://www.mof.gov.cn/index.htm

Ministry of Construction: http://www.chinamor.cn.net/

Ministry of Communications: http://www.moc.gov.cn/

Ministry of Information Industry: http://www.mii.gov.cn/mii/index.html

Ministry of Water Resources: http://www.mwr.gov.cn/

Ministry of Public Security: http://www.mps.gov.cn

Ministry of Agriculture: http://www.agri.gov.cn/

Ministry of Commerce: http://www.mofcom.gov.cn/

Ministry of Health: http://61.49.18.65/2.htm

People's Bank of China: http://www.pbc.gov.cn/

National Audit: http://www.audit.gov.cn/

China Customs: http://www.customs.gov.cn/YWStaticPage/default.htm

State Environmental Protection Administration: http://www.zhb.gov.cn/

State Administration of Radio Film and Television: http://www.chinasarft.gov.cn/

General Administration of Sport of China: http://www.sport.gov.cn/

State Administration for Industry and Commerce: http://www.saic.gov.cn/

General Administration of Quality Supervision, Inspection and Quarantine: http://www.aqsiq.gov.cn/

State Food and Drug Administration: http://www.sda.gov.cn/WS01/CL0001/

State Administration of Work Safety: http://www.chinasafety.gov.cn/

New China/ Xinhua News Agency: http://www.xinhuanet.com/

Chinese Academy of Science: http://www.cas.ac.cn/

Chinese Academy of Social Science: http://www.cass.net.cn/

Council for Social Security Fund: http://www.ssf.gov.cn/web/index.asp

National China Banking Regulatory Commission: http://www.cbrc.gov.cn/chinese/home/jsp/index.jsp

State Bureau of Surveying and Mapping: http://www.sbsm.gov.cn/

China Post: http://www.chinapost.gov.cn/

Selected Bibliography – Further Reading

All references in the text can be found in the endnotes. They are not necessarily part of this recommended reading material in which we list only English language books of particular interest to the reader.

Blackman Carolyn, *Negotiating China. Case Studies and Strategies*. Allan & Unwin, 1997

Bond, M.H., *Beyond the Chinese Face*. Oxford University Press, Hong Kong, 1991

Buckley Ebrey Patricia, *Cambridge Illustrated History China*, Cambridge University Press, 1996, 2004

Chow Rey, ed., *Modern Chinese Literature and Cultural Studies in the Age of Theory: Reimagining a Field*. Duke University Press, Durham, London, 2000

Cohen Myron, *Kinship, Contract, Community, and State. Anthropological perspectives on China*, Stanford University Press, 2005

De Mente Boye Lafayette, *Chinese Etiquette & Ethics in Business*, NTC Business Books, 1994

De Mente Boye Lafayette, *The Chinese Have a Word for It. The Complete Guide to Chinese Thought and Culture*, Passport Books, 2000

Deng Rong, *Deng Xiaoping and the Cultural Revolution. A Daughter Recalls the Critical Years*, transl. Sidney Shapiro, Foreign Language Press Beijing, 2002

Denton Kirk, ed., *Modern Chinese Literary Thought. Writings on Literature, 1893–1945*, Stanford University Press, Stanford, California, 1996

Dutton Michael, *Street life China*, Cambridge University Press 1998, 2000

Eberhard Wolfram, *A Dictionary of Chinese Symbols*, Routledge, London, NY 1986

Edmonds Richard Louis ed., *Managing the Chinese Environment*, Oxford University Press, 1998, 2000

Fang Lee Cooke, *HRM, Work and Employment in China*, Routledge, London, New York, 2005

Fang Tony, *Chinese Business Negotiating Style*, International Business Series, Sage Publications, Thousand Oaks, London, New Delhi, 1998

Fernandez Juan Antonio, Underwood Laurie, *China CEO. Voices of Experience from 20 International Business Leaders*, John Wiley & Sons (Asia) Pte Ltd, Singapore, 2006

Friedmann John, *China's Urban Transition*, University of Minnesota Press, Minneapolis, London, 2005

Fu Genqing, *The Classical of Filial Piety*, Shandong Friendship Press, 1998

Fung Yu-lan, *A Taoist Classic, Chuang-tzu*, Foreign Language Press Beijing, 1991

Gao Ge, Ting-Toomey Stella, *Communicating Effectively With the Chinese*, Sage Publications, Thousand Oaks, London, New Delhi, 1998

Gao Jianping, Wang Keping, *Aesthetics and Culture, East and West, Meixue yu wenhua, dongfang yu xifang*, Anhui Jiaoyu Chubanshe, 2006

Gilmore Fiona, Dumont Serge, *Brand Warriors China. Creating Sustainable Brand Capital*, Profile Books, London, 2003

Gold Thomas, Doug Guthrie, Wank David, *Social Connections in China. Institutions, Culture, and the Changing Nature of Guanxi*, Cambridge University Press, 2002

Goldman Merle, Ou-Fan Lee Leo, *An Intellectual History of Modern China*, Cambridge University Press, Cambridge 2002

Gunn Edward, *Rendering the Regional. Local Language in Contemporary Chinese Media*, University of Hawaii Press, Honolulu, 2006

Gray John Henry, *China. A History of The Laws, Manners, and Customs of the People*, Dover Publications, Inc. Minneola, New York, 2002 (reprint by Macmillan & Co, London, 1878)

Haley George, Haley Usha, Chin Tiong Tan, *The Chinese Tao of Business: The Logic of Successful Business Strategy*, John Wiley & Sons (Asia) Pte Ltd, Singapore 2004

Hampden-Turner, C., Trompenaars, F., *Riding the Waves of Culture: Understanding Diversity in Global Business*, McGraw-Hill, 1998

Hartzell Richard, *Harmony in Conflict. Active Adaptation to Life in Present-day Chinese Society*, Caves Books, Taipei, Taiwan, 1988

Hofstede Geert, *Cultures Consequences, Comparing Values, Behaviors, Institutions and Organizations Across Nations*, Sage Publications, Thousand Oaks, London, New Delhi, 2001

Hodge Bob, Louie Kam, *The Politics of Chinese Language and Culture. The Art of Reading Dragons*, Routledge, London, New York, 1998

Hu Wenzhong, Grove Cornelius, *Encountering the Chinese. A Guide for Americans*, Intercultural Press, Yarmouth, Boston, London, 1999

Huang Quanyu, Leonard Joseph, Chen Tong, *Business Decision Making in China*, International Business Press, New York, London, 1997

Kynge James, *China Shakes the World: The Rise of a Hungry Nation*, Orion Publishing, 2006

Ledderdose Lothar, *Ten Thousand Things*, Princeton University Press, 2001

Li Xiaodong, *Dancing Dragons. Chinese Aesthetics since 1979*, Drills Publishing, Utrecht, 2000

Lieberthal Kenneth, *Governing China. From Revolution Through Reform*, W Norton & Company, New York, London, 2004, 1995

Lieberthal Kenneth, Graham John, Lam Mark, Zeng Ming, Williamson Peter, Yan Rick, Vanhonacker Wilfried, Xin Katherine, Pucik Vladimir, Ghemawat Pankaj, *Harvard Business Review on Doing Business in China*, Harvard Business School Press, 2004

Lin Yutang, *My Country and My People, Wu Guo yu Wu Min*, Foreign Language Teaching and Research Press, Beijing, 1998

Liu Kang, *Globalization and Cultural Trends in China*, University of Hawaii Press, Honolulu, 2004

Liu Lydia, *Translingual Practice. Literature, National Culture, and Translated Modernity China 1900–1937*, Stanford University Press, 1995

Luo Yadong, *Guanxi and Business*, World Scientific, Singapore, New Jersey, London, Hong Kong, 2000

Luo Zhiye, *Sun Tzu's The Art of War, Zhongguo waiyu fanyi chuban gongsi*, Beijing, 1995

Ma Ke, Li Jun, ed., *China Business*, China Intercontinental Press, Beijing 2004

Mackeras Colin, *The New Cambridge Handbook of Contemporary China*, Cambridge University Press 2001

Michaelson Gerald, *Sun Tzu, The Art of War for Managers*, Adams Media Corporation, Avon, Massachusetts, 2001

Murphy Rachel, *How Migrant Labor is Changing Rural China*, Cambridge University Press, Cambridge, 2002

Overmyer Daniel, ed., *Religion in China Today*, The China Quarterly Special Issues, New Series, no. 3. Cambridge University Press, 2003

Pei Minxin, *China's Trapped Transition. The Limits of Developmental Autocracy*, Harvard University Press, 2006

Peng Shiyong, *Culture and Conflict Management in Foreign-invested Enterprises in China. An Intercultural Communication Perspective*. Peter Lang, European University Studies, Vol. 369, 2003

Perkins, Radelet, Snodgrass, Gillis, Roemer, *Economics of Development*, W.W. Kortom & Company, 2001

Qu Sanqiang, *Copyright in China*, Foreign Language Press, Beijing, 2002

Ren Jiyu, *A Taoist Classic. The Book of Lao Zi*, Foreign Languages Press, Beijing, 1993

Sheh Seow Wah, *Chinese Leadership. Moving from Classical to Contemporary*. Times Editions, Singapore, 2003

Smith P., Bond M. H., Kagitcibasi C., *Understanding Social Psychology Across Cultures. Living and Working in a Changing World,* Sage Publications, London, Thousand Oaks, New Dehli, 2006

Spence Jonathan, *In Search for Modern China*, Northon & Company, New York, London, 1990, 1999

Starr John Bryan, *Understanding China*, Second Edition, Profile Books, 2001

Steger Ulrich, Fang Zhaoben, Lu Wei, *Greening Chinese Business. Barriers, Trends and Opportunities for Environmental Management*, Greenleaf Publishing, 2003

Stevens Keith, *Chinese Mythological Gods*, Oxford University Press, 2001

Studwell Joe, *The China Dream. The Elusive Quest for the Greatest Untapped Market on Earth*. Profile Books, London 2002, 2003

Waley Arthur, *Confucius. The Analects*, Wordsworth Editions Limited, 1996, waiyu jiaoxue yu yanjiu chubanshe, 1997

Wang Ban, *The Sublime Figure of History. Aesthetics and Politics in Twentieth-Century China*. Stanford University Press, Stanford, California, 1997

Wedeman Andrew, *From Mao to Market. Rent Seeking, Local Protectionism, and Marketization in China*, Cambridge University Press, Cambridge, 2003

Widmer Ellen, Wang Der-wei David, *From May Fourth to June Fourth. Fiction and Film in Twentieth-Century China*, Harvard University Press, Cambridge, Massachusetts, London, 1993

Wilkinson Endymion *Chinese History: A Manual, Revised and Enlarged*, Harvard University Asia Center for Harvard-Yanching Institute, Cambridge, London, 2000

Xu Chao, Lao An, *The Book of Rites (Selections). Translation of Confucian Classics*, Shandong Friendship Press, 1999

Yan Sun, *Corruption and Market in Contemporary China*, Cornell University Press, Ithaca, London, 2004

Yang Bojun, Waley Arthur, *The Analects*, Hunan People's Publishing House, Foreign Languages Press, Beijing, 1999

Yang Mayfair Mei-hui, *Gifts, Favors, & Banquets. The Art of Social Relationships in China*, Cornell University Press, Ithaca, London, 1994

Zhang Dainian, *Key Concepts in Chinese Philosophy*, Foreign Language Press, Beijing, Yale University Press, New Haven, London, 2002

Zhang Xudong, *Chinese Modernism in the Era of Reforms*. Duke University Press, Durham, London, 1997

Zinzius Birgit, *Doing Business in the New China. A handbook and Guide*, Praeger, Westport, Connecticut, London, 2004

Index of Chinese Characters

Bai hua	百花	Hundred Flowers
Bai hua qifang Bai jia zhengming	百花齐放 百家争鸣	Let a hundred flowers bloom, let a hundred schools contend
Baihua	白话	Colloquial Chinese
Bai jia jiangtan	百家讲坛	Hundred philosopher's forum
Bainaohui	百脑会	Shopping mall for electronics
Bao	报	Reciprocity
Bao Ma	宝马	BMW
Bazi	八字	Eight Characters
Bu fangbian	不方便	Not convenient
Bu zai	不在	Not in
Bu zhidao	不知道	I don't know
Changmian	场面	Public face
Chi de ku zhong ku Fang wei ren shang ren	吃得苦中苦 方为人上人	To be able to eat the most bitter of bitterness elevates a human being to a higher level
Chiru de bainian	耻辱的百年	Century of humiliation
Chun jie	春节	Spring Festival
Chun Qiu	春秋	Spring Autumn
Cun	村	Village
Cun tianli, mie renyu	存天理灭人欲	The heavenly ethical principle needs to be observed, individual desire needs to be destroyed
Da Xue	大学	Great Learning
Da yue jin	大跃进	Great Leap Forward
Daiye	待业	Waiting for employment
Dang'an	档案	Personal file
Danwei	单位	Work Unit

Daodejing	道德经	The Way and its Power
Dao	道	The Way
Dao de	道德	Moral dignity
Daqing	大庆	Model Commune Daqing
Datong	大同	The Great Togetherness
De	德	Power/Virtue
De cai jianbei	德才兼备	Integrity and ability are equally important
De zhi ti	德智体	Virtue, Wisdom, Health
Di	地	Earth
Di san fang	第三方	Third party
Di yi ci xindong	第一次心动	The First Heartbeat
Duanwu jie	端午节	Dragon Boat Festival
Falungong	法轮功	Falungong
Fan	返	Withdrawal/reversal
Fan tizi	繁体字	Non-simplified/traditional characters
Fan you pai douzheng	反右派头争	Anti-Rightist campaign
Fei .. bu	非 ... 不	Not ... not
Fei .. bu ke	非 ... 不可	Not ... cannot
Fei .. bu xing	非 ... 不行	Not ... cannot
Fengshui	风水	Wind Water
Fu	福	Wealth
Fu	蝠	Bat
Fu dao	福到	Wealth arrives
Fuwuyuan	服务员	Service provider
Fu xiao, de zhi ben ye, xiao zhi suo you sheng ye	夫孝，德之本也，孝之所由生也	Filial piety is the foundation of all virtues and the fountainhead whence all moral teachings spring

Gan zhi	干支	Stem Branch
Ganbei	干杯	Ad fundum
Ganqing shen, yi kou men; ganqing qian, tian yi tian	感情深,一口闷,感情浅,舔一舔	If your feelings are deep, finish the wine in one swallow, If your feelings are shallow, just take a lick
Guangming Ribao	光明日报	Guangming Daily
Guanxi	关系	Relationships
Guanxi wang	关系网	Relationship network
Gui	鬼	Ghost
Guilao'er	鬼老儿	Old Ghost
Gongwen	公文	Official Letters
Guo cui	国粹	National Essence
Guomindang	国民党	Nationalist Party
Guo qing	国情	National Characteristics
Guo xing	国性	National Character
Guoyu	国语	National Language
Han	汉	Han dynasty
Hanlin Yuan	翰林院	Hanlin Academy
He	和	Harmony
Heshang	河殇	River Elegy
Hong bao	红包	Red envelop
Hukou	户口	Household registration
Hui	回	Hui minority
Hui	会	Society/Association
Huibao	回报	Reciprocity
Huang	皇	Emperor
Huang	黄	Yellow
Huang He	黄河	Yellow River

Ji	计	Stratagem
Jia	家	Family
Jia le fu	家乐福	Rich and happy family/ Carrefour
Jia ren	家人	Family member
Jian tizi	简体字	Simplified character
Jihua shengyu	计划生育	Birth planning/One child policy
Jing jiu	敬酒	To propose a toast
Jingshen wuran	精神污染	Spiritual Pollution
Jiu li	旧历	Old Calendar
Jun jun chen chen fu fu zi zi	君君臣臣父父子子	A king is a king, a subject is a subject, a father is a father, a son is a son
Junzi	君子	Noble personality
Kaolu kaolu	考虑考虑	We will reflect on it
Ke kou ke le	可口可乐	Coca Cola
Keqi	客气	To be polite
Kexue fazhan guan	科学发展观	Scientific Development Concept
Kou tou	叩头	Kowtow
Lao bai xing	老百姓	Common people/hundred names
Laowai	老外	Foreigner
Laozong	老总	The boss
Le shi	乐事	Lays
Li	李	Minister Li
Li	礼	Rite(s)
Li dang wei gong	立党为公	The Party is founded for the interest of the People
Lian	脸	Face

Liji	礼记	Records about Rites
Lu	鲁	State Lu
Luhua nong	露花浓	Revlon
Lun	伦	Differentiation of individuals and their relationships
Lun Yu	论语	The Analects
"Lun Yu" Xin De	"论语" 心得	Understanding "The Analects"
Lushan	庐山	Mount Lu
Mao Zedong wan sui	毛泽东万岁	Long Live Mao Zedong
Meihua xiang zi ku han lai	梅花香自苦寒来	Fragrance of plum blossom origins in bitter cold
Mianxiang	面相	(Science of) Face
Mianzi	面子	Face
Ming	命	Life/fate
Ming	明	Ming dynasty
Minzhu dangpai	民主党派	Democratic parties
Mo sheng ren	陌生人	Strangers
Nei	内	Inner
Neibu	内部	Internal/inside/indoor
Nong li	农历	Farmer's calendar
Pingxing	平行	Equal level
Putonghua	普通话	Standard language
Qi	气	Vital force of life
Qiang da chu tou niao	枪打出头鸟	The bird that sticks up his head is shot
Qiang xue hui	强学会	Study Society for Self-Strengthening
Qiangxue bao	强学报	Become Stronger
Qin	秦	Qin dynasty

Qin Shi Huangdi	秦始皇帝	First Emperor of Qin
Qing	清	Qing dynasty
Qing	情	Feelings
Qing	请	To invite
Qingmian	情面	Face of the feelings
Qingming jie	清明节	Tomb sweeping day
Ren	仁	Benevolence
Ren	人	Human being
Ren duo liliang da	人多力量大	The more people the stronger China becomes
Renminbi	人民币	People's Currency
Renmin Ribao	人民日报	People's Daily
Renqing	人情	Human feelings
Renqing wang	人情网	Network of human feelings
Renwen	人文	Humanities
San min zhuyi	三民主义	Three Principles of the People
Sange daibiao	三个代表	Three Representatives
Shang	商	Shang dynasty
Shang shan xia xiang	上山下乡	Go to the mountainous and rural areas
Shangxing	上行	Towards the top
Shang you zheng ce; Xia you dui ce	上有政策 下有对策	A policy is imposed from above; A counter policy is executed from below
Shehui diwei	社会地位	Social position
Shenbao	申报	Shenbao Newspaper
Shi	十	Ten
Shiji	史记	Historical Records
Shijing	诗经	Book of Odes

Waidi	外地	Outside area
Wan wu	万物	Ten thousand things
Wei	为	Conscious action
Wenhuare	文化热	Cultural Fever
Wenyan	文言	Classical Chinese
Wo ye mei you banfa	我也没有办法	It is beyond my control
Wu	武	Emperor Wu
Wu Jing	五经	Five Classics
Wu si yundong	五四运动	May Fourth Movement
Wu wei	无为	Non-action
Wu wei	五味	Five Flavors
Wu xing	五行	Five Elements
Wu zang	五脏	Five Organs
Xi bu da kaifa	西部大开发	Development of the West
Xia shou	下首	Lower
Xiaxing	下行	Towards the bottom
Xiao	孝	Filial piety
Xin	信	Credibility
Xinhua	新华	New China News Agency
Xin qingnian	新青年	New Youth
Xin Wenhua Yundong	新文化运动	New Culture Movement
Xin xue	新学	New Learning
Xue hai wu ya ku zuo chuan	学海无涯苦作舟	To study the boundless sea of knowledge one needs to sail the boat with bitterness
Yamen	衙门	Government compound
Yan	言	To speak, say, tell
Yanjiu yanjiu	研究研究	We will look into it
Yang	阳	Yang

Yangguizi	洋鬼子	Spirit from across the water
Yi	义	Righteousness
Yili	仪礼	Rules and Rites
Yi Jing	易经	Book of Changes
Yi lun	议论	Gossip
Yi shi yi er shi er	一是一，二是二	1 = 1, 2 = 2
Yin	阴	Yin
Yin li	阴历	Moon calendar
Ying bi qiang	影壁墙	Screen wall
You dian kunnan	有点困难	A bit difficult
You pai	右派	Rightist
Yu	鱼	Fish
Yuan	元	Yuan dynasty
Yuan fen	缘分	Fate
Yunqi	运气	Luck
Zhang zhe wei zun zhang zhe wei xian	长者为尊 长者为先	The oldest is the most esteemed, the oldest goes first
Zhi yao gongfu shen tie chu mo cheng zhen	只要功夫深 铁杵磨成针	Only thorough skill can ground an iron pestle down to a needle
Zhigong daibiao dahui	职工代表大会	Staff and Workers' Representative Congresses
Zhong	忠	Loyalty
Zhongjian ren	中间人	Intermediary
Zhongyong	中庸	Doctrine of the Mean
Zhou	周	Zhou dynasty
Zhou Li	周礼	Rites of Zhou
Zhu shi	主食	Staple food
Zichan jieji ziyou zhuyi	资产阶级自由主义	Bourgeois Liberalism
Zi jia ren	自家人	One's own family

Zi Yue : "Bu zai qi wei, bu mou qi zheng" Zengzi yue: "Junzi si bu chu qi wei."	子曰: "不在其位, 不谋其政" 曾子曰: "君子思不出其位."	When the master said, "He who holds no rank in a State does not discuss its policies," Master Zeng said, "A true gentleman, even in his thoughts, never departs from what is suitable to his rank."
Zou zi ben zhuyi daolu de dang quan pai	走资本主义道路的当权派	Capitalist Roaders

Chinese Names – People and Locations

Yan'an	延安
Yang Liwei	杨利伟
Yang Shangkun	杨尚昆
Yao Ming	姚明
Yu Dan	于丹
Zhang Yimou	张艺谋
Zhao Ziyang	赵紫阳
Zheng Xiaoqiong	郑小琼
Zeng Qinghong	曾庆红
Zhou Enlai	周恩来
Zhou Yang	周扬
Zhou Zuoren	周作人
Zhuangzi	庄子
Zhu Rongji	朱镕基
Zhu Xi	朱熹

Chinese Refernces in Notes

Fu Genqing, Liu Ruixiang, Lin Zhihe, *The Classical of Filial Piety*, Shandong Friendship Press, 1998

傅跟清， 刘瑞样，林之鹤 "孝经" 山东友谊出版社 1998

---

http://news.sina.com.cn/z/hukou/index.shtml 'guanzhu zhongguo huji zhidu gaige'

关注中国户籍制度改革

Lin Yutang, *My Country and My People, Wu Guo yu Wu Min*, Foreign Language Teaching and Research Press, Beijing, 1998

林语堂 "吾国与吾民" 外语教学与研究出版社 1998

Lin Yutang, *Zhongguo Ren*, Xue Lin Chubanshe, Shanghai, 2000

林语堂 "中国人" 学林出版社 2000

Mianxiang. Toushi ni yi sheng de xingfu, Beijing Zhongti Yinxiang Chuban Zhongxin chuban Faxing

"面相。 透视你一生的幸福" 北京中体音像出版中心出版发行

Ren Jiyu, *A Taoist Classic. The Book of Lao Zi*, Foreign Languages Press, Beijing, 1993

任继愈 "老子" 外文出版社北京 1993

Shen Ji, *Shanghai Godfathers* (Shanghai Daheng), Xue Lin Chubanshe, Shanghai, 2001

沈寂， "上海大亨" 学林出版社， 上海, 2001

Xie Weidong, *Aolin pike jingshen. Aolin pike jingshen yu zhonghua minzu jingshen de wanmei tongyi*. Zhonghua gong shang lianhe chubanshe, Beijing 2007

谢卫东 "奥林匹克精神与中华民族精神的完美统一" 中华工商联合出版社 北京 2007

Xu Chao, Lao An, *Li Ji, Book of Rites*, Shandong Friendship Press, 1999

徐超，老安， "礼记" 山东友谊出版社 1999

Yang Bojun, Waley Arthur, *Lun Yu, The Analects*. Hunan People's Publishing House, Foreign Language Press, 1999

杨伯峻，韦利， "论语" 湖南人民出版社，外语出版社 1999

Yu Dan, Yu Dan *"Lun Yu" Xin De*, Beijing Zhonghua Shuju, 2007	于丹，于丹"论语"心得，中华书局，北京2007
Yu Dan, Yu Dan *"Zhuangzi" Xin De*, Zhongguo Minzhu Fazhi Chubanshe, 2007	于丹，于丹"庄子"心得，中国民主法制出版社，北京 2007